AF603695

PRAISE FOR *ONE DAY IN SEPTEMBER*

"Scott Reich's *One Day in September* is the best baseball book, the best history book, the best book period that I have read in a long while...Reich joins an elite group of writers exploring the intersection of American sport, culture, and history. "

— David Eisenhower, bestselling author
of *Eisenhower at War: 1943-1945*

"I've known of New England's first true chronicler of baseball—Tim Murnane—for decades. But until Scott Reich's extraordinary telling...I had never heard of the story of the Murnane All-Star game. This book...is a true tapestry of baseball and American history."

— Keith Olbermann, Award-winning
journalist and broadcaster

"Through meticulous research and vivid storytelling, Reich uncovers a forgotten chapter of baseball history that feels both surprising and essential. By the final page, you'll wonder how this remarkable story remained untold for so long."

— Darren Rovell, Emmy Award-winning
sports business reporter, ESPN & CNBC

"A forgotten game, a remarkable cast, and a world at war. Scott Reich tells this story with the care it deserves...You will wonder how such a glorious afternoon stayed buried so long."

— Rob Neyer, West Coast League commissioner
and award-winning author

"Scott Reich's *One Day in September* is a lovely, elegiac book... Lavishly illustrated, carefully researched, and affectionately told, it brings to life not only a game, but America and the game of baseball at a crossroads."

—Kevin Baker, author of *The New York Game:
Baseball and the Rise of a New City.*

ALSO BY SCOTT D. REICH

The Power of Citizenship:
Why John F. Kennedy Matters to a New Generation

One Day in September

Baseball, Brotherhood, and the Birth of the All-Star Game

By Scott D. Reich

One Day in September is a work of non-fiction. References to historical events were researched and depicted to the best of the author's ability. The descriptions of all individuals are done with the utmost respect by the author.

Published by Compass Rose Publishing
228 Park Ave. S #620056 New York, NY 10003-1502

Hardcover ISBN: 979-8-9941958-8-8

Softcover ISBN: 979-8-9941958-7-1

Cover design by Madeline Mafilios

First Edition

To Emelia, Eli, and Dylan—

Always stay true to who you are.
I love you, and I'm so proud to be your dad.

CONTENTS

PROLOGUE

1 THE RISE OF MURNANE'S GAME 7
ARRIVAL AT FENWAY

2 THE SILVER KING OF BASEBALL 25
THE WARM-UP

3 BOSTON, FENWAY & THE RISE OF THE RED SOX 51
A PAGEANT OF SKILL

4 THE ROAD TO MURNANE DAY 71
OPENING SALVOS

5 THE STARS WHO CAME 85
CHESS ON GRASS

6 TRUST, BETRAYAL & THE BIRTH OF A NEW TRADITION 101
FIRE & RESOLVE

7 THE FIRST ALL-STAR GAME 123
THE GREAT FINISH

8 AFTER THE APPLAUSE 159
TWILIGHT AT FENWAY

9 THE MEMORY WE CARRY 169
AFTERMATH

EPILOGUE: THAT INNOCENT PROMISE

APPENDIX

NOTES

BIBLIOGRAPHY

INDEX

ACKNOWLEDGMENTS

ABOUT THE AUTHOR

Baseball is America's poetry.

I see great things in baseball. It's our game, the American game. It will repair our losses and be a blessing.

—Walt Whitman

And here is one of its forgotten guardians.

What 'Tim' Murnane doesn't know about baseball isn't worth knowing, for there is not another man in the United States who has had so much experience with the great national game as he has had.

—*Boston Globe*, July 14, 1907

A baseball carries no memory of the moment it helped create. Only later—after the cheering fades and the score is known—does the ball become an artifact of history.

PROLOGUE

The sun hung low over Boston, casting rich autumn hues across the infield grass of Fenway Park. It was a Thursday afternoon in late September 1917, the kind of day that lives forever in memory—a radiant canvas of gold and green, when the air was crisp and the shadows long—in an America that, in the decades after the Civil War, had finally begun to recapture the promise of her founding. It was a day when Americans found themselves, once again, stitched together by deep and simpler virtues.

By that autumn, Americans were learning what it meant to live with uncertainty. The old assurances of progress and stability, of distance from the world's troubles, had begun to erode. War pulled the nation outward, grief pulled families inward, and the country searched for signs that its shared life still held. In moments like these, Americans have always turned to places where the nation gathers without instruction—where meaning emerges not by decree, but by participation.

Beyond the park's brick walls, the Great War pressed in on the city. Millions of young Americans had answered the call to service. Boston's streets bustled with men in uniform. South Station swallowed and released whole platoons; the Navy Yard and the docks seemed to hum at all hours. Posters for enlistment lined shop windows, and newspapers carried casualty lists alongside editorials on duty and resolve. The country braced for sacrifices it was only beginning to understand.

Public life had grown heavy with obligation. Even leisure felt provisional, borrowed. And yet, on this day, people gathered the way they always had when they needed to feel like themselves again: by taking the trolley, climbing the steps, finding their seats, and turning their faces toward a patch of grass that still promised rules, rhythm, a fair chance—and the quiet belief that some institutions endured, even as the world seemed to tilt off its axis.

Inside Fenway Park, the mood reflected that faith. A brass band pushed out patriotic airs, bunting and flags snapped in the breeze, vendors threaded the aisles with programs under their arms. More than 17,000 gathered. Not for a pennant race or a championship, but for something quieter, nobler, and deeply American: a ballgame played for a cause.

The Red Sox took the field, fresh off another pennant and anchored by a twenty-two-year-old left-hander named Babe Ruth. But across from them stood no ordinary opponent. Instead, a hand-chosen constellation of stars gathered in what one reporter called "the fanciest picked team that ever trotted out from any bench." Ty Cobb, Tris Speaker, "Shoeless" Joe Jackson, Buck Weaver, Ray Chapman, Walter Johnson, and others had assembled from rival clubs and rival cities, with the legendary Connie Mack and Hughie Jennings as managers. In an extraordinary show of unity, these men had skipped their regular season games to come to Boston, laying down rivalries and record books for one afternoon of generosity. Writing afterward, Francis Eaton would call it simply "the greatest baseball show on earth."[1]

Before a single pitch was thrown, the afternoon announced itself as something more than a game. The field filled with motion as a series of skills contests unfolded—tests of speed, strength, and touch that felt part carnival, part fellowship. Arms were uncorked and balls sent arcing across the grass, the kind of throws that make a crowd murmur even when nothing officially counts. Precision followed power as pitchers took aim at distant targets for the most accurate throw, and runners broke from the line in flashes of white flannel, circling the bases with a blur of urgency that pulled the crowd forward in its seats. And then there was Ruth—still known to many more for his arm than his bat—lifting fungo after fungo into the autumn air, the ball climbing higher than seemed reasonable, long enough aloft to draw wonder before it fell back to earth. One writer would later admit he had never seen a ball rise quite like that.

It was more than a game. It was an event. Actress and comedian Fanny Brice moved through the aisles selling programs. Actor and entertainer Will Rogers—rope in hand—rode a horse and performed lasso tricks around the field, drawing laughter and delight. And coaching first base for the Red Sox, in a cameo only that era could offer, was the retired heavyweight boxing champion John L. Sullivan, barking instructions like a field general and playfully challenging others to slugfests.

At stake was no trophy, no title. The beneficiary of all this spectacle was the family of Tim Murnane—a name little remembered today, but a major figure in the early baseball world.

Murnane had been a ballplayer in the game's unruly early years, patrolling the infield with grit in the 1870s before moving to the outfield, managing clubs and leagues, and even serving occasionally as an umpire (and "in a very impartial manner" at that, wrote one editor).[2] But it was after he hung up his spikes that his influence deepened. As the longtime baseball editor of the *Boston Globe*, Murnane became one of the sport's most passionate advocates and its steadiest internal critic, chronicling its rise with warmth, wit, and a stubborn insistence that the game's honor mattered. He wrote not just about the box scores, but about the sport's character—what it rewarded, what it excused, and what it ought to demand.

When Murnane died suddenly of a heart attack at age sixty-five in February 1917—collapsing in the foyer of Boston's Shubert Theatre while waiting for his wife to check her coat—he left behind a widow and four young children still under his roof. Two older daughters from his first marriage were grown, but the household he had rebuilt late in life still depended on his pay and his name. There was no pension, no tidy institutional protection—just rent due, mouths to feed, and a blank space where tomorrow's column should have been. What he left was a reputation, and a baseball public that understood what he had given it.

Nearly $15,000 was raised—a tremendous sum in 1917, when the average home in Boston sold for around $5,000—but money was not the only currency that changed hands.[3] What happened that day was something richer: a public act of presence. People came, and in coming affirmed—together—that obligation could be joyful, and that baseball could serve as both national pastime and national conscience. As the world waged what President Woodrow Wilson called "the most terrible and disastrous of all wars, civilization itself seeming to be in the balance," the game offered solace, unity, and joy.[4] There were no broadcast rights to sell and no corporate banners to satisfy—just sunlight, a crowd, and a shared purpose that felt, for an afternoon, uncomplicated.

In every sense, what happened that afternoon was indeed extraordinary. While there had been earlier benefit games, never before had so many of baseball's greats gathered on so public a stage, with such deliberate spectacle, and in the shadow of a world at war. It was, in essence, the first modern All-Star game—years before the term would become official—and it revealed something fundamental about the sport: that baseball, at its best, is not only competition but communion. Not a metaphor, either—just thousands of people agreeing, for a few hours, to care about the same thing in the same place.

That communion was not symbolic; it was practiced. It required bodies in seats, money in hands, time set aside, and attention freely given—as well as programs purchased, scorecards folded, and voices spent. It asked nothing abstract of its participants, only that they show up, together, in public, for someone else. What feels distant now is not the generosity itself, but the habit of enacting it so visibly, so collectively, and so without any expectation of return.

And yet, to those who lived it, the day did not feel unusual. Benefit games were not novelties; they were civic reflexes. When loss struck, people gathered—quickly, publicly, without much debate—and turned spectacle into service. The question is not why they did this in 1917. The question is why it no longer feels like the obvious answer in modern times—and what we traded away when we let that instinct go quiet.

Today, when tragedy strikes, our responses tend to fragment. We grieve privately, donate digitally, send a message, and keep moving, often because life demands it. None of this is wrong. But it is different. What has faded is the instinct to gather at scale—to transform public pleasure into public care, and to let comfort carry an obligation with it. What this afternoon leaves behind is not a judgment about our generosity but a quieter uncertainty: whether we still have a common place in which to practice it together.

Such a gathering did more than raise money. It instructed. It reminded Americans, not through speeches or laws but through repetition, what was expected of them when misfortune struck. Children watched their parents buy a program, neighbors recognized one another in the aisles, the next day's paper recorded not only the score but the turnout. To attend was to participate in a shared moral life—to learn, almost by instinct, that care was more than a private virtue. It was also a public responsibility.

In time, baseball would grow richer, flashier, and more commercial. It would survive scandals and strikes, segregation and slow repair, becoming both a mirror of America's divisions and a witness to its aspirations. But on that afternoon in 1917—before television, before free agency, before the sport learned how to market its myths—baseball revealed something essential about its character, and about the country that had shaped it. Long before baseball learned how to celebrate itself, it learned how to care for its own.

This is the story of that afternoon—of a forgotten moment in a remembered place. Of the players who came, the man they honored, and the country they carried with them onto the grass. Of a sunlit, singular day when baseball reminded America of its better angels, and when the old park's brick and iron held something like a civic vow. One game, played for honor and for love, helped give rise to a tradition that still echoes more than a century later.

Even amid the upheaval of the Civil War, Americans carried their games with them. Soldiers played baseball in camps and prison yards alike, spreading a pastime that was fast becoming a shared national language.

1

THE RISE OF MURNANE'S GAME

By the turn of the twentieth century, America had a national language, a national currency, and, unmistakably, a national pastime. Baseball, once a ragged curiosity played on open fields and city commons, had grown into something sturdier: a republic built on muscle and merit. In prairie towns and factory cities alike, boys threw balls against barn doors, while their fathers carried batting averages in their heads like scripture—recited, disputed, defended. In mill towns, men argued strike zones on trolley platforms; in farming counties, box scores arrived folded inside catalogues and mail-order circulars. The game had not only taken hold of the American imagination; it had become one of the instruments through which the country understood itself. In a nation still deciding what kind of power it would be, baseball offered something astonishingly rare: common measure.

It had not always carried such weight. Before the Civil War, baseball was local and fluid, played under competing codes that could shift between neighboring towns. New York clubs standardized the version that would endure: ninety feet between bases, nine men to a side, nine innings to settle a contest. New England held to its own traditions, including the bracing right to retire a runner by striking him with the ball—an act that felt more like frontier improvisation than parliamentary order. The New York code, cleaner and easier to reproduce, proved best suited to leave its local roots behind and ride the currents of a country in motion—rail lines expanding, populations shifting, cities swelling.

Ironically, it was the war that gave baseball its first national platform. Regiments played wherever they camped—on scrubby fields outside Washington, in muddy clearings along the Potomac, sometimes even on the White House lawn—finding in baseball a welcome order amid chaos. A Rhode Island soldier wrote in December 1861 that baseball offered the men "a revival of their school days," and that such amusements sustained their health and spirits.[1] In Alexandria, Texas, a Union game was interrupted by Confederate fire that wounded and captured the center fielder. When the skirmish ended, one soldier remarked grimly that they had lost not only their comrade but also "the only baseball in Alexandria."[2] Even captivity carried the pastime forward: Union prisoners taught the game in Southern camps, and guards learned it by watching. By the war's end, baseball had traveled wherever Americans had gone. Amid patriotic fervor, one Brooklyn contest opened with the Star-Spangled Banner, quietly binding the young pastime to the nation's civic identity.[3] The rules had been standardized before and during the war; afterward, they offered a common language.

In the decades that followed, the game scaled with the country itself. Railroads connected distant cities, professional leagues emerged and collapsed and emerged again, and box scores appeared beside commodity prices and election returns. Ballparks rose as civic landmarks, gathering clerks and laborers, merchants and mill hands, under the same wooden grandstands. Immigrants found in the game a grammar of belonging. Italian, Irish, and Jewish players stepped into lineups that mirrored the churn of tenement streets, and the stands reflected the same mosaic. For a few hours, differences were absorbed into a common ritual—the same calls disputed, the same pennants chased, and the same curses hurled at umpires. And like so many shared American rituals, baseball soon revealed a deeper instinct: to formalize, to codify, to turn custom into institution.

Americans had a habit of organization. It was once joked that whenever three men met by chance, they elected a president, a vice president, and a treasurer—and, if time allowed, drafted a constitution.[4] Baseball proved no exception. Like the country around it, the game built institutions wherever it went.

Leagues formalized. Schedules lengthened. The casual game of camp and commons hardened into institution. It could be written about in newspapers, wagered upon in saloons, and followed with the same fervor as politics or revival meetings. Clubs charged admission, players were paid, owners quarreled over territory and gate receipts. For the first time a man with a bat in his hands could dream of earning a livelihood from the game—though not without risk. Contracts dissolved. Franchises folded. Salaries vanished midseason. Baseball promised opportunity, but it did not yet promise stability. That too was part of its American quality.

Writers helped transform that risk into narrative. Baseball did not merely happen on the field; it unfolded in print, where bats and balls became episodes in a larger American story. In smoky press boxes, newspapermen stitched scattered contests into something coherent and continuous. A Tuesday loss in St. Louis could be made to echo in Philadelphia by Wednesday morning. A rookie's three hits in Detroit might be framed as the first stanza of a career. They made heroes out of men and seasons into sagas, turning standings into suspense and statistics into character studies. They were romanticists at heart, hemming together stories that made ordinary contests feel epic—each season another song in a republic still composing itself. Their prose soared when a double split the gap, lingered when a pitcher bent his will against a batter, and rose when the crowd swelled into one voice. These writers—part reporter, part advocate, part poet—gave baseball its mythic dimension, ensuring that players lived on not just in memory but in national imagination.

Making Heroes of Men

Tim Murnane stood at the forefront of this Homeric school. In the offices of the *Boston Globe*, where he would serve as sports editor and writer for thirty years, he cut a distinctive figure—red and black blazer, silver hair beginning to assert itself—nearly buried beneath a mound of newspapers from across the country. A pen rested between his fingers, stained with ink.

He worked quickly, almost playfully, as if composing rather than reporting, leaning back in his chair to consider a turn of phrase before driving it home. The *Globe* once described him as "playing a merry tune" while grinding out his "witty base ball squibs."[5] The desk might be cluttered, but the voice was clear. From that crowded corner of the newsroom, Murnane helped turn a sprawling sport into a shared conversation.

Early Stars Emerge

As leagues stabilized, the game began producing its first true hero class—figures whose reputations traveled by train and headline alike. Adrian "Cap" Anson, broad-shouldered and commanding, emerged as the sport's initial superstar. A prolific hitter and field general, his influence helped formalize the professional game—even as his role in hardening baseball's color line cast a long and corrosive shadow over its early structure. The Delahanty brothers offered another glimpse of the sport's expanding promise: from a single Cleveland household came five major leaguers, their shared ascent suggesting baseball's power to turn private aspiration into public inheritance. Honus Wagner, the "Flying Dutchman," carried the compact power of the industrial age; Christy Mathewson lent the mound a gentlemanly composure that reassured middle-class sensibilities; Cy Young seemed less spectacle than monument, his endurance a standard against which others were measured.

Walter Johnson, the "Big Train," arrived with a different kind of authority. Tall, spare, and unflappable, he hurled a fastball so swift and true that hitters often seemed reduced to spectators. Over two decades in Washington, he paired velocity with remarkable control, rewriting the possibilities of pitching dominance. If Young was a monument to stamina, Johnson was modern force incarnate—precision and power fused into something almost mechanical, a harbinger of the century's coming velocity.

"Nap" Lajoie brought grace to second base and such popularity that Cleveland named its club after him, his smooth swing emblematic of a game learning refinement. "Wee" Willie Keeler, all five feet four inches of him, mastered precision over force and lived by the creed he made famous: "Hit 'em where they ain't." Mordecai "Three Finger" Brown, his damaged hand the relic of a childhood accident, turned deformity into advantage, baffling hitters with curveballs that danced across the plate. Native American "Chief" Bender pitched with intelligence and poise despite the jeers that followed him, winning with quiet command. And Rube Waddell—brilliant, mercurial—might strike out a lineup only to wander off moments later in pursuit of a passing fire truck, a reminder that genius and instability often shared the same dugout bench. Greatness in those years came in many temperaments, but it accumulated the same way: season by season, until a name could fill a ballpark far from where it had first been chanted.

For all its emerging polish, the era still possessed a rough edge. When Cleveland once tried a trick—its first baseman shoving runners off the bag as a pick-off throw arrived—they discovered quickly that Wagner was the wrong man to try it on. Pushed off first, he turned and decked the fielder, dropping him in the dirt.[6] Baseball was becoming organized, but it was not yet polite. Codes of conduct existed more by custom than enforcement, and justice was often delivered with a forearm rather than a fine.

In truth, the sport's early decades were harsher than nostalgia prefers to remember. As historian Bill James observed, the tactics of the 1880s were aggressive; by the 1890s, they had grown violent.[7] Players slid "spikes up," yanked runners off bases, and treated umpires as adversaries rather than arbiters. John Heydler, later president of the National League, recalled Baltimore players to be so ruthless they would maim a rival or official if it advanced their cause. Umpires, he said, sometimes "bathed their feet by the hour" after being spiked through their shoes.[8] Crowds too could turn feral. Bottles flew. Language coarsened. Baseball was learning discipline, but it had not yet mastered restraint. The myth of gentlemanly sport would come later; the apprenticeship was bruising.

Murnane understood why. "No class of men living are as hard to handle as a lot of ball players," he wrote, noting that even the most virtuous manager would "have enemies in his club if he were a saint," unless players were committed to condition and effort. His solution was pragmatic rather than sentimental: "The best way after all is to handle the men as a team, and not as individuals."[9]

As the sport entered its second generation, the talent

deepened and sharpened. Tris Speaker roamed the outfield with cerebral precision, positioning himself not merely by instinct but by calculation, playing angles as if he were solving a geometry problem in motion. Shoeless Joe Jackson swung with a fluid grace that seemed borrowed from another era, his bat traveling through the zone as if guided by memory rather than muscle. Ty Cobb played with an edge that electrified and unsettled in equal measure—brilliant, relentless, forever testing the limits of gamesmanship and decency. And a young Babe Ruth hinted at a transformation that would soon redraw the game's geometry entirely, lifting the ball into spaces it rarely occupied.

These were not distant legends frozen in sepia. They were living presences, their exploits arriving by train and telegraph, filling newspapers and ballparks across the country. Boys imitated their stances in vacant lots. Men argued their merits in barber chairs. By 1917, baseball's stage was crowded with stars, and the public had learned how to adore them.

And yet the sport mirrored the country in more ways than one. Baseball was fiercely segregated—an unbroken color line barred Black players from the major leagues even as the game proclaimed itself national and democratic. The exclusion was neither accidental nor temporary. It hardened into custom, then into quiet law.

Amid the rigid segregation of the era, Black baseball flourished with brilliance and defiance. Pioneers like Andrew "Rube" Foster—player, manager, executive, evangelist—organized teams that thrilled African-American communities from Chicago to Kansas City. In 1920, he founded the Negro National League, the first sustained professional Black league in the United States, building an institution where none had been permitted to exist. His Chicago American Giants became a standard-bearer, showcasing a caliber of play that rivaled any major league roster. John Henry "Pop" Lloyd, often called the "Black Wagner" in reference to Honus, fielded and hit with elegance that drew admiration even from white contemporaries who could not share a diamond with him. Pete Hill ranged across the outfield with tireless speed. Cristóbal Torriente struck fear with a bat that could change a game in a single inning. Bill Foster, Rube's brother, pitched with intelligence and command that reflected a deep study of hitters and circumstance.

They forged a vibrant, fiercely competitive world—barnstorming across state lines, drawing integrated crowds even when leagues were not integrated, proving daily that excellence did not require permission, even when opportunity was denied. If the major leagues called themselves national, the Negro leagues quietly demonstrated what national talent truly meant.

In an age dominated by robber barons, sweatshops, and the relentless drone of industrial machines reshaping cities and lives, baseball retained a homespun quality—or at least the comforting illusion of one. Steel mills roared. Assembly lines quickened. Skyscrapers rose from mud and ash. Yet inside the ballpark, time seemed to move differently. It was chalk dust and coal smoke, hand-sewn gloves and woolen uniforms, box scores inked beside war headlines and market reports.

It was the crack of a bat cutting cleanly through summer air, the smell of roasted peanuts drifting above cigar smoke, the mingling of fresh-cut grass and damp earth. The sun-dappled afternoons at the ballpark offered a momentary refuge from the upheavals of modern life. Here, regardless of origin or station, Americans gathered under open sky to witness a contest governed by rules everyone could recite and outcomes no one could predict. The illusion of fairness—clear boundaries, equal innings, impartial umpires—felt like reassurance in a world hurtling toward complexity.

As the sport matured, it faced a quiet challenge: how to remain alive rather than calcified. Growth exposed imbalance. Pitching at times overwhelmed hitting. Tempers flared. New strategies strained rules drafted for simpler contests. Crowds grew louder, money more visible, incentives sharper. The game risked hardening into something brittle—either too rigid to adapt or too reckless to endure.

For baseball to survive as more than entertainment, it would have to evolve without losing itself. It would need custodians as well as competitors—men who understood that reform was not betrayal but preservation.

Murnane believed it could. He argued that its genius lay in balance—between motion and stillness, power and restraint, individuality and obedience to rule. When pitching gained too great an advantage, he championed reform. In an 1888 column titled "BETTER FOR THE BATTER," he warned that "the pitching is getting far ahead of the batting," insisting that progress was not sacrilege but stewardship.[10] The public, he believed, deserved competition rather than domination.

He advised umpires with the practicality of a former player. "Measure your man," he urged, so that crouching hitters or towering sluggers could not manipulate the strike zone with theatrics or stretching. (In 1917, the strike zone ran from the knees to the shoulders, taller than the mid-torso zone used today.) He mentored younger officials who would carry the standard forward.[11] He pressed for rules that protected both spectacle and fairness. The game, like the nation, required vigilance. Left unattended, it could tilt toward imbalance; guided carefully, it could renew itself.

By the early twentieth century, baseball had woven itself into daily life with the quiet persistence of habit. Local businesses sponsored teams whose uniforms bore the names of breweries and hardware stores. Opening days drew parades with brass bands and bunting. Children gathered on street corners to trade tobacco cards and debate the relative merits of pitchers they had never seen in person. Barbershop windows posted lineups in chalk. The sports page became a kind of daily catechism, transforming box scores into narrative and players into familiar presences.

Baseball appeared in novels and vaudeville routines, on postcards and sheet music. Its language slipped into common speech—"out of left field," "batting a thousand," and "three strikes"—until the grammar of the diamond echoed far beyond it. In mill towns and city neighborhoods, Sunday leagues offered laborers a brief taste of distinction. Baseball was not simply spectacle. It was repetition—an agreed-upon return. In these ways, the myths of the game bled into daily life, lending a hint of heroism to the ordinary.

Young immigrant boys in the teeming streets of New York memorized batting averages between selling papers and dodging trolley cars. For them, baseball was more than pastime; it was passport—a shared language in a city where accents collided and words often failed. Entire towns paused when World Series updates were piped into public squares through megaphones, factories slowing as crowds gathered to hear the next inning announced. News traveled in bursts of static and rumor, each cheer relayed and reinterpreted.

The game moved by retelling, each miraculous catch or walk-off swing replayed and embellished until what happened on the field mattered as much in memory as it had in the moment. Baseball did not merely occur; it circulated.

The game also created community as naturally as it generated statistics. Ballparks offered an afternoon sanctuary from the pressures of a changing country. Rituals multiplied: box seats for bosses, bleachers for boys, Cracker Jack for everyone, opening day with a cherished family member. Rooting for a team meant belonging—to a city, a neighborhood, a shared memory carried from season to season. Even failure had its consolation. Fans discovered one of sports' quiet mercies: the eternal promise of "wait till next year." Hope, unlike pennants, was renewable.

In parallel, ballparks rose in steel and concrete, announcing that the game intended to stay. Shibe Park in Philadelphia. Forbes Field in Pittsburgh. Comiskey in Chicago. These were not temporary wooden grandstands liable to burn or sag. They were statements—cathedrals of brick and girders, built to endure.

And in 1912, Fenway Park opened in Boston, its cramped geometry and looming left-field wall declaring that baseball could bend to a city's contours rather than erase them. The Green Monster did not yet bear that name, but it already signaled personality over uniformity. These parks were civic landmarks as much as sporting venues. Inside, a factory worker might sit beside a banker, an immigrant beside a Yankee Brahmin,* rising in unison for the same long fly drifting toward the wall. The tickets were affordable. The heroes flawed. The proximity intimate enough that a foul ball could still change hands without ceremony. The connection felt unmanufactured.

By 1917, the game had entered what felt like its golden adolescence—old enough to know itself, young enough to remain unguarded. It was untouched by television and massive corporate sponsorship. Radios were only beginning to crackle in scattered communities; most Americans still received their

---

*A Brahmin refers to a member of Boston's old, established, upper-class Protestant families—the city's historic social elite who traced their roots back to colonial New England and often dominated banking and commerce, politics, Harvard and intellectual life, and cultural institutions.

baseball in ink, the morning paper carrying yesterday's drama folded beneath an arm. Players rode trains and shared rooms. They tipped their caps to hecklers they might see again at the station. The boundary between celebrity and familiarity remained thin enough to cross.

The season carried ritual weight. Rivalries—the Dodgers and the Giants, the Cubs and the Cardinals, the Tigers and the White Sox—returned like recurring chapters in a continuing story. Each year added a footnote, a grudge, a remembered slight—collectively inviting comparison, commemoration, and anticipation. These contests unfolded in nine-inning increments, where character—discipline, nerve, restraint, resolve—revealed itself gradually rather than in bursts. Rivalry was not spectacle for its own sake. It trained spectators in patience. It taught them to compare, to remember, to measure this September against the last. Baseball schooled its audience in continuity.

World on Fire

Yet even as baseball perfected its rhythms, the wider world began to fracture. In June 1914, an assassin's bullet in Sarajevo struck not only an archduke but a continent balanced precariously on alliance and pride. What followed was less a conflict than a convulsion. Treaties tightened like snares. Armies mobilized. Within weeks, Europe was at war.

"On history's clock, it was sunset," wrote Barbara Tuchman in *The Guns of August*, "and the sun of the old world was setting in a dying blaze of splendor never to be seen again."[12] The old assumptions—about honor, empire, inevitability—burned quickly. The new century, barely adolescent itself, turned savage.

Across the Atlantic, Americans watched with fascination shaded by unease as reports of carnage arrived in fragmented telegrams and grainy photographs. Headlines spoke of trenches, gas, machine guns—terms that seemed both modern and medieval. For many the war appeared distant, a European calamity unfolding far from ballparks and Main Streets where life continued under clear summer skies.

Yet beneath that surface calm, something tightened. The scale of destruction defied precedent. The vocabulary of slaughter expanded. The knowledge settled slowly: no nation of consequence would remain untouched. The United States, ascendant and industrial, could not indefinitely pretend the Atlantic was insulation rather than corridor.

For nearly three years America clung to neutrality, even as its economic and cultural ties bound it ever closer to Britain and France. President Wilson urged restraint. Many citizens agreed. Europe's quarrels, they argued, need not become America's inheritance.

But neutrality grew harder to sustain with each passing month. German U-boats prowled the Atlantic, their policy of unrestricted submarine warfare collapsing the distinction between combatant and civilian. In May 1915, the sinking of the *Lusitania*—with more than one hundred Americans among the dead—shocked the nation. Newspapers printed the names. Editorials darkened. What had seemed distant suddenly felt proximate. The ocean no longer appeared wide enough to guarantee safety.

The war's pace accelerated beyond comprehension. In 1916, the German army targeted the French fortress city of Verdun, intent to grind France down through attrition. The battle endured for ten months, an industrial harvest of youth, artillery pulverizing earth until the landscape itself seemed wounded. Nearly a million casualties accumulated in increments too large for imagination.

That summer, along the River Somme, British forces advanced into machine-gun fire and were cut down in numbers that stunned even a hardened continent. Tens of thousands fell on the first day alone.[13] By winter, more than a million men had been killed or wounded there as well.[14] The war had become a machine, and it consumed without pause.

Americans read the figures in disbelief. They remained abstract until one pictured the emptied classrooms, the shuttered shops, the silence where a generation's voices should have been.

Murnane, speaking at a social club in 1916, reached instinctively for baseball as a counterargument. If nations were bound together by a shared baseball league, he suggested with a half-smile, they might chase pennants rather than trenches. "I, for one, would like to be the first president of such a league," he said, adding that he would be ready for heaven "feeling that at least I had accomplished something good and great for the only game of games."[15]

The humor carried longing. Beneath the jest lay conviction that competition governed by rules was preferable to slaughter without restraint—that the discipline and fellowship of the sport carried civic lessons worth exporting.

Admiration followed him into clubrooms and banquets. He became known as the white-haired sage of baseball, quoted with deference, toasted with affection.[16] Yet admiration did not guarantee security. There was no pension for a columnist's loyalty, no institutional cushion for decades of service. Writing later, the *Boston Journal* noted that Murnane's worries were not abstract. It had long been his "great ambition," the *Journal* wrote, "that all of his children should be able to go to college when they were old enough"—an aspiration still uncommon in an era when higher education remained the province of the few.[17] Baseball had grown vast and profitable, but its chroniclers still lived by the next edition. The disparity was not unusual for the era. It was simply fact.

By early 1917, neutrality had thinned as submarine warfare intensified. Discovery of the so-called Zimmermann Telegram revealed Germany's secret overture to Mexico, proposing alliance against the United States. Public patience frayed. In April, only months after winning reelection under the slogan "He Kept Us Out of War," Wilson stood before Congress and asked for a declaration. "The world must be made safe for democracy," he insisted.[18]

History did not inch forward; it pivoted. Within days, the United States entered a conflict already soaked in blood.

On the eve of America's entry into the conflict, baseball remained refuge and ritual even as the world convulsed beyond its gates.[19] The national game had grown strong enough to bind a continent—strong enough, perhaps, to steady it for an afternoon. Crowds still rose for the seventh-inning stretch. Box scores still carried order into breakfast conversations. The diamond remained a measured square in a world losing its bearings.

Whether that square could withstand what was coming was not a question a box score could answer. It was a question history would ask of everyone.

And so, the story moves in two directions at once: backward into the life of the man whose name would summon a nation's stars, and forward toward the September afternoon when those stars would gather beneath the Boston sky.

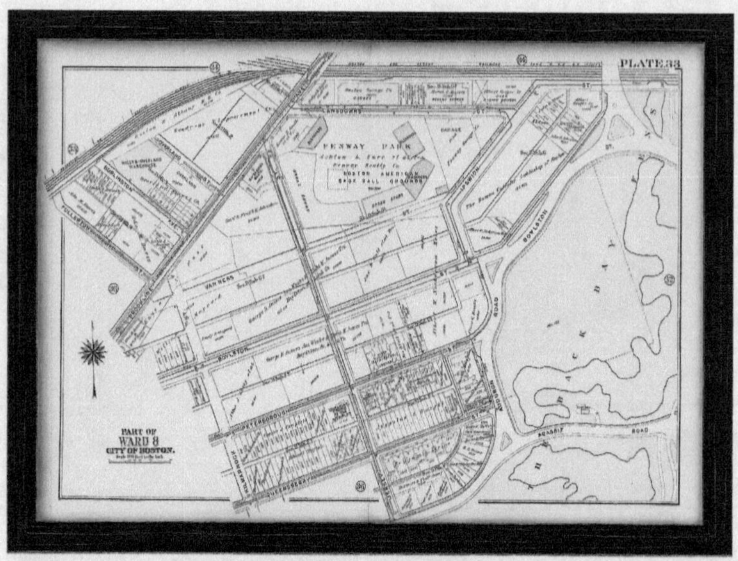

Fenway Park opened in 1912, set within a Boston neighborhood of streets and rail yards bordering the marshlands known as the Fens. Its first season proved magical, as the Red Sox christened their new home with a dramatic walk-off World Series championship.

ARRIVAL AT FENWAY

September 27, 1917: Game Day

The morning broke soft and gold over the Fens, laying a sheen of light across the grandstand roof as if blessing the day in advance. Before the gates opened a small crowd gathered on Jersey Street, drawn by curiosity, patriotism, and the need to witness something joyful. When the first stars appeared, the mood shifted. A murmur rolled through the line as Walter Johnson, his great right arm tucked calmly at his side, walked toward the ballpark's entrance. Tris Speaker, beloved former Red Sox turned rival, drew cheers from onlookers. Ty Cobb, unmistakable even at a distance, the most feared and celebrated hitter of his generation, invited a reaction that mixed awe, wariness, and admiration.

Inside the clubhouse, wool uniforms hissed as they slipped from lockers—creased from travel, faintly scented with leather and dust, some not even freshly cleaned. Well-worn cleats clacked against the cement floor in uneven rhythm. Canvas bags sagged open at players' feet, their contents rumpled and familiar: gloves darkened by seasons of use, spare laces, a change of socks pulled free and dropped without ceremony. Cigar smoke curled lazily toward the rafters. The chatter carried a note of amused disbelief: rivals compared grips, rehashed old matchups, and discovered with warm surprise how quickly competition could give way to camaraderie. Reporters hovered near the doorway, scribbling early notes, already weighing which angle would carry their lede: patriotism, celebrity, charity, or simply the rare magnetism of seeing so much greatness sharing one room.

By the time the band found its opening note, the park was awake, alive, ready for a gathering that felt—if only for a day—like the pulse of the nation had shifted to this small corner of Boston.

The crowd thickened along Jersey Street with a kind of quiet expectation. Men arrived in jackets and ties, felt hats tipped back as they conversed with each other. Women wore long skirts and pinned hats, some with gloves on. Soldiers home on leave or not yet shipped off mixed with factory hands who had traded a day's wages for a ticket, mothers guided children craning for their first glimpse of greatness, old men talked knowingly about Cobb's temper or Johnson's fastball as though discussing the weather. Vendors took their posts behind wooden carts, arranging peanuts, scorecards, and programs. From the ticket windows came the steady, metallic clatter of coins, punctuated by a rising hum of anticipation—this, after all, was a gathering unlike any Boston had seen: the champions of the American League against a galaxy of handpicked stars, all assembled to honor a man who had spent his life chronicling the soul of the game.

Out on the field, the park settled into its purpose. Groundskeepers dragged the infield dirt until it lay smooth as parchment under the watchful eye of Jerome Kelly, the longtime groundskeeper whose hands had shaped this surface from its first season and who tended it still with near-religious care. Chalk men traced the baselines in crisp strokes that glowed in the late-morning sun. The faint smell of linseed oil floated from the dugouts, mingling with cigar smoke drifting from the grandstand. Over the center field wall, an American flag snapped in the breeze, its folds catching the light with each gust. When the Red Sox finally emerged for warmups, the crowd responded with a rolling cheer that spread like a tide across the stands.

It was, unmistakably, the sound of a nation pausing to catch its breath—just long enough to remember itself.

Walter Johnson arrived at Fenway Park on Murnane Day as baseball's most overpowering pitcher—the "Big Train," whose blazing fastball and quiet dignity made him one of the game's first national icons. He would go on to lead all of Major League Baseball in strikeouts during the 1917 season, further cementing his place as the era's most feared arm.

Tim Murnane: ballplayer, manager, writer, scout, umpire, league organizer, executive, and one of baseball's earliest guardians. Few figures shaped the game's early public voice more than the thoughtful Boston journalist whose death would inspire the gathering of stars at Fenway Park in 1917.

2

THE SILVER KING OF BASEBALL

When Tim Murnane died in February 1917, baseball did not merely lose a writer. It lost its conscience.

In the days that followed, tributes poured in from players, managers, and executives in both leagues. They did not speak of him as a columnist or even as a former ballplayer. They spoke of him as something rarer: a guardian. Someone who had been inside the game from its rough beginnings and had helped shape what it became.

The benefit game that would be played in his memory that September did not arise from sentiment alone. It arose from standing, from trust—because for nearly half a century Murnane had given baseball more than ink. He had given it meaning.

To understand why major leaguers stepped away, uncompensated, from pennant races to honor him—why owners consented, why crowds came, why the afternoon felt less like an exhibition than a consecration—the explanation lies in the life that preceded the loss. Not to linger in biography for its own sake, but to see what Murnane represented at a moment when baseball and the nation were under strain.

An immigrant boy who found in baseball both livelihood

and language. A journeyman present at the birth of the major leagues. An organizer who helped impose order on a chaotic sport. And, most of all, a writer whose pen carried the weight of public trust. By 1917, no figure better embodied baseball's claim to be America's game. When he died, the sport felt obliged to respond.

An Immigrant Finds His Game

Timothy Hayes Murnane was likely born June 4, 1850, in a small rural village southwest of Dublin, though some sources list his birth year as 1851. He was the eldest son of Patrick and Bridget Murnan. The family name did not yet carry its final "e"; that would come later, as Tim reinvented himself in print. When he joined the *Boston Globe* staff in 1887, the spelling changed decisively. "Murnan" became "Murnane," and his byline soon shifted to the more formal "T. H. Murnane." Boston was not free of suspicion toward its Irish Catholic population in those years. Whether the alteration was strategic, aesthetic, or simply convenient, it smoothed the edges of his origins. The deep brogue remained, but on the printed page he appeared slightly remade. Baseball was not the only institution learning to professionalize. So were the men who narrated it.

Like many Irish families of the era, the Murnanes crossed the Atlantic in search of steadier prospects. Tim was almost seven when he arrived in New York in 1857.[1] By 1860, his father was dead, and the boy became man of the house.

Responsibility arrived early. So did baseball.

In Connecticut towns along the Naugatuck River, amid factory whistles and the rhythms of immigrant labor, young Murnane found in the game something larger than recreation. Baseball offered structure in a life already unsteady. It demanded discipline and rewarded cooperation. It allowed a boy of modest means to measure himself in public and to belong without pedigree.

If baseball offered Murnane structure, it soon offered spectacle—an afternoon that revealed what the game might become.

The Afternoon that Became Legend

On June 14, 1870, in Brooklyn, twenty-year-old Tim Murnane stood among roughly 15,000 spectators to witness the most anticipated contest professional baseball had yet staged. The Cincinnati Red Stockings—the sport's first openly professional club—arrived undefeated, their incredible sixty-five-game winning streak stretching back through the previous season across every town they visited.[2]

Across the field stood the Atlantics of Brooklyn, determined to puncture the aura of inevitability Cincinnati carried from town to town. The crowd pressed close, forming a living semicircle deep around the outfield. There were no firm boundaries between spectators and spectacle; the field felt communal, volatile. Alive.

MLB official historian John Thorn would later call it "the greatest game ever played," not for polish, but what it revealed about the sport's future.[3]

Cincinnati surged ahead early. Brooklyn answered. By the ninth inning, the score stood tied at 5–5. In that era, extra innings required mutual agreement, and the umpire assumed the contest would end in a draw. The Atlantics' captain began toward the clubhouse. But Cincinnati's Harry Wright insisted on continuing. The umpire was recalled, the players returned, and baseball discovered, almost accidentally, that suspense could be extended.[4]

In the tenth inning came a moment that would echo for decades. With runners aboard, Cincinnati's George Wright deliberately let a pop-up fall untouched, then turned a quick double play on confused baserunners. There was no infield-fly rule yet; strategy had outpaced structure.[5]

In the top of the eleventh, Cincinnati claimed a new lead. The crowd braced for restoration of order, but instead came chaos. In the bottom of the inning, a wild pitch advanced a runner. A drive into the outfield disappeared into the crowd, and one overeager Brooklyn spectator leapt onto the outfielder's back in an effort to prevent a clean retrieval. The fan was arrested, but a run scored. Then the Atlantics' Bob Ferguson—right-handed by habit and seeking to hit the ball to the right side of the field to advance a runner—shifted to bat left-handed, becoming baseball's first switch hitter. He singled. An error followed and Brooklyn won, 8–7. The invincible had been beaten.

The consequences were swift: spectator interest in Cincinnati's team waned after that single loss, investors withdrew, and within months the club folded. Harry and George Wright soon relocated to Boston, laying foundations that would shape the game's institutional future—and taking the Red Stockings name with them.

For Murnane, the afternoon was revelation. Baseball was not static; it was improvisational, democratic, volatile. It could shatter myths and mint new ones in the span of an inning. It could force rules into existence by sheer ingenuity. It could enthrall a city and humble it before sundown. He would spend the rest of his life trying to give language to that alchemy.

Learning the Game from Inside

Leaving the game after witnessing such a transformation was never likely. What he had seen from the crowd, he now wanted to learn from inside the lines.

He was no prodigy—five foot nine and a half inches, solidly built but unremarkable—Murnane would never be the kind of player crowds traveled to see. He rotated through infield and outfield positions with the reliability managers prized. But he understood tactics, hustled, and endured. Later writers even credited him with helping to popularize the bunt as an offensive tactic, reflecting the tactical imagination he brought to baseball's early game.[6] Once he stole second by leaping entirely over a crouched second baseman attempting a tag, earning the nickname "the hurdling baserunner."[7]

There was toughness in him long before the press box made him famous. Years earlier, when a traveling circus offered fifty dollars to any man willing to wrestle a caged gorilla, Murnane stepped forward. The bout was brief and punishing; he emerged scratched and bloodied, grinning anyway. "I didn't beat him," he told his friends, "But I sure gave the beast a battle."[8]

In 1872, he broke into the National Association of Professional Base Ball Players with the Middletown Mansfields, a club that would not last the year but gave him entry into the professional circuit.[9]

Those were brutal years in professional baseball's infancy.

Gloves were thin, fields uneven, contracts unreliable. Teams dissolved midseason. Salaries vanished. Players drifted between leagues that appeared and collapsed with dizzying speed. Murnane learned how quickly enthusiasm could outrun structure, how fragile ambition could be without governance.

Two years later, while playing for the Philadelphia Athletics, he embarked on a midseason barnstorming tour of Europe—a remarkable undertaking for a still-young professional game.[10] The trip revealed baseball as export and experiment beyond American shores. In Manchester, England, Murnane made a running catch local newspapers called "masterly."[11] The reception amused him. An English spectator, he joked, might watch a fielder misplay a routine ball and call out, "Well tried, old chap!" An American fan, witnessing the same error, would bellow, "Take him out, the bonehead!"[12]

He belonged to baseball's formative turbulence, and he never forgot it.

Present at the Creation

Baseball did not stabilize overnight. By the time Chicago businessman William Hulbert—impatient with gambling scandals, runaway contracts, and the disorder of the National Association—moved to remake professional baseball in his own image, organizing the National League in 1876 and insisting on discipline where there had been drift, Murnane was already inside the game. Hulbert's reforms—franchises tied to cities, limits on player movement through the reserve system, which effectively tied players to one club, and the elevation of league authority over individual clubs—gave baseball its first durable framework. It was, in effect, the sport's Constitution, replacing the fragile Articles of Confederation that had preceded it.

Murnane joined the Boston Red Stockings—now the Red Caps—for the league's inaugural season, hitting .282. He stayed one more year and shared in Boston's championship, then departed for Providence the following season. Just before that season began, he married Frances Manning in Boston. Not long after, he gave up his playing days and opened a billiards room to support his growing family. Yet he never truly left the game. If his bat was set aside, his voice was not. Even as he tended tables and balanced accounts, he wrote, observed, and remained entangled in baseball's affairs—his mind fixed on standings, reforms, and the restless future of the sport.

For nearly two decades, Frances anchored the part of Murnane's life that did not appear in print. While leagues collapsed and reorganized—while he moved between the billiards room, club meetings, and eventually the press box—home remained the one constant. Two daughters, Mary Adelaide and Emma Louise, grew up amid the rhythms of a game not yet secure enough to guarantee a living.

Then, in August 1895, Frances died at the age of thirty-five after suffering from Bright's Disease, a slow and merciless kidney disorder that, in that era, was little more than a diagnosis without remedy. The loss struck as baseball itself was wobbling through economic turbulence. Murnane sent his daughters to school and buried himself in work. What had once been vocation became necessity. The game was no longer merely something he loved. It was what stood between his family and uncertainty.

Murnane was a "good, all-around ball player" in the words of baseball's first superstar, Cap Anson, but Murnane would never become a headliner. His statistics—respectable but unspectacular, a career .269 hitter in the National League—tell only part of the story. What mattered more was his vantage point. He watched baseball strain toward legitimacy: owners quarreling, gamblers intruding, loyalties shifting as leagues rose and fell. The enterprise was ambitious but brittle, its future anything but assured.

Yet even amid that brittleness, a new class of leadership was taking shape. By the turn of the century, the manager was no longer merely a field captain but a strategist, financier, and public emblem of discipline. As Murnane observed in surveying the game's leading figures, success required more than clever plays; it required one to be "a student of human nature," a man capable of steady command and personal discipline.[13] That judgment, he insisted, had to begin early, especially when scouting new players. "In picking out a youngster," Murnane warned in one column, "great care should be taken in finding out if the boy is level headed in an emergency."[14] The most prominent managers—Hanlon, Comiskey, McGraw, Clarke—were no longer drifting professionals but established men of means, many of them Irish-born or Irish-descended, whose ascent mirrored the game's own climb toward respectability. Baseball did not simply offer diversion to immigrants. It offered authority—and, in some cases, permanence.

Murnane chronicled that ascent closely, often with the eye of someone who had once sought such authority himself. He understood that the sport's future depended not only on rules and revenue but on character in positions of power—and that character, once compromised, was difficult to restore.

The instability was not merely financial; it was statistical and moral. Clubs accused one another of manipulating turnstiles to undercount attendance and shortchange visiting teams, who were entitled to a fixed share of the day's gate receipts. One owner later admitted he had added forty base hits to a player's ledger to lift his average above .300 and inflate his resale value.[15] Distrust ran so deep that a Brooklyn executive once remarked that he never entered a league meeting without first checking his money and valuables at the hotel desk.[16] Gambling flourished openly, in clubhouses, hotel corridors, and the shadows of the grandstands. The game's numbers, like its loyalties, could be bent. And everyone knew it.

From those years, Murnane carried a conviction that would define his second career: the game required order, and it required advocates willing to defend that order. The sport had to answer not only to profit, but to principle.

When his playing days ended in the early 1880s, he did not drift far. He reentered baseball through the press box and meeting hall, first launching his own publication, then joining the *Boston Globe* as sporting editor. The transition was not reinvention but continuation.

In later years, with a mane of silver-white hair and a high forehead that made him instantly recognizable, he became known as the "Silver King." The nickname carried more than description. In an era of industrial acceleration and civic upheaval, his great shock of white hair suggested continuity. He seemed to embody memory itself—a living link between baseball's unruly infancy and its institutional adulthood. In league meetings and press boxes alike, the Silver King presided less by authority than by accumulated trust. Men who disagreed with him still deferred to him. Younger writers watched how he framed a controversy before deciding how to frame their own.

In February 1898, he married again—Mary Agnes

Dowling—and the house filled with noise once more. Three sons and a daughter followed in quick succession. Friends observed that the second family seemed to restore him. Whether restoration is too neat a word, the effect was visible. His writing gained urgency. His involvement in minor-league governance deepened. He was no longer simply preserving baseball's memory. He was trying to secure its future, aware that the game's solvency and his household's stability were intertwined in ways he could not ignore.

Baseball's First Homer

In Murnane's columns, box scores became dramas. A clever steal revealed nerve. A pitcher's collapse exposed temperament. Heroes did not form themselves; they were shaped in prose, repeated until their qualities hardened into legend. For Murnane, promise alone was insufficient. "An ambitious novice," he wrote, "must be a student of the game and anxious to improve his weakness."[17] The immigrant slugger, the farm-boy pitcher, the cunning baserunner—these figures became archetypes through repetition and elevation. Murnane's style balanced lyricism with scrutiny. He liked to suggest that his prose contained just enough romantic fire to elevate the game without obscuring it. "I don't put much Shaksper [sic] or Longfellow into my gossip," he once wrote, with a wink at his own ambitions, "but I drop in a little Byron and a good deal of go-as-you-please, and I make the baseball folks know that I am getting after them."[18]

Part of what made Murnane's style special was indeed the way he lingered not just on outcomes, but on the emotional pitch of a moment. Describing a tense at-bat in 1888, he wrote, "Every Boston player was on his feet yelling encouragement to Nash; the third baseman shut his teeth, gripped the bat like a vise and shook it at the new pitcher from the South." The scene, charged with anticipation, collapsed in a single instant: "He was a shade too anxious, however…and the Bostons were losers."[19] The flourish attracted readers while the firmness kept the game honest.

Later writers would refine the form. Grantland Rice cloaked athletes in Olympian grandeur, writing of the "One Great Scorer" who marked not victories but character. Damon

Runyon infused the ballpark with Broadway cadence and gambler's wit: "The race is not always to the swift, nor the battle to the strong, but that's the way to bet." Fred Lieb chronicled the game's architecture and preserved its memory in detail, christening Yankee Stadium as "The House That Ruth Built." But Murnane came first. He was baseball's original epic voice, singing the game into national consciousness before others refined the melody.

He wrote not as distant observer but as former participant. His authority derived from dirt-stained hands and firsthand knowledge. When he praised, readers listened. When he criticized, owners felt it. His pen could celebrate, but it could also expose—reminding league officials that legitimacy required fairness. That dual capacity—affection and rebuke in the same column—made him difficult to dismiss.

In this way, Murnane helped establish a template for American sportswriting: lyrical but accountable, romantic but exacting. Baseball could be exalted, but it could not be lied about.

Trading a Bat for a Pen

If Murnane had been only a journeyman player—one more sturdy figure in the game's unruly first decades—his death would have drawn respectful notices and then been swallowed by the churn of the season. The outpouring in 1917 came because, after he left the field, Murnane became something baseball did not yet know it needed: a voice capable of translating the game to the public while holding it accountable to itself.

Back in the 1880s, baseball remained intimate enough that the boundaries between participant and chronicler were porous. Writers traveled with clubs. They sat close enough to hear the arguments. They knew which managers were bluffing, which owners were pinching, which players were nursing injuries in silence. The press, in other words, was not simply an observer of baseball's growth; it was one of the engines of it, shaping how the public understood a game still in the process of becoming America's.

Murnane also understood something else that many executives did not: baseball belonged to the people who argued about it. It belonged to the boys who memorized averages and the working men who crowded into wooden grandstands at the end of a shift. It belonged to the immigrants who learned the language of the country through the language of the box score. And yet that obligation ran both ways. "A little encouragement when the boys are in bad luck costs nothing," he wrote in one column, predicting that a supportive crowd could "go a great ways to brace them up for one more effort."[20] Spectatorship, to Murnane, was not passive—it carried responsibility. That sense of shared ownership—widely felt, rarely articulated—was one of the game's quiet miracles. Murnane made it visible.

He wrote with candor, but not cruelty. He could be plainspoken without being petty, and firm without expressing indignation. When he praised, readers believed him because he did not flatter; when he criticized, it carried weight because it was never merely for sport. An 1889 description captured his reputation: he was "clear and judicial in his judgment," quick to detect weakness, yet "just as ready to say kind words where praise is merited."[21] In an age when sporting pages could be a carnival of bluster, the steadiness stood out.

Murnane's columns did not read as if composed from a distance. They read as if written by someone who had been in the room—because he often had. In winter, when most sportswriters retreated, he visited ballplayers at home, sometimes staying long enough to learn the details that would color his writing months later: the way a pitcher trained when no one was watching, the ailments a hitter concealed, the small habits that revealed character.

One such visit took him to the Oklahoma cotton farm of Red Sox pitcher George "Rube" Foster, who warned Murnane in advance that he lived "the simple life and eat[s] plain food."[22] Foster had earned $9,000 the season before, yet Murnane quickly understood the claim after seeing him "in the role of pioneer farmer, enthusiastic over his hard work." The visit became an adventure, including horse and buggy rides through overhanging branches that repeatedly knocked Murnane's cap off, which he described in detail. "After 20 minutes (to me it seemed like a week)," Murnane reported, "we reached the top of the hill." Foster's wife would prepare a meal Murnane never forgot. "I have dined at many places from Chinatown in San Francisco to Boston," he wrote, "but never found any food that tasted quite as good as that cold lunch…eaten with a keen relish, sitting on a pile of new boards in the open field." This was the real focus of his trips: getting to know people outside the game. There was a reason for that discretion. "I make it a point not to ask any questions or encourage baseball talk while visiting ball players in the Winter [sic] time," he wrote. Trust, like authority, had to be earned by restraint.

His own home, meanwhile, depended upon the same care. The stability he urged upon the sport was the same stability he sought for his children.

Decades after his death, a reader wrote to the *Globe* recalling those winter dispatches—how she had followed his sleigh rides through deep New England snow to the homes of ballplayers who seemed distant and unknowable in summer. He had made their private worlds legible. "I hope some day the *Globe* will find another Tim Murnane," she wrote, not knowing it never quite would.[23] He also functioned as an early scout, traveling widely and steering clubs toward promising players—an eye that proved prophetic more than once.[24]

That intimacy also shaped the way he understood baseball as a game. He called it "a game for thinking men," a phrase that carried more than a hint of creed. Baseball's pauses mattered to him—the space between pitches, the time a crowd had to argue, to instruct, to imagine. The game did not demand constant attention; it invited interpretation. Its drama unfolded in spurts and silences, requiring both patience and perception. Murnane believed that balance was part of baseball's genius, and he was alert to anything that threatened it.

His standing quickly grew tangible and spilled beyond the boundaries of journalism. In August 1888, when Boston's club searched for a new manager, the *Globe* invited readers to weigh in. Letters poured into the sporting department. No fewer than forty-five correspondents wrote in favor of one name: Tim Murnane.

The episode is revealing not because he took the position—he did not—but because the public imagined him in it as naturally as they might imagine a respected captain at the helm of a ship. Some praised his discipline and eye for talent. Others wrote that his experience with men made him the ideal guide for a team that needed steadiness. One called him "without a peer" as a judge of players.[25] That so many readers would nominate a newspaperman to manage their club says something important about baseball's scale in those decades. Authority did not flow only from title; it flowed from trust. As one newspaper wrote the following year, Murnane was a man who would "call a spade a spade."[26]

Characteristically, Murnane declined the implied honor and even used his column to advance another man's name. Yet the moment lingered. It suggested that he had become more than a chronicler. He had become, in the public imagination, a guardian of the sport—someone whose judgment carried civic weight.

That is the key. Baseball was professionalizing, commercializing, and hardening into an institution, but in those transitional years it still carried the feel of a community endeavor. The sport had owners, to be sure. It had contracts, salaries, and disputes that grew more ferocious with each season. Yet it also had a public that felt entitled to care, to argue, to claim it as part of their lives. Murnane did not sneer at that entitlement. He validated it. In doing so, he helped keep baseball from drifting entirely into the realm of mere commerce.

His influence spread beyond the daily column. He organized. He advised. He led minor leagues as an executive. In 1891, he assumed the presidency of the New England League. The circuit had faltered and gone dormant, but under Murnane it regained stability and stature, serving as a proving ground across Massachusetts and Maine. He remained at its helm for nearly a quarter century, guiding it through the uncertainties that swallowed so many minor leagues. By the time it reconstituted as the Eastern League in 1915, Murnane had become as synonymous with its steadiness as he was with the Boston press box.

Yet not all of Murnane's convictions aligned with the old New England orthodoxy. When the question of Sunday baseball stirred public controversy, he resisted the claim that the game's integrity depended upon Sabbath prohibition. To Murnane, baseball's moral character rested not in the calendar but in its honesty—its freedom from gambling, its fairness of play, its discipline of rules, its access. He did not mock religious scruple; he simply refused to locate the game's virtue in abstinence alone. That position placed him at odds with powerful voices who saw Sunday contests as desecration rather than recreation.

The debate did not remain confined to league meetings. In

1908, the controversy spilled into the national press when aptly-named Billy Sunday—a former major league outfielder turned leading American evangelist, whose revival meetings drew crowds rivaling pennant races—publicly rebuked Murnane. Sunday accused him of belittling opposition to Sabbath play and insisted that baseball's honor depended upon restraint. "I have always been against playing baseball on Sunday," Sunday wrote in reply to Murnane's criticism. "Baseball is the cleanest sport in America," he maintained, precisely because it had been kept "out of the hands of gamblers." To permit Sunday baseball, he argued, would be to lower the game in the eyes of thousands who believed the Sabbath sacred.[27]

That a revivalist of Sunday's stature felt compelled to answer a sportswriter testified to Murnane's reach. This was no parochial dispute. It was an argument about whether modern America could make room for recreation without surrendering reverence.

The exchange was more than theological sparring. It revealed baseball's place in the nation's moral argument. Murnane was not merely commenting on policy; he was participating in a broader debate over how modern America would reconcile commerce, recreation, and conscience. Even those who disagreed with him understood that his voice carried weight beyond the sports page. In a country still negotiating its Protestant inheritance and its urban future, the baseball diamond had become one of the arenas where that negotiation played out.

Time, however, has a way of sanding down sharp edges. By October 1915, the tone had shifted. The *Boston Globe* carried a report from Omaha, where Billy Sunday was conducting a revival. The evangelist who had once warned that Sabbath play imperiled baseball's honor now conceded his own misjudgment in another matter and spoke approvingly of the Boston sportswriter whose views had so irritated him years before. "Billy Sunday Was All Wrong," the headline announced, noting that he liked Murnane's baseball because "he gives good stuff."[28]

The phrasing was unmistakably Sunday's—plainspoken, unsentimental. It was not an apology. It was something more durable: respect. That turn says as much about Murnane as any column he wrote. His arguments could provoke, but they did not diminish him. Even a revivalist inclined to guard the Sabbath could recognize integrity in a man who believed that the game's virtue rested in fairness and discipline rather than abstinence alone. That integrity was not confined to his opinions. It was built into the scaffolding of the sport itself.

Murnane helped shape the game's infrastructure in a period when infrastructure was still being invented. Guides and instruction manuals may sound quaint now, but in a country where the sport was still growing into itself, the dissemination of rules and ideas mattered. Baseball had to be taught. It had to be standardized. It had to be made legible to communities that wanted to play it and to readers learning how to watch it.

Murnane became one of the men who made that possible. He wrote not just to entertain but to educate; not just to memorialize games already played but to expand the game's future footprint. The details of those publications matter less than what they reveal: the breadth of his relationships, the respect he commanded across leagues, and the way he thought about baseball as a public good.

In an age before centralized commissioners and television contracts, authority traveled through print and persuasion. The manuals Murnane authored were less rulebooks than instruments of cohesion. They helped distant towns imagine themselves part of something larger.

His authority extended beyond publication and presidency. Murnane served on the Board of Arbitration of the National Association of Minor Leagues—the body charged with resolving disputes across more than fifty leagues. In that role, he mediated contract conflicts, player movements, and interleague grievances that might otherwise have splintered fragile organizations. The work required discretion and credibility; owners and players alike had to believe that his judgment rose above faction.

But the association itself was not inevitable. It had been born of crisis. In September 1901, as the National League and the new American League edged toward open warfare, minor-league presidents met in Chicago to avoid being crushed between them. From that meeting emerged the National Association of Professional Baseball Leagues—a collective framework meant to bind disparate circuits into something durable. Murnane did not simply referee its disputes; he helped imagine its necessity. What he had witnessed as a player—leagues dissolving overnight, contracts unenforceable, careers uprooted by whim—he now sought to prevent at scale. The modern lattice of minor-league baseball bears his imprint.

And through it all, the former player never disappeared. His writing carried the imprint of someone who knew the field as a physical place and the clubhouse as a human one. "I write from memory," Murnane noted in one of his early columns—a quiet declaration of method.[29] He understood the grueling travel, the injuries played through, the unease of uncertain job security. If he wrote about honor and fairness, it was not in the abstract. It was because he had seen how quickly those values could be compromised when money, ambition, and resentment took hold.

Indeed, he treated baseball's governance as something the public had a stake in, which was a radical posture in a period when owners increasingly wanted the sport to feel like a private enterprise with a captive audience. Murnane did not see it that way. He saw baseball's legitimacy as inseparable from competitive fairness, and he understood how quickly legitimacy could corrode when commerce overwhelmed principle.

Nowhere was that clearer than in 1901, at the fragile birth of Ban Johnson's American League. The league was new, ambitious, and hungry for status, eager to present itself as a peer to the National League rather than a mere upstart. It was also political. In the midst of this uncertainty, Murnane quietly let slip to the press that Johnson preferred the pennant winner emerge from one of the great urban markets—Boston, St. Louis, Philadelphia, or Chicago.[30] The disclosure landed like a spark in dry grass. What should have been a competition governed by play on the field suddenly sounded vulnerable to commercial gravity. The implication was subtle but dangerous: that markets might matter more than merit. It was a suspicion that would linger in professional sports long after the American League's fragile beginnings.

Murnane knew exactly what he was doing. He had played. He had managed. He had sat in meetings. He understood how narratives hardened into policy. If a league hoped to claim the public's trust, it could not be seen to nudge outcomes toward the cities that sold the most papers and filled the most seats. His leak was not gossip. It was a warning shot, a reminder that baseball's moral contract with its audience mattered, and that even a new league with noble rhetoric could be tempted by expedience.

The episode clarified something essential about his influence. Murnane was not aligned with factions; he was aligned with the game's credibility. In a period when baseball was professionalizing at breakneck speed—money increasing, markets expanding, rival leagues maneuvering—he insisted that legitimacy rested not on spectacle but on fairness. If championships could be steered, even subtly, the republic of baseball would curdle into commerce alone. That, to him, was corruption in embryo.

Nor were such concerns theoretical. In league meetings, Murnane recorded debates over alleged "sign tipping bureaus"—organized efforts to steal opponents' signals. In one such case involving the New York Highlanders (later the Yankees), an investigation cleared the club, but the resolution adopted by league officials was unequivocal: any manager or official found guilty of operating such a scheme would be barred from baseball for life. The severity of the language reflected how acutely owners understood the fragility of public trust—an anxiety that would prove prophetic within a decade.[31]

Murnane's willingness to prick power did not make him an outsider. It made him, paradoxically, more central. Baseball was still close enough to its origins that a trusted voice could function as a kind of informal regulator, reinforcing norms that rulebooks alone could not enforce. Players knew it. Owners knew it. Readers sensed it. When Murnane defended an umpire's honesty against a howling crowd, he was not merely taking a side; he was protecting the game's claim to integrity. At times, his defense of order took on a cutting edge. When a player named Tim Flood assaulted an umpire, Murnane did not soften his response. Flood, he wrote, "has a new record, and will now be in a position to go back to his trade and give up the game he was unfitted for." He similarly praised a Canadian judge who had jailed a ballplayer for attacking an official and urged American courts to do the same. "It wouldn't take many decisions of this kind," he argued, "to drive the bad men out of the sport." Baseball, to Murnane, was not a refuge from law; it was bound by it. A man who would "take a running jump...with his spiked shoes" at an umpire forfeited any claim to the game's fraternity.[32] Errors could be forgiven; contempt could not.

Murnane was not reflexively defensive of umpires, but neither was he blind to their failures. After witnessing what he considered a poor officiating performance, Murnane remarked that he "could pick little boys up on the street who would render more intelligent decisions" than the umpire in question.[33] Fairness, in his view, required restraint on both sides.

By the 1910s, his byline had become a kind of civic marker. His intimacy with the game never became abstract. In 1916, on the field before a Boston Braves game, he presented a gold watch to Brookline native Jack Keliher in celebration of the young player's arrival in the major leagues.[34] The gesture was small, but it revealed how thoroughly Murnane remained woven into baseball's living present—chronicling careers, yes, but also marking their beginnings.

The *Globe* was not merely his platform; it was, in many ways, his extended household. His daughter Louise, who joined the *Globe* staff after his death and worked there for years, grew up within its orbit. When she died in 1931, the paper marked her passing with the solemnity reserved for one of its own.[35] The boundaries between profession and private life had long since dissolved. Baseball and the *Globe* were not assignments. They were inheritance, and the institution he had served had quietly become kin.

For Boston readers, his account of yesterday's game was almost as essential as the game itself—not because he could recite the box score, but because he could supply what the box score could not: atmosphere, motive, consequence, character. He gave baseball, day after day, a moral vocabulary. In a country growing louder, faster, and more commercial, that vocabulary carried unusual force.

Architect of the Game

The conscience he gave the game in print, he also embedded in its structure. Beginning in the 1880s, Murnane authored and edited a succession of instructional manuals and organizational guides that carried his standards into clubhouses, sandlots, and league offices around the country. These were practical handbooks for a nation learning how to build baseball in towns and cities where professional clubs did not yet exist.

In 1884, while managing and playing in the Union Association, he authored *Guide to Base Ball,* emphasizing the emerging idea of baseball as national pastime.[36] He explained fundamentals that now seem obvious—level infields, visible foul poles, orderly recordkeeping—but were essential in a young sport still defining itself.[37]

His 1903 volume *How to Play Base Ball* enlisted leading figures such as Nap Lajoie and Cy Young to instruct readers in the craft, while Murnane's own contributions blended mechanics with principle. Players were urged to practice relentlessly, to abstain from liquor during the season, to subordinate personal records to team success. In companion volumes—*How to Umpire, How to Captain a Team, How to Manage a Team, How to Coach, How to Organize a League*—he addressed the architecture of the sport itself. Competitive balance required vigilance. Managers deserved financial investment in their clubs. Gambling had no place on ball grounds. Games should begin promptly and move with purpose.

These works were revised, reissued, and disseminated nationally through annual guides and sporting libraries. The guides were not slim pamphlets of advice. They were encyclopedic. Murnane compiled statistics not only for league leaders but for every player in every organized circuit he could track, major and minor alike. He tabulated gate receipts, charted standings twice monthly so readers could trace the arc of a season as it unfolded, and preserved records from towns most Americans would never visit. The depth bordered on obsessive. To Murnane, no league was too small, no box score too provincial to deserve preservation. The game's integrity depended upon the record—and the record belonged to the public.

In his 1911 guide, Murnane framed the annual volume in language that revealed how he understood the game itself. "Like the flowers that renew their old form and flavor each spring to gladden the hearts of humanity," he wrote, "this little book, filled with baseball exotics, makes its annual appearance this year for the delectation of every lover of a country's glorious pastime." Baseball, he insisted, "belongs to all sections and classes." Not all could be champions, "but we can all do our best."[38]

The sentiment was not ornamental. It was creed. He believed it in part because he lived it. Baseball's promise of renewal was not abstract to a widower who had rebuilt a household and staked his children's security on the sport's endurance. Baseball's value lay in renewal, participation, and effort. The game united classes and regions. Victory mattered, but striving mattered more.

One of his later volumes distilled decades of observation into a compact catalog titled "Murnane's Don'ts."[39] The list reads like portable instruction for players and citizens alike: arrive early, hustle, avoid cheap talk, accept the umpire's ruling, do not blame equipment for failure, think independently, never assume defeat before it is declared. The tone is direct, steady, and unmistakably earnest. The lessons concern effort, restraint, and accountability.

The early twentieth century bore Theodore Roosevelt's imprint—his rhetoric of vigor, discipline, and moral seriousness shaping public life beyond politics. Industrialization had altered the scale and speed of American existence. Immigration and urbanization transformed neighborhoods. The frontier was declared closed. In response, Roosevelt advanced a vision of citizenship built on strenuous effort, fair play, and personal responsibility. National strength, he argued, depended upon character.

Roosevelt did not invent those ideals, but he embodied them more visibly than any other figure of his generation. His voice set the tone of the age.

Murnane's writing operated within that atmosphere and reflected it. The discipline he prescribed on the diamond mirrored the discipline reformers sought in civic life. Hustle signaled seriousness. Self-command under provocation suggested maturity. Respect for the umpire affirmed faith in ordered authority. The ballfield became a proving ground in miniature, a place where habits of fairness and restraint could be practiced before being carried into factories, offices, and polling places.

Baseball was ascending toward its status as the national pastime during this same period, and its rise carried symbolic weight. The sport promised merit within structure, competition bounded by rules, freedom tempered by fairness. Through books as well as columns, Murnane reinforced those promises. He did not merely describe the game; he personified the era's belief that disciplined effort could forge both strong men and a stable republic.

And so, the September 1917 benefit game presents a deeper question, one that rests beneath the day like a foundation stone: why did so many people, across so many rivalries and interests, feel compelled to honor this one man?

National Scripture

By 1917, baseball was more than pastime. It had become a metaphor, a kind of national scripture—still holding an aura of honest purity, unshaken yet by the scandal that would erupt two years later and darken the sport's innocence. It remained democratic in the deepest sense: playable in streets and pastures, accessible to immigrants and natives alike, a shared language in a rapidly modernizing nation. Other sports offered spectacle. Baseball offered belonging.

Few embodied that civic dimension more completely than Tim Murnane, whose standing was rooted in lived experience, sharpened by judgment, and sustained by trust. He had played the game when its contracts were fragile and its leagues unstable. He had witnessed its transformation into institution. He had helped codify its rules, defend its fairness, elevate its heroes, and preserve its stories.

Even in the lean years of the Depression, his name remained shorthand for baseball's conscience. In 1932, a *Globe* columnist praising Red Sox president Bob Quinn wrote that not since "the *Globe*'s own beloved baseball writer and champion, the late Tim Murnane," had the city known so ardent a defender of the national game and its integrity.[40] Fifteen years after his death—and for years after that—Murnane was still the benchmark, and the comparison was not casual. In hard times, Boston measured its stewards against the memory of the Silver King.

When that authority vanished in the winter of 1917, the loss was not merely personal. It felt structural—as though one of the beams holding the game upright had been quietly removed. Baseball had grown prosperous; its chroniclers had not. There was no pension waiting, no institutional cushion, no commissioner's office prepared to assume responsibility. The man who had defended the sport's integrity for nearly half a century left behind a household still dependent upon his work. In a game that had learned how to sell spectacle and measure profit at the turnstile, a different kind of reckoning arrived. The obligation now turned inward.

Into that moment came an idea—not for standings or statistics or profit, but for honor. For memory. For gratitude made visible. The proposal did not emerge from a formal league mandate or marketing calculation, but from within the game's own circles—players, writers, and club officials who understood what Murnane had meant to them. They would assemble the finest talent the game could offer, suspend rivalry for an afternoon, and turn the receipts toward his family.

Thus emerged the plan for a benefit game on September 27, 1917—not merely to commemorate a writer, but to answer him. To prove that the game he had defended still recognized its debts. That it could pause its pennant races and remember the man who had insisted it stood for something larger than the score.

Baseball's early twentieth century was filled with outsized personalities and extraordinary talent. Here, Ty Cobb of the Detroit Tigers and Shoeless Joe Jackson of the Chicago White Sox stand together during warm-ups on Murnane Day.

THE WARM-UP

September 27, 1917: Pre-Game, High Noon

The park took on an almost conversational hum as the players spread out across the field—bats cracked in rhythmic intervals, outfielders called to one another across the widening green, pitchers grunted softly as they loosened their arms.

Walter Johnson walked slowly to the bullpen mound, each stride measured, his shadow long against the outfield wall. The first throw left his hand with a sound that was less a pop than a low, heavy snap, like a branch giving under its own weight. Even from the grandstand fans leaned forward involuntarily, as though witnessing a feat of nature.

Closer to home plate, Ruth cracked jokes with players on both teams, twirling a bat lazily in hand before sending a few towering fly balls toward the bleachers, each one greeted with a ripple of amazement. Shoeless Joe Jackson—in for the game and risking injury despite being in a pennant race—jogged in from center field. He glanced with approval at the outfield grass—worn thin in the high-traffic lanes but carefully tended all the same. Speaker squatted in short center, glove poised, studying the angles of the park as if reading a familiar scripture. The dugout chatter—some playful, some pointed—carried across the field, a reminder that beneath the spectacle these were the fiercest competitors of their age, temporarily bound together by purpose.

From the stands, fans called out names and were rewarded with nods, tipped caps, an exaggerated stretch that held a beat too long for effect. The closeness surprised them. How near the great ones were. How ordinary they seemed in these moments—shoulders loose beneath worn jerseys, laughter breaking through the practiced severity of game faces. These were not pristine costumes but working clothes, shaping the men inside them into something accessible, even familiar.

On the dugout steps, players paused to watch one another

loosen up. A pitcher rolled his shoulder, then tested it with a sharper throw. A hitter took a few short strides, then stopped to stretch again. Someone mimicked another's warm-up motion and drew a grin. Rivalries hovered, but lightly. For now, the game was still gathering itself.

There were moments when nothing happened at all. Men stood with hands on hips, breathing evenly. Others brushed dirt from their palms with the hems of their pants. Conversation wandered—to the train ride in, to mutual acquaintances, to places played and places still unseen. Someone remarked on the weather. Someone else agreed that it finally felt like fall.

The crowd sensed the rarity of it without quite naming why. They were watching the game before it became itself—seeing how it assembled, how it began. The structures that governed the season—leagues, standings, obligations—had not yet asserted themselves. In their place was something sustained simply by choice and habit.

At moments, the sound thinned to a murmur. A breeze crossed the outfield and lifted the loose fabric at a sleeve. The band adjusted its tempo. Light slid across the grandstand roof and settled into the infield. Fenway seemed to hold the afternoon rather than press it forward.

Later, as coats were gathered and programs folded again, this part of the day was already slipping from view. It would not appear in box scores or headlines. It would survive only in fragments—in the memory of a tossed ball, a laugh carried on the breeze, the feeling that something had briefly opened before it took form.

The field quieted again. The railing stood empty. Above it all, the park waited, absorbing what it had been given. The day had found its early rhythm. The spectacle was ready to unfold.

Ray Chapman and Walter "Rabbit" Maranville loosen up before the festivities at Fenway Park on September 27, 1917. Beloved for their hustle, quickness, and spirited play, the two infielders embodied the lively, hard-nosed style that defined baseball's Deadball Era.

Boston's famed "Golden Outfield"—Harry Hooper, Tris Speaker, and Duffy Lewis—patrolled Fenway with a combination of speed, instinct, and intelligence that helped define the Red Sox dynasty of the 1910s.

3

BOSTON, FENWAY & THE RISE OF THE RED SOX

The Murnane Game did not take place at Fenway Park by accident. It could not have happened anywhere else.

By 1917, the park had become more than a field; it was a civic stage where Boston rehearsed its divisions and its reconciliations. The Red Sox too were no ordinary club. They embodied the city's tensions—old and new, Brahmin and immigrant, establishment and insurgent. To understand why the baseball world gathered in Boston that September afternoon, one must first understand the theater in which it unfolded—and the lineage that made such a gathering feel less arranged than ordained.

The Red Sox we know today were not the first to bear the name, nor the first professional club to represent Boston. When the Cincinnati Red Stockings—baseball's first fully salaried team—disbanded after the 1870 season, their player-manager, Harry Wright, carried both the name and the professional model eastward, establishing the Boston Red Stockings and planting the city firmly in the game's earliest institutional soil.

Wright was more than a transplant; he was a builder of systems and expectations. In Cincinnati he had organized, played for, and managed the first fully professional club, and in Boston he carried forward both its structure and its ambition. He experimented with defensive positioning based on hitters' tendencies, an early recognition that the game rewarded study as much as strength. Even its rituals were taking shape. In 1869, Wright described how spectators would rise between halves of the seventh inning to "extend their arms and legs and…enjoy the relief afforded by relaxation from a long posture upon the benches."[1] One apocryphal story traces the stretch's emergence to a 1910 game when President William Howard Taft stood up and stretched in the middle of the seventh inning. Thinking he was ready to leave, the story goes, others in the crowd stood up in a show of presidential respect.[2]

Wright embraced professionalism without apology. He recruited talent aggressively and paid above-market rates to secure it—most notably to his younger brother George, who became the club's star. Both men would later enter the Hall of Fame, their careers emblematic of the sport's early shift from pastime to enterprise.

In time, the Boston Red Stockings joined the newly formed National League (NL). As rival clubs revived familiar names and sportswriters sought distinctions, Boston's team cycled through identities—Red Caps, Rustlers, Bees, Doves (coined by Tim Murnane himself after the team's owner, George Dovey), and eventually the Braves—before relocating decades later to Atlanta. But whatever the nickname, Boston remained embedded in the game's institutional foundation. Long before Fenway Park, the city had already established itself as one of baseball's proving grounds.

The AL Emerges

In 1901, the American League (AL) declared itself a major league, and Boston once again found itself at the center of baseball's evolution. A new club revived the Red Stockings, at times called the Puritans or the Plymouth Rocks, while the older NL team—soon to be known as the Braves—continued its own lineage.[3] For more than half a century, Boston would host two major league identities: Nationals and Americans, two visions of the same game competing for the city's allegiance.

No figure shaped this new order more forcefully than Byron Bancroft "Ban" Johnson, a Midwesterner with the instincts of a reformer and the ambition of a statesman. Founder, president, and quiet power broker of the AL, Johnson saw baseball not merely as competition but as civic theater. Where the NL tolerated unruly benches and combustible tempers, Johnson promised discipline. It would not be acceptable, for instance, for an umpire responding to fans' taunts to hurl a bat into the stands and hit a boisterous spectator. (This happened during a Philadelphia Phillies game in 1884, and though the umpire was arrested after the game, the charges were later dropped.)[4] His league would be orderly enough for women and children: cleaner, more regulated, more respectable. If baseball were to become a national institution, it would need to look like one.

Johnson also understood leverage. With the NL enforcing a rigid salary cap, he offered freedom from it. The result was immediate: established National Leaguers crossed over, bringing credibility and star power with them. The new league did not feel experimental for long; it felt inevitable.

Boston's Americans quickly validated the gamble. After finishing second in 1901 and third in 1902, they captured the AL pennant in 1903 and faced the Pittsburgh Pirates in a best-of-nine inaugural "World's Series," as it was often styled at the time, between the NL and AL champions. Boston won five games to three, staking an early claim to supremacy in the young rivalry between leagues.

At the center stood Denton True "Cy" Young, who had defected from St. Louis to join the AL. Young's greatness lay less in mystique than in mastery. He did not overwhelm; he out-thought. He altered arm angles, varied speeds, and disguised intent with surgical precision, keeping hitters perpetually uncertain. Across both leagues he would amass 511 victories—290 in the NL, 221 in the AL—an achievement so monumental that the sport's annual pitching honor would eventually bear his name in each league.

Team ownership shifted in 1904 when John I. Taylor (known affectionately as "John I.")—son of the *Boston Globe's* publisher, General Charles Taylor—purchased the club.[5] With a newspaper empire behind them, the Taylors grasped that baseball was as much narrative as it was numbers. They rebranded the team the "Red Sox," a shorter, headline-friendly variation that echoed

Chicago's recent "White Sox" moniker, and continued to invest in talent.

The Americans defended their pennant in 1904, but the championship series dissolved when John McGraw's NL Giants refused to participate, dismissing the AL as inferior despite Boston's win the prior year over Pittsburgh. Public backlash forced a reckoning. Beginning in 1905, the World's Series became an annual fixture—a formal truce in what had begun as open warfare.

The Red Sox played at the wooden Huntington Avenue Grounds, a venue as eccentric as the era itself. Its deep center field stretched to improbable distances, and fans sometimes stood in fair territory. There, in 1904, Cy Young threw a perfect game before 10,267 spectators—an event Tim Murnane observed firsthand, predicting fans would "hand down the story [for] generations to come."[6] Even then, the game was accumulating memory.

But lumber ballparks were vulnerable. Fires consumed several across the country, sometimes mid-season. In that vulnerability, Boston's ownership saw opportunity: a modern, fireproof stadium worthy of a franchise—and a city—on the rise.

A Team Ascendant, A Park Takes Shape

The Taylors' new park would not be another wooden experiment vulnerable to flame and decay. It would rise from steel and concrete on the reclaimed marshland known as the Fens—a permanent structure for a game seeking permanence. When Fenway Park opened in April 1912, it was not yet a shrine. But to Boston it felt modern, muscular, and slightly defiant, its irregular angles and sloping embankments already suggesting that this would be a field that shaped its players as much as it housed them.

John I. understood that ballparks were more than backdrops; they were assets, anchors in brick and steel. Owning the field meant controlling the surrounding real estate and anchoring the franchise to a physical center of gravity. Built in less than a year at a cost of $650,000, Fenway was both investment and declaration: baseball was no longer provisional.

On April 20, 1912, the New York Highlanders came to town

for Fenway's first major league game. Mayor John "Honey Fitz" Fitzgerald—grandfather of future President John F. Kennedy—threw out the ceremonial first pitch. The Red Sox won 7–6 in eleven innings. The moment competed with headlines of the *Titanic's* sinking five days earlier, a reminder that even as Fenway opened, history pressed in from beyond the foul lines.

What followed made the new park feel consecrated. The 1912 Red Sox won 105 games, powered by "Smoky" Joe Wood, whose thirty-four victories and 1.91 ERA gave the season the glow of legend.[7] But it was September 6 that fixed Fenway in the city's imagination, burning it there permanently. Wood faced Walter Johnson—thirty-three victories and a 1.39 ERA that season—in a duel that felt less like a game than an event. Tickets went on sale two hours before first pitch; by game time, fans spilled onto the field itself and refused to give up their hard-earned viewing positions. Mounted police had to clear space so play could begin. Players could not even access the dugouts because fans blocked the entrances, so the batting team was forced to stand idly in foul territory while their teammates swung.

"No other game in the history of the franchise," wrote Glenn Stout, "would ever have a bigger impact" on the ballpark itself.[8] Wood prevailed, 1–0, before nearly 29,000 spectators—twice the prior game's crowd—who watched as if the fate of the season rested on every pitch. Fenway had discovered its appetite for drama.

The World's Series that October deepened the bond. Boston faced John McGraw's New York Giants in a hard-fought contest that stretched to a deciding Game 8 after one game ended in a tie. Attendance dipped amid cold winds and a feud between Boston ownership and the Royal Rooters—the Irish-American fan club, of which Mayor Fitzgerald was a member, that had long marched into games behind a hired band, singing their trademark song "Tessie" and wagering funds with equal enthusiasm. Denied their customary ticket block, they boycotted the finale.

Even without them, the ending was operatic. Tied after nine, the Giants took a 2–1 lead in the tenth with victory in reach. In the bottom half, the Sox answered—first with a single to tie, then a sacrifice fly to win. A walk-off World's Series victory in Fenway's inaugural season transformed the park from structure to symbol.

By 1917, Fenway was no longer new. It was memory layered upon memory—a civic amphitheater where Boston's pride, rivalries, and rituals converged. When the baseball world gathered there to honor Tim Murnane, it did so in a place already seasoned by triumph, tension, and collective belief. The park was ready for a national moment because it had already learned how to hold one.

The Golden Outfield

Boston's brightest star in that enchanted 1912 season was Tristram "Tris" Speaker, the "Gray Eagle"—"Spoke" to teammates—one of the finest outfielders the game has ever known. He would finish his career a .345 hitter with a staggering lifetime WAR* of 134.9, but numbers only hint at the instinct that defined him. In 1912 he batted .383, stole fifty-two bases, and seemed to glide toward every ball struck in his direction. "I always could hit," Speaker later shrugged. "Really, I couldn't tell you how I hit. I just hit 'em."[9]

If Speaker was the headline, Harry "Hoop" Hooper and George "Duffy" Lewis were the exclamation points. Together they formed the "Golden Outfield," a trio widely regarded as the best defensive alignment of its era. George R. Holmes of the United Press labeled them the best outfield of all time.[10] They did not merely patrol Fenway; they reimagined it, treating oddities as advantages rather than inconveniences.

Hooper, slight and cerebral, possessed what one paper called "the most unerring [arm] in the American League."[11] In the decisive Game 8 of the 1912 World's Series, he produced a play that entered folklore. To accommodate extra spectators, a temporary two-and-a-half-foot fence had been erected inside the regular right-field wall, shrinking the playing field for profit. In the fifth inning, Giants second baseman Larry Doyle launched a drive to deep right-center. On contact, Hooper immediately

---

*WAR (Wins Above Replacement) is a catch-all statistic designed to capture a player's overall value, estimating how many more games his team wins with him than it would with an average player. The higher the WAR, the more valuable the player.

sprinted toward the wall without looking back. He reached the low, temporary barrier at full speed, glanced once over his shoulder to spot the ball, and leapt—miraculously snaring the ball in his bare hand as his momentum carried him over the wall and into the crowd. The Giants protested, complaining that the ball had gone over the wall and should be a home run, but the umpire upheld the catch. Joe Wood called it "almost impossible to believe even when you saw it."[12]

Speaker's genius was different. He played center field daringly shallow, trusting his speed to retreat on deep drives while positioning himself to double off runners on sinking liners that would fall safely against more cautious fielders. His anticipation turned the outfield into a chessboard.

Hooper, meanwhile, treated the rulebook as an instrument. A trained engineer, he exploited the language governing tag-ups, at times letting a fly ball brush his glove before securing it—freezing runners just long enough to double them off.* He even used momentum to carry catches into dead-ball territory (which would stop play), preventing advancement. His most consequential act, however, may have come off the field: he persuaded manager Ed Barrow to convert Babe Ruth from pitcher to everyday outfielder, ensuring that Ruth's bat would shape the sport's future.[13]

---

*Incidentally, Harry Hooper was at first more excited about a career in engineering than baseball. He worked as a surveyor for the Western Pacific Railroad earning $75 a month. The owner of a local team in the California State League asked him if he would play baseball for his club during his senior year of college with the understanding, as Hooper later wrote, "that he'd give me my release as soon as I got out of college." The owner soon sold him to another club in Sacramento, managed by Charlie Graham, where he was promised an engineering job alongside his baseball gig. Graham came to Hooper and asked if Hooper would be interested in playing for the Red Sox, mentioning that then-owner John I. Taylor would be in town the following week. Initially Hooper demurred, reaffirming that he simply wanted to be an engineer. Hooper agreed to meet Taylor for drinks that week, a warm August day in 1908. Over beers, Taylor told Hooper he understood that he was an engineer and that he'd be building a new ballpark in Boston and could use his services. Hooper said he was interested, at which point Taylor pulled the switch: "At the moment, however, we are not in immediate need of engineering assistance. Considering that for the time being at least we would only require your services as a ballplayer, I was also wondering how much money you might want." Hooper, advised by Graham, was told $2,500 would be a reasonable salary, but that he should ask for $3,000 that they might compromise at $2,500. Hooper proceeded to request $3,000; Taylor countered with $2,500 but quickly offered to compromise at $2,800—and Harry Hooper joined the Red Sox.

And then there was Duffy Lewis, master of Fenway's peculiar left field. Where other parks offered flat warning tracks, Fenway presented a sloping embankment rising toward a twenty-five-foot wall. Fans sometimes stood on that incline during games, in fair territory. Lewis practiced caroms obsessively, learning the angles and rhythms of what became known as "Duffy's Cliff." He did not adapt to Fenway; he domesticated it.

Long before the wall was raised to its modern height and painted green, it already had a personality, and Lewis was fluent in its dialect.

Yet beneath the trio's brilliance ran a current of tension that mirrored Boston itself. The city's political and cultural power remained lodged in the hands of upper-crust Protestant families. The Red Sox outfield told a different story: Lewis, Irish Catholic and working-class; Hooper, a Californian outsider; Speaker, a Texan whose Southern identity set him apart from Beacon Hill's Brahmin restraint. Their ascent did not simply entertain Boston. It unsettled its hierarchy.

Fenway was becoming more than a ballpark. It was a meeting ground—of regions, classes, religions, ambitions. And the Golden Outfield stood at the edge of that field, turning fly balls into theater while a city learned to see itself in their arc.

A City and Team in Conflict

By the turn of the twentieth century, Boston had been remade by immigration. The Irish famine had sent waves of Catholic families across the Atlantic, and many settled in South Boston, Charlestown, and other tight-packed neighborhoods that echoed the tenements of New York's Lower East Side. They labored in mills in Lowell, stitched shoes in Brockton, and filled the factories that powered the city's industrial growth.

Their arrival unsettled Boston's Protestant establishment. The Irish brought a devotional Catholicism rooted in parish life and neighborhood loyalty—an ethos that clashed with the city's Brahmin restraint. Shut out of finance, academia, and elite law firms, Catholics found employment in city government, joined the police and fire departments, and built political machines that traded patronage for votes. Social exclusion hardened into parallel societies—separate clubs, separate schools, separate neighborhoods—two Bostons sharing a single map.

The Red Sox clubhouse reflected the same fault lines, compressed into one narrow room.

In the team's early years, the Red Sox were often associated with Boston's Protestant elite, while the crosstown Braves drew more working-class immigrant support. Inside the Red Sox roster, religious and cultural loyalties divided the clubhouse into camps. Tris Speaker, "Smoky" Joe Wood, and third baseman Larry Gardner led a Protestant faction that called itself the "Masons." Duffy Lewis, Harry Hooper, and catcher Bill "Rough" Carrigan were aligned with the Catholic "Knights of Columbus." The nicknames were half-humorous, half-serious, but the tensions beneath them were real. Even if, as Murnane admiringly wrote, Gardner possessed "a disposition as sweet as the wild flowers that grow on the mountains of Vermont," from where Gardner hailed.[14]

Religion was only part of it. Region and memory mattered, too. Speaker, a proud Texan, openly embraced the mythology of the Old South and even acknowledged membership in the Ku Klux Klan. To Carrigan, a son of Maine, and to Lewis, steeped in Boston's Irish Catholic world, such affiliations were more than eccentricities. They were affronts.

The animosity between Speaker and Lewis was particularly raw. In 1913, Lewis—self-conscious about recent hair loss—asked Speaker to stop snatching his cap during pregame warmups. Speaker persisted. Lewis warned him. When the taunting continued, Lewis grabbed a bat and swung at Speaker's shins, leaving him sprawled in pain. For a full season thereafter, Speaker scarcely spoke to Lewis or Hooper—two-thirds of the celebrated Golden Outfield. Meanwhile, across town, the Braves surged to a 1914 World's Series title.

Publicly, however, the trio maintained decorum. After the Red Sox won the 1915 World's Series, Speaker penned a newspaper column praising Lewis and Hooper's play. The harmony was performative, but necessary. Boston prized excellence more than intimacy.[15*]

By 1915, the Red Sox had become baseball's model franchise. A new force had joined them: George Herman "Babe" Ruth, a broad-shouldered, irreverent, left-handed pitcher whose appetite for life matched his talent. Still more pitcher than slugger, Ruth was already impossible to ignore. Alongside him stood Hubert "Dutch" Leonard, owner of a devastating curveball and a microscopic 0.96 ERA in 1914.**

Ruth's arrival did nothing to calm the clubhouse divide. If anything, it magnified it.

Smoky Joe Wood despised him. During one pregame warmup, Wood's errant pitch rolled away; Ruth made an exaggerated show of retrieving it. Words escalated. Teammates separated them before blows landed. According to contemporary accounts, Ruth's Catholicism—and his refusal to defer—deepened the resentment within the Protestant wing. When Ruth later discovered that his bats had been sawed cleanly in half, no one claimed responsibility—but the episode lingered, another quiet mystery in a season already thick with rivalry.[16]

The fractures would not remain contained. In 1916, amid simmering resentment and management's impatience with clubhouse discord, Speaker was sold to the Cleveland Indians.[17] Officially, the move was framed as financial necessity. Unofficially, it marked the breaking point of a partnership that had never been as harmonious as its statistics suggested.

Boston lost its Gray Eagle. Cleveland gained a franchise cornerstone.

When Speaker returned to Fenway in September 1917 for the Murnane Game, he did so not as the face of the Red Sox, but as a visiting star—an exile of sorts. The crowd still recognized the gait, the shallow positioning in center, the quiet authority.

---

*In the same newspaper column, Speaker told a quirky story tacitly hinting that there may have been something amiss in the umpiring of the deciding game. Speaker wrote of a telegram delivered mid-game to Bill Klem, the legendary "Old Arbitrator," who umpired from 1905 to 1941, worked eighteen World Series, and was posthumously inducted into the Baseball Hall of Fame. Speaker wrote that he asked Klem what the telegram said, but Klem said "it wasn't anything much." Speaker went on to write, "It is an unusual thing to deliver a telegram during a big league ball game of any kind, let alone a world's series scrap. It is figured that the news may upset a ball player or umpire.Therefore I thought there must be something important in it. Whatever it said, Klem did not seem to be as sure of himself as usual during the next few innings. There may be a good story in that telegram." Whether he was hinting at a gambling-related threat being made to Klem or something else is not clear, but it was quite an observation to make public the day after winning the World's Series.

**Hubert "Dutch" Leonard is not to be confused with Emil "Dutch" Leonard, a right-handed hurler who pitched for several teams between 1933-1953.

But he belonged elsewhere. The moment carried the faint ache of what had been won together—and what had splintered apart.

The 1917 Campaign

The 1917 Red Sox were a study in contradiction: reigning champions, still talented, still combustible. Old alliances lingered. Old resentments smoldered. The hope of a three-peat flickered.

At twenty-two, Babe Ruth shouldered the staff. He threw 326 innings, won twenty-four games, and posted a 2.01 ERA while hitting .325 at the plate. The force within him was unmistakable. Three years later, he would hit fifty-four home runs in a single season and alter baseball's geometry. In 1917, the revolution was still gestating.

Carl Mays emerged as the club's steadiest arm, winning twenty-two games with a 1.74 ERA, his submarine delivery confounding hitters. Dutch Leonard faltered after prior brilliance. Ernie Shore and George "Rube" Foster (not to be confused with Andrew "Rube" Foster, the pioneering Negro League leader) filled out a capable rotation. The outfield remained anchored by Hooper and Lewis, though Tris Speaker was now in Cleveland, his absence a reminder that the Golden Outfield's harmony had been more statistical than sentimental.

Jack Barry managed while playing second base, steady but light-hitting. Everett "Scoot" Scott, the original "Iron Man," appeared daily at shortstop, extending the consecutive-games streak that would one day pass to Lou Gehrig. The offense was not fearsome. But the club was resilient.

By late summer, Boston had hovered near the top of the standings, spending weeks in first place and riding a ten-game winning streak. They finished 90–62–5—strong, but second to the Chicago White Sox, who would go on to win the World's Series.

If the statistics suggested steadiness, the season itself did not.

In June, a game against the first-place White Sox devolved into chaos. Ruth faced Chicago ace Eddie Cicotte under gathering storm clouds. The White Sox took an early lead. Rain began to fall. In the right-field bleachers, gamblers—"sporting men"—saw opportunity. If the game were called before it became official, bets could be salvaged. They rushed the field under the pretense of seeking shelter, but in reality, they were simply trying to halt play. When the rain intensified in the fifth inning—just shy of official status—hundreds more stormed the grass. Police were nowhere to be found. The umpire threatened forfeiture if Boston couldn't corral its fans. Fights nearly broke out between fans and players. "All hell broke loose," one account recalled.[18] Chicago ultimately prevailed in what *The Sporting News* deemed "one of the most disgraceful scenes ever witnessed in a major league ball park."[19]

The following week, Ruth supplied a different kind of spectacle. After umpire Brick Owens issued a walk to the Senators' lead-off batter, Ruth rushed to home plate to argue balls and strikes. Owens threatened to eject Ruth if he didn't stop arguing and return to the mound. "If you chase me [from the game]," Ruth threatened, "I'll punch your face."[20] Owens ejected Ruth, and sure enough, Ruth proceeded to punch Owens twice in the head. His teammates sprinted in from the infield to forcibly restrain him, and Owens ejected catcher Pinch Thomas for good measure, too. Ernie Shore, who had pitched five innings just two days before, entered in relief with Sam Agnew serving as the other half of the new battery. Agnew would go three-for-three on the day with two RBIs on the way to victory, but that wasn't the big storyline. Instead, it was that Shore proceeded to pitch *a perfect game* and recorded twenty-seven consecutive outs in relief. So Ruth, having not recorded an out, shared a no-hitter with his teammate, and the one walk he threw was the reason the game itself was not perfect—though Shore was.[21] Ruth received a ten-game suspension.

Such was the temperature of the moment: volatile, theatrical, combustible, and always one argument away from fracture. Baseball was institution and improvisation at once.

By the time September waned, the Red Sox were playing out the schedule's final measures. They had just split a two-game set with Cleveland when the calendar turned toward September 27. The season had not delivered a pennant. The clubhouse still bore old fractures. The city remained politically and culturally divided.

And yet, on that afternoon, the game paused. The arguments quieted. The resentments cooled.

When Boston gathered at Fenway to honor Tim Murnane, it did so after a year that had revealed both the sport's disorder and its power. Champions and ex-champions. Teammates and exiles. Ruth the firebrand. Speaker the departed star returning in a different uniform. A city restless with war and politics.

For a few hours, rivalry yielded to remembrance.

To read the box score is to see names. To stand in Fenway that day was to feel something larger: a game capable of drawing its own scattered forces back to a single diamond—not for standings, but for tribute. For gratitude. For memory.

Will Rogers—cowboy, humorist, and one of America's most beloved entertainers—often joked that baseball captured the national character better than politics ever could. He offered memorable entertainment on Murnane Day.

A PAGEANT OF SKILL

September 27, 1917: The Contests Begin

The long-distance throwing contest came first, designed to determine who could hurl a baseball the farthest. The late-September sun hung unseasonably warm but not oppressive—the temperature reached a high of seventy-eight degrees—filtered through a faint haze that softened the edges of the grandstand roof.[22] *A light breeze drifted lazily, tugging at flags and carrying with it the mingled scents of cigar smoke, roasted peanuts, and the damp earth of the outfield grass.*

Players were gathered in center field near the flagpole that was just past the outfield wall. Secured by steel tape, a string was placed from the pitcher's mound to home plate, which measured 375 feet from the outfield marker where the contestants stood.

Clarence "Tilly" Walker of the Red Sox opened with a heave of more than 383 feet, rousing the hometown crowd into appreciative cheers. His teammate Duffy Lewis thrilled them even more: his line-drive toss, low and true, landed 384 feet away—barely eclipsing Walker's effort and drawing an even louder roar. Walker jogged over, laughing as he gestured at the margin of defeat, and Lewis grinned back, the sort of friendly competition that warmed the crowd. Tris Speaker launched a throw that would have hit the catcher's glove on a single bounce, that's how straight it was—but his toss didn't have enough distance. Sam Jones of the Red Sox couldn't beat his teammates either.

Along both dugouts players leaned on railings, caps tugged low against the sun. Some swatted at the dust with their spikes. Others tossed a ball absently from hand to glove. A few men near the top step traded easy banter—speculating who had the best arm, ribbing each other for their warm-up throws and how the newspapers might rank their performances. A rumbling of lively chatter drifted outward: someone compared the feel of Fenway's outfield grass to the hard-packed turf of municipal fields, another teased that Lewis's toss carried more luck than muscle. The soundscape was layered—vendors hollering "Ice-cold lemonade!" and "Peanuts, peanuts!", cheers from the bleachers, the brass band letting off a short flourish as the crowd settled between applauses.

But then Joe Jackson stepped forward—quiet, unshowy, his cap pulled low. Most players favored a powerful, limited-arc trajectory. Jackson, as ever, defied convention. He accepted the ball without ceremony, took a smooth, unhurried stride, and unfurled an arm that seemed borrowed from mythology. The throw rose in a great, ascending arc—higher than any before it—carried for a moment by the mild afternoon breeze before descending toward the distant rope line. When it thudded into the turf at 396 feet, 8 inches, a sound rippled through the park like a collective gasp. A few players exchanged looks of disbelief; even Ty Cobb, arms folded and jaw set, gave a curt nod of respect. Jackson, the contest's winner, merely tipped his cap and walked away, an accidental showman revealing what his body could do.

The bunt-and-run contest followed, a test that bordered on mischief. Before it began, players gathered near the first base line, swapping jokes and stories as they waited for the groundskeeper to smooth the batter's box. The air carried a faint sweetness from crushed grass, stirred up by players warming along the baselines.

Mike McNally—reserve infielder, beloved teammate of Ruth's both in Boston and later in New York, and a player whose reputation rested more on grit than folklore—kicked off the contest, surprising nearly everyone. With a perfectly deadened bunt and a sudden burst of speed, he reached first in 3.2 seconds, tying the existing record. Red Sox utility infielder Hal Janvrin, Ty Cobb, the Braves' Walter "Rabbit" Maranville, and Harry Hooper each clocked a fifth of a second slower, while Cleveland's Ray Chapman finished last. But McNally remained unmatched. Months later, newspapers would still marvel at his time, wryly noting that if he knew anything about the art of running, he might have been even faster.

A home run derby by another name followed. Players were given a few balls each to toss up in the air for themselves to swat at. As players waited their turn, they shaded their eyes with their caps and watched each fungo arc into the pale blue. Small placards were staked into the outfield to mark where each ball landed, their white squares catching the sun. With each toss and swing, the crowd collectively drew in a breath.

Walter Johnson, more famous for the ferocity of his arm than his bat, lofted a ball 360 feet. Boston's Carl Mays sent one 373 feet. "Just plain, ordinary nervousness and stage fright" caused some veterans to pop the balls straight up or even miss them altogether, the Boston Journal later noted.[23]

And then Ruth stepped in. He grasped his bat and accepted a ball, setting his feet close together at first, almost narrow, his usual stance. A hush rippled through the crowd—not silence, exactly, but a tightening of attention, as if the whole park leaned forward together, on the cusp of a moment that would soon slip into story. He tossed the ball skyward, and in a swift, steady motion, he unfurled the great force that only the Bambino could muster: his feet shifted forward, the might of his body offering every ounce of strength to punish the ball. The fungo rose high, spinning against the brightening sky. His first attempt soared 402 feet, 8 inches, easily good for first prize. Fans gasped at both the distance and the height; the ball climbed into a powder-blue sky far beyond anything the park had seen before. "I doubt if I ever saw a ball hit so high," one Boston Globe reporter would write.[24] *A few pitchers exchanged rueful looks, as if to say, "We're supposed to get this guy out?"*

The sprinting contest came next: 360 feet, four bases, pure speed. In the lull before the race, players joked about who rounded bases like a runaway locomotive and who cornered like a grocery wagon with one loose wheel. The band struck up a jaunty march; the breeze carried its brassy notes across the field, mixing with the rhythmic clapping floating from the grandstand.

Again McNally fared well, circling the diamond in 14.6 seconds, good for third place—he had put his best efforts into the bunt-and-run contest. Harry Hooper edged him out at 14.4. But Ray Chapman—on his way to a career-best fifty-two stolen bases that season—won decisively in 14.0 seconds flat.

At last came the accuracy throw: a wooden barrel placed on a box at second base, one perfect strike the only requirement for victory with contestants placed behind home plate. Between attempts, players lounged on the infield grass, trading small boasts and playful ribbing.

"You're aiming for Worcester, not second base."

"Not surprised you can't even come close."

Vendors threaded through the stands, their shouts merging with the rustle of programs and the hoots and howls that followed each near miss. The breeze had freshened slightly, stirring dust from the basepaths toward the outfield.

Tris Speaker took a few attempts and came very close to hitting the barrel, but he couldn't do it. Tilly Walker hit the bottom of the barrel, which put him in the lead. Then, with a quiet intensity, Red Sox pitcher Dutch Leonard stepped forward. He studied the barrel for a moment, exhaled, and delivered a throw so true it seemed guided by invisible rails. The ball hit dead center, punching through the back of the barrel with a sharp crack that drew gasps—a perfect union of precision and force.

Winners in each contest received a ceremonial loving cup—a large, decorative, two-handled trophy—its arches gleaming in the sun. It was a small prize but, in the moment, a symbol of mastery. Shoeless Joe would go on to pose for photographs with his cup the rest of his life, one of his most-prized achievements.

Between events, the afternoon loosened its tie. Will Rogers filled the idle moments with rope tricks and sly, mischievous patter, teasing players and pretending to corral them as if they were cattle rather than ballplayers. Cobb and Tris Speaker—now with Cleveland but slipping back into his old Red Sox road jersey for the day—took turns on Rogers's horse and lasso, drawing laughter from the railbirds and knowing smirks from teammates unaccustomed to seeing either man so unguarded. Fanny Brice and the chorus girls of the Ziegfeld Follies drifted through the aisles selling programs, collecting smiles as readily as coins, conveniently "forgetting" to give customers collectively over $500 in change to swell the day's proceeds. From the coaching box, John L. Sullivan barked mock challenges, pounding his *fists into his palms as if the ring—and not the diamond—might call him back at any moment. Fenway had become a carnival—an oasis from the uncertainty that hovered beyond its walls. Everywhere, people leaned into the pleasure of it: the laughter, the applause, the shared astonishment at what elite athletes could do when freed from standings and statistics.*

And then, almost as quickly as it began, the festivities dissolved into a gentle settling of the park. The echo of Leonard's splintered barrel faded. Players collected their gloves. Rogers coiled his rope. The band fell quiet as the afternoon sun edged past its zenith, sharpening the shadows that stretched from the grandstand roof. A different kind of anticipation drifted across the crowd—quieter, more focused, more reverent.

The hour of spectacle had passed. Ahead lay the contest that mattered, not for pennant races or personal records but for honor, remembrance, and the rare joy of seeing the greatest ballplayers in America gathered as one.

The afternoon sunlight brightened the infield, catching motes of dust that floated briefly before settling. Outfielders strolled to their positions. Ruth walked out to the mound.

In that brief, breath-held silence before the first pitch, the entire park—players, soldiers, children, newspapermen—felt suspended in a single, unbroken moment.

Now, at last, the game could begin.

Newspapers announced the Murnane benefit game as a rare spectacle. The Boston Red Sox would take the field against a handpicked team of baseball's best for a single afternoon at Fenway Park.

4

THE ROAD TO MURNANE DAY

On February 7, 1917, Murnane stood in the *Globe's* offices with his friend and fellow writer, Emory H. Talbot, as he finished up his column. He spoke eagerly of his plans to travel south with the Red Sox for spring training in Hot Springs, Georgia, anticipating once more the ritual of shaping early storylines. He predicted, with typical confidence, that "all 16 of the big league teams" would someday make the resort their spring home.[1]

After a hurried dinner, he set out to meet his wife, Agnes, at the Shubert Theatre on Tremont Street in Boston's theater district. The evening's attraction was a new comedic opera, *Eileen,* expected to delight the city's Irish community. Murnane would have relished its cheerful conclusion, but sadly he would not live to see it.

He met Agnes at the Boylston Street subway entrance near his office and the two walked toward the theater, pausing often to greet acquaintances along the way. When they entered the theater, Agnes walked downstairs to drop her coat at a coat-check near the ladies' room, with Tim waiting for her in the foyer. A few minutes later, when she entered the ladies' room, she found a crowd gathered around a body laid out on the floor.

It was Tim. In a few short moments, he had collapsed in the foyer and been carried below, where a physician in attendance was beckoned to revive him. Three priests hurried to administer last rites. Within minutes, the doctor pronounced him dead. The medical examiner soon attributed the cause to a heart attack.

The death of the Silver King—"old sport," he called himself—stunned not only baseball but Boston and beyond. Murnane had been more than a columnist. He was a trusted witness, a steady interpreter, a man whose pen carried authority without conceit. Readers recognized in his prose a reflection of themselves and a version of the country they hoped to improve. He was the game's conscience, and his sudden passing felt jarring, almost indecorous in its swiftness. The mourning assumed the character of a civic observance.

That instinct had already found expression beyond Boston. In July 1917, as the United States began sending troops overseas, members of Congress gathered in Washington for their annual baseball game, with proceeds benefiting the American Red Cross. Lawmakers set aside party and committee to take the field together before a crowd that understood the symbolism without needing it explained. Baseball offered a grammar of cooperation at a moment when unity felt newly urgent. The game did not resolve debate or erase division, but it provided a shared language—rules everyone accepted, effort everyone could see, and an outcome that mattered less than the act of taking the field together. Indeed, baseball had already become one of the country's most familiar ways of gathering in moments of uncertainty.

Boston would soon find its own expression of that same impulse, shaped not by politics but by loss. What followed was not spontaneous but deliberate: an effort by players, writers, and executives to translate private grief into a public act worthy of the man they had lost.

Tributes Pour In

News of Murnane's death traveled swiftly through clubhouses and editorial rooms.

In the *Boston Globe,* his professional home, Murnane was remembered as "the dean of the baseball writers"—though, the paper added, "no one ever knew it from him."[2] He had seen the sport from within and without, and familiarity had not hardened him. He believed in baseball as "a former of character," and that it refined the habits of both players and spectators.[3]

Across baseball, the tributes echoed one another. AL president Ban Johnson called the loss untimely and deeply shocking. Pittsburgh owner Barney Dreyfuss praised Murnane's "straightforwardness and integrity."[4] Clark Griffith, owner of the Senators, declared that no man had done more to elevate the game with a pen. Tigers' owner Frank Navin credited Murnane with helping to shape the game itself. Rival executives, managers, and players spoke not as competitors but as custodians of a common inheritance. Murnane had been fair. He had been principled. He had been the game's conscience. He possessed, as one put it, an entirely lovable character.[5]

Boston's mayor, James Michael Curley, captured the sentiment in a letter to Agnes: "A bright and shining star of the National game has fallen, honest sport has lost a brilliant advocate and I have lost a cherished friend."[6]

The funeral at St. Aidan's Church drew politicians, newspapermen, and ballplayers alike. Curley and Congressman James A. Gallivan—political adversaries—helped carry the coffin. Babe Ruth attended. The *Globe* devoted generous space to the floral tributes, marveling at Murnane's hold upon "human hearts."

Yet beneath the eloquence lay a harder truth. Agnes and six children, two from his first marriage and four still young at home, faced uncertain means. There was not even sufficient money for a proper gravestone. Baseball in 1917 remained more fraternity than institution. It celebrated its servants but did not pension them. Sympathy flowed freely. Stability did not.

As winter yielded to spring, the nation itself moved toward conflict. On April 2, 1917, President Woodrow Wilson asked Congress for a declaration of war. He pledged the dedication of America's "blood and her might for the principles that gave her birth and happiness and the peace which she has treasured. God helping her, she can do no other."[7] Americans were summoned to unity, sacrifice, and purpose. Factories ran through the night. Enlistment offices filled. The country's search for common purpose intensified.

In that atmosphere, honoring Murnane carried significance

beyond sentiment. It was practical, and it was timely—perhaps even providential.

A benefit game could provide for a bereaved family. But it could also do something else. It could gather rival leagues, rival players, and rival constituencies in a common cause at a moment when the nation itself was being asked to close ranks. It could suggest that competition need not extinguish fellowship, that Americans could assemble peacefully under shared rules and memory, even as the world fractured.

Those who began discussing such an exhibition understood this instinctively. The event would not simply memorialize a man. It would affirm what he had spent a lifetime arguing: that baseball was a civic instrument capable of binding a divided public.

Thus the conversation took shape in earnest. The question was not only how to honor Tim Murnane, but how to do so in a manner worthy of his family and his faith in the game.

Precedents and Limits

Baseball had rallied for its own before. It had simply never done so with this degree of structure or scale.

When beloved Philadelphia Athletics' catcher "Doc" Powers died soon after crashing into a concrete wall while chasing a foul ball in 1909—in the first game ever at Philadelphia's Shibe Park—players organized a benefit exhibition to aid his widow. The afternoon included skills contests, but the structure remained loose. The game lasted six innings. Players rotated positions inning by inning. Only four clubs were represented. The gesture was generous and sincere, but informal.

Two years later, Cleveland staged the Addie Joss memorial game to remember the thirty-one-year-old star pitcher who took ill midseason and died unexpectedly.* Joss's death had shaken the American League, and stars assembled in his honor before a substantial crowd. Yet the contest remained confined to one league. There was no National League presence and no broader competitive design. It was tribute without synthesis.

Barnstorming tours likewise showed that fans would

---

*Addie Joss won a stunning 160 games across just nine seasons, with a career ERA of 1.89—second best all-time.

pay to see rival stars share a field. But those gatherings were commercial ventures, staged after the season and detached from institutional purpose.

What these occasions lacked was deliberate structure.

In 1915—less than two years before Murnane's death—*Baseball Magazine* editor F.C. Lane had already imagined something more formal. He proposed an annual inter-league exhibition featuring the sport's leading players, not as novelty but as affirmation of baseball's national stature—also an acknowledgment that no prior game had achieved this. Lane's vision suggested that the sport could gather its brightest figures, suspend rivalry, and present itself ceremonially to the public as the "real grand opera of baseball."[8]

The Murnane Game did not replicate that proposal directly. Instead, it demonstrated that such a concept could function. It united tribute, spectacle, elite selection, and structured competition in a single civic moment. Earlier benefits had been uneven or regional. This one carried intention. It would be staged as public ritual in a wartime city seeking cohesion.

The Powers game showed fraternity. The Joss game showed reverence. Barnstorming revealed possibility. Lane articulated the vision.

At Fenway in 1917, those strands converged. Sixteen years later, when Major League Baseball formalized the All-Star Game, the architecture felt familiar—not because it had sprung from nowhere, but because it had already been tested in service of something larger than the standings.

A Game for Tim

The date was soon set: September 27, 1917. And where else but Fenway Park, where Murnane had chronicled triumph and folly in equal measure, where he had praised the game's grace and scolded its lapses, where he had watched a young franchise grow into a power and a young ballpark assume civic meaning.

The choice was intentional. Fenway was Murnane's terrain. From the press box he had shaped the way Boston understood its team and the country's understanding of Boston. If baseball was to honor him, it would do so on ground he had helped consecrate with ink.

The plan moved quickly from sentiment to structure.

Proceeds would go to Agnes and the children. The Red Sox would take the field. Opposing them would be a roster drawn from across the major leagues, players willing to travel, to interrupt their seasons, and stand together in tribute. Managers lent their authority. Club officials gave approval. What began as grief took on organization.

The nation, meanwhile, was at war. By September, American troops were training in earnest, Liberty Loan drives crowded the streets, and newspapers carried dispatches from Europe beside box scores. Public life had tightened with purpose. In that atmosphere, even baseball was being asked to justify itself.

The Murnane Game answered that question before it was fully posed. This would not be a mere exhibition or a simple passing of the hat. It would assert that rivalry could yield to respect, that competition could coexist with unity.

Murnane had long argued that baseball formed character and nurtured citizenship. Now the game would test whether it believed him. Invitations were sent. Commitments followed. The city prepared.

Boston in 1917 was no serene backdrop for sentiment. It continued to simmer with rivalry, class against class, Brahmin restraint against Irish insurgency, old Protestant hierarchy against rising Catholic power. Mayor James Michael Curley—up for reelection in December—stood squarely in that turbulence, champion of working-class wards, scourge of Beacon Hill propriety, builder and brawler at once. To admirers he embodied democratic ascent. To critics, he signaled disorder.

War sharpened every tension. Shipyards along the harbor churned day and night. Prices rose. Strikes flickered and faded. Immigrant neighborhoods bristled under questions of loyalty while the old elite fretted over the city's direction. Even the approaching mayoral election promised fresh division.

Yet amid political, cultural, and moral strain, something unusual occurred. Leaders across factions lent their names to the Murnane Game. Rivalries eased. For one afternoon, the city accustomed to argument would settle on agreement: Tim Murnane deserved honor.

That convergence was deliberate. The benefit sought not only to aid a widow and her children, but to display what baseball, and Boston, could be at their best: competitive without cruelty, partisan without rancor, proud without fracture.

In a city inclined to take sides, Fenway would hold them together, if only briefly.

The Game Takes Shape

On September 2, 1917, the *Globe* announced the plan beneath a bold headline: "Big League Stars Play Here On 'Tim Murnane Day,' Sept 27." A subheading promised that the Red Sox would meet "some of [AL President] Johnson's and [NL President] Tener's best" in a memorial contest.[9]

The date fit neatly into the World Champion Red Sox schedule, though other games were scheduled across the league that would have half the teams in action. The design was ambitious. Boston would face an All-Star aggregation drawn from both leagues, supplemented by contests in hitting, throwing, and running. All proceeds, the paper announced, would be placed in trust as an educational fund for Murnane's children, three of whom were still minors.[10]

The framework revealed intent. A committee of newspaper writers along with former Red Sox owner John I. would select the roster. They met at Braves Field in Boston on September 5, with John I. having already received commitments from team owners that they would make available any players that were selected by the committee.[11]

Ban Johnson and John Tener were the first to purchase box seats, each sending $100 checks in support. An executive committee—Colonel Harry E. Russell as chairman; John F. Morrill as treasurer; John I. as secretary; and an array of club officials, civic leaders, and Murnane's longtime associates—would oversee the day's arrangements. The gathering was to be both ceremonial and organized, not a loosely assembled showcase.

Invitations quickly went out to players across the leagues. The proposed outfield alone of Tris Speaker, Ty Cobb, and Shoeless Joe Jackson suggested an extraordinary concentration of talent. The National League pledged participation, though circumstances would later narrow that presence.* Nonetheless, the intention remained clear: the leagues would converge in spirit, if not in full roster.

Benny Kauff of the Giants—once hailed as "the Ty Cobb of the Feds"—was among those selected, still riding the promise that had followed him from the Federal League after the Giants acquired him for $30,000.[12] Grover Cleveland Alexander, who won thirty games for Philadelphia that 1917 season, was chosen.[13] Heinie Zimmerman (a triple crown winner), Johnny Evers (a league MVP), and Cincinnati's Edd Roush (future Hall of Famer and the NL batting champ that season) rounded out the list. Whatever controversies later shadowed some of these men—Kauff and Zimmerman were both later banned for fixing games—belonged to the future. In September 1917, they assembled at the height of their reputation.**

Adjacent columns in the *Globe* underscored how closely baseball and national life intertwined. One report detailed Babe Ruth's injured ankle yet noted he remained the final man off the field at batting practice, driving balls through steady rain. Players' tolerance for injuries in those days was different. Earlier that month Tris Speaker, playing for Cleveland, had attempted to steal home against Detroit when his teammate unexpectedly swung and hit the ball directly into Speaker's face as he approached home plate. As the *Globe* reported, "Through the courtesy of Manager [Hughie] Jennings of Detroit, [Speaker] was allowed to remain out of the game one inning while the cut was sewed up, and then resumed his place in center, which was temporarily filled" by a different player.[14] Another article described Ban Johnson's effort to quicken the pace of play and curb arguments that stretched games beyond two hours. Still another explained plans to devote World Series funds to equipment for American troops abroad.[15]

Baseball, in other words, was not retreating from the war—it was adapting within it.

Across the Charles River, Harvard Yard was thinning. Students such as Quentin Roosevelt, John Dos Passos, E.E. Cummings, and Archibald MacLeish exchanged lecture halls

---

*This was in part because the NL games before and after September 27 were far away: Brooklyn was in Chicago, the Braves were in Cincinnati, Philadelphia was in Pittsburgh, and the Giants were in St. Louis. Whereas in the AL, Cleveland was already in Boston, the Yankees were hosting the Tigers, the Philadelphia Athletics had the Browns in town, and the Senators were home against the White Sox, meaning all AL teams were on the East Coast.

**For the reader wondering why Honus Wagner did not make the cut, 1917 was his last season as a player, and it had already been a few years since he was a premier player. He only played seventy-four games for the Pirates in 1917, ending the season with a mediocre .265 batting average.

for enlistment lines, bound for ambulances, artillery, and aviation. War pressed into classrooms, factories, and churches. It reshaped the city that would soon gather at Fenway.

Against that backdrop, the benefit game assumed a layered meaning. It was plainly an act of charity. It was also an affirmation of continuity. Institutions built for leisure and learning yielded their young men to service, yet the ballpark remained a place where thousands could assemble under familiar rules. The exhibition did not deny war. It unfolded within it.

For those who anticipated September 27, the promise was thus not escape but reassurance. Champions whose names filled columns would stand shoulder to shoulder in tribute. Skills contests would celebrate the craft Murnane had spent a lifetime elevating. The afternoon would show that baseball could summon its finest for a purpose beyond rivalry.

The symbolism was unmistakable. The armies forming abroad drew from varied ancestry and region. Sons of dockworkers and sons of bankers stood in the same draft lines. The same mixture would fill Fenway's seats: businessmen, machinists, students, immigrants, politicians. Baseball had long mingled difference on its fields. The nation would now do so overseas.

The day promised spectacle, bright uniforms, booming drives, the novelty of shared stardom beyond World Series fame. It also carried weight. Charity and competition merged into ceremony. The benefit was practical, yes, but it was declarative as well. The game would honor its own, and in doing so assert something about the country that sustained it.

When September 27 arrived the weather cooperated, clear and brisk, summer yielding to early autumn. More than seventeen thousand filled Fenway Park. Politicians appeared. Former owners and rival executives took their seats. Teammates and adversaries reunited for a common cause.

For a man like Murnane—who could remember a player's face decades later and recall the smallest detail of a long-forgotten game—the turnout was fitting.[16] He had linked generations through memory and respect. That afternoon, those generations returned the gesture. They gathered not only to raise funds, but to demonstrate what the sport could achieve when it assembled with purpose.

The game was ready to begin.

In 1917, Babe Ruth was still best known as a dominant pitcher for the Boston Red Sox. He went 24-13 that season with a 2.01 ERA while batting .325. Within a few short years, he would transform the game with a power the sport had never seen.

OPENING SALVOS

September 27, 1917: The Game Begins, 0-0

The warmup contests were good sport, a dazzling prelude that left the crowd buzzing, but the afternoon's true marvel—the long-awaited matchup between the Boston Red Sox and the All-Stars—was ready to begin. Boston Globe sportswriter and Murnane colleague, John Hallahan, called out the names of the players into a megaphone as they took the field, each introduction greeted by cheers that rolled from grandstand to bleachers like waves cresting along a shore. Even visiting players—rivals, normally—received cheers of appreciation.

The Red Sox went with their usual lineup, the one that had won two consecutive championships and performed well throughout the 1917 campaign. Harry Hooper led off and played right field; player-manager Jack Barry batted second and played second base; Dick Hoblitzell filled the three-hole and played first base; Duffy Lewis hit clean-up and played left field; Walker filled Tris Speaker's old territory in center field and hit fifth; Gardner played third base and hit sixth; Scott was at shortstop and hit seventh; Agnew played behind the plate and hit eighth; and the Great Bambino, Babe Ruth, pitched and hit ninth.

The All-Stars led off with the shortstop, Rabbit Maranville. Ray Chapman hit second and played second base; Ty Cobb, Speaker, and Shoeless Joe Jackson batted third, fourth, and fifth while rotating through the outfield positions; Stuffy McInnis hit sixth and played first base; Buck Weaver hit seventh and started at third base; Steve O'Neill started behind the plate and was eighth in the order; and Urban Shocker of the Yankees got the start.

Maranville of the crosstown Boston Braves led off the game, stepping from the visitors' dugout with the easy confidence of a man accustomed to commanding the moment. He was small by big-league standards, wiry and restless, with a quick grin and quicker feet—an athlete whose very posture suggested mischief, which his big, storytelling grin did little to alleviate. As he approached the plate, a murmur rippled through the crowd; many there had watched the five-foot-five-inch Maranville dance and dart his way through National League seasons nearby at Braves Field, turning routine plays into acrobatics and tight games into theater. Now he would open this extraordinary contest.

In front of him, Ruth stood on the mound, shoulders loose, eyes locked on his catcher's signals. The young left-hander, still trim in those days, twirled the ball in his hand, his expression composed but alert, as the faintest glint of challenge flickered beneath the brim of his cap. He knew Maranville personally and by reputation—knew he was no ordinary leadoff man, but a sparkplug capable of unsettling even the steadiest pitcher. The Red Sox infield shifted subtly, cleats crunched lightly on the groomed dirt as they readied for anything: a bunt, a slap single, a cheeky attempt to stretch a routine grounder into trouble.

As Maranville entered the batter's box, he tapped the plate with his bat with the slow assurance of a man entering familiar territory. The dirt was loose beneath his spikes, still soft, and he ground his back foot in a small, deliberate circle until he felt it catch just right. A faint puff of dust rose at the motion, drifting across the plate before the breeze pulled it away. He slid his front foot forward, carving a shallow groove in the clay, lifting another small spray of dirt at the heel's turn. He angled his bat upward, settled his shoulders, and lifted his chin toward the mound.

For a moment—before the pitch, before the swing, before the noise—there was only the quiet ritual that every ballplayer knows: the scuff of leather spikes against packed earth, the creak of wood in his hands, the subtle shift of weight as he roots himself into the box. The stance wasn't just preparation; it was possession. He had made this patch of dirt his, if only for a fleeting moment.

Fenway, noisy only moments earlier, now seemed to fold in on itself, every sound sharpening—the rustle of clothing, the chirp of an umpire signaling it was time to begin, the low rustle of the American flag in the outfield.

Ruth exhaled, rocked back, and delivered the first pitch.

The line between spectacle and competition had vanished in an instant. The game—this rare contest of champions and heroes—was alive.

Maranville then hit a sharp grounder to Barry at second and was retired for the game's first out. Chapman entered the box and performed his own ritual, then slapped a single past Everett Scott at short for the first hit of the game. With one out and Ty Cobb at the plate, the speedy Chapman decided to test Ruth's delivery and broke for second. Ruth delivered a strike, but Thomas couldn't hurl the ball fast enough to second, and Chapman slid in safely in what was described as a "marvellous [sic] fade-away slide."[17] *Ruth went on to strike out Cobb—Ruth's only one of the day. The crowd erupted as Cobb made an angry face, revealing his intensity and the seriousness with which the players took the game. Ruth got the ball back from Agnew and tried to nab Chapman walking off second base after the strikeout, but the throw went wide and into the outfield, allowing Chapman to get to third. With the pressure on, Ruth got his old teammate Speaker to line out to Duffy Lewis in left field to escape the top of the first unharmed.*

For one afternoon, baseball's brightest names shared the same field, with the All-Stars (above) taking on the reigning World Series Champion Red Sox (below). The gathering at Fenway Park transformed a simple exhibition into a living tableau of the game in its golden age.

5

THE STARS WHO CAME

The box score alone cannot capture what unfolded at Fenway Park that September afternoon. Nor can the lineup card, though it carried the familiar weight of champions: the reigning World Series Red Sox, assembled one more time before war and time dispersed them, sharing the field with an array of the finest players the game could summon. The day's electricity derived not only from who played, but who appeared and for what purpose.

They came from every corner of American public life. Ballplayers stepped off trains and out of rival clubhouses, setting aside standings, contracts, and caution to honor a man whose influence transcended uniforms. Veterans of the game—umpires, managers, promoters, writers—took seats beside civic leaders and cultural figures who had little professional reason to attend. Business leaders paid their respects too. They came because Tim Murnane had mattered.

Fenway felt less like a stadium than a meeting ground. The contest on the field was one dimension; the assembly in the stands was another. Baseball's past and present shared the same air. So did Boston's working neighborhoods and its drawing rooms. The stage met the diamond. The prize ring approached the dugout. The afternoon disclosed the reach of Murnane's world and, in doing so, disclosed something essential about baseball.

There were luminaries, men whose names alone could draw applause.

Some stood on the field: Ruth, Johnson, Speaker, Cobb, names destined to echo long after Fenway's wooden seats gave way to steel and concrete. Others settled into the grandstand, instantly recognized even among ordinary spectators. This chapter concerns those men and women, the figures who attended not for salary or publicity but from loyalty and regard, and from a belief, still common in 1917, that baseball remained one of the few institutions capable of binding Americans in unsettled times. To grasp the meaning of Murnane Day, one must look beyond innings and totals to the dugouts, the boxes, and the aisles, to the faces that chose to be present.

Their attendance signaled that the occasion had expanded beyond a simple benefit. It was memorial and reunion, declaration and reaffirmation that the game's connective tissue endured.

The Personalities

Attendees descended on the ballpark from far and wide, representing every corner of the baseball world and well beyond it. Among the first noted by the *Boston Globe* was baseball veteran John Paul Santiago Kelley, credited with introducing the game to South America, who came to honor his longtime friend. A fixture since the Civil War era, Kelley had umpired some of the earliest organized contests and was said to be the only person ever to celebrate the fiftieth anniversary of his first umpiring assignment by officiating another.[1]

Kelley's presence carried more than ceremony. In 1917, baseball remained young enough that its pioneers still mingled with active players. Kelley thus embodied a living link to the sport's beginnings, and his presence affirmed that the afternoon concerned inheritance as much as stardom. Murnane had chronicled evolution. Kelley had witnessed its origins.

In a nearby box sat George Wright: pioneering shortstop, future Hall of Famer, and publisher of several of Murnane's books through the Wright and Ditson firm, which also served as ticket agent for the event. He attended with his sons, Beals and Irving, accomplished tennis champions. Beals, thirty-eight, had claimed the 1905 U.S. National Championship and two gold medals at the 1904 St. Louis Olympics before, of all things, a foul ball at a baseball game hit him and curtailed his career. Irving, thirty-five, had captured the 1907 Long Island Lawn Tennis Championship and would later secure mixed doubles titles at the U.S. Nationals in 1917 and 1918.

Their attendance reflected the Wright family's enduring sporting lineage. George's brother, Harry, had earlier assembled and managed the pioneering Cincinnati Red Stockings before founding the Boston Red Stockings. The Wright name was structural, not decorative. That they appeared together, publisher and sons, suggested how thoroughly sport and family intertwined in that era.

Joining the Wrights was painter and educator Joseph DeCamp, a leading figure of the Boston School, whose canvases fused Impressionist light with the discipline of traditional form. His presence felt less ceremonial than symbolic. For the painters of his circle, light was never fixed; it shimmered, softened edges, transformed the ordinary into something briefly luminous. Fenway that afternoon seemed to behave the same way. White uniforms flared against the green field like strokes of paint; the crowd rose and settled in waves of color and sound; the September sun laid a warm glaze across the diamond. An artist's attendance was no accident. It suggested that the day, like a canvas, was meant to be witnessed and held—its atmosphere as important as its outcome. Baseball and Boston's cultural life did not sit in separate frames. They shared a palette. And Murnane, attentive to mood as much as score, had long understood how to render the game in light as well as line.

Other familiar faces filled the stands. Walter Maranville's father journeyed from Springfield to watch his son. The venerable John Morrill, former infielder-manager of the Boston Beaneaters and close friend of Murnane, appeared as one of the city's most respected elder statesmen. Nearby was Miah Murray, longtime trainer of the Boston Americans and Red Sox, remembered for his steady presence during the club's championship years.

Charles A. Marston—celebrated as the man who discovered Nap Lajoie in New England's textile leagues—was there, as was Sport Hermann, a well-known baseball promoter and occasional journalist who frequently appeared at major exhibitions. Tom Barry, the former Boston baseball writer and prominent sporting editor, was likewise noted in the stands.

Major Frank Briggs, nationally known sportsman and future member of multiple U.S. Olympic Committees, attended. Archie Hurlburt, Boston political insider and friend of the future president Calvin Coolidge, was present as well.

Politics too claimed its place in the grandstand. Congressman James A. Gallivan attended beside Mayor James Michael Curley despite their rivalry, just as they had done as pallbearers at Murnane's funeral. Their presence signaled that Murnane Day had crossed beyond sport into civic ritual, drawing the city's political class deeper into its orbit.

Read in sequence, the names can feel like an accumulation. Yet the accumulation is the point. The sport's elders, intermediaries, and public figures converged not out of obligation, but out of recognition. Murnane's influence had reached across these circles for decades. The benefit game brought those circles into view.

The Entertainers

The constellation of entertainers who appeared that afternoon reflected just how much weight the day carried. Chief among them was Will Rogers—a name that still rings faintly familiar to older readers, though the sheer scale of his fame has long since receded into history. In his prime, Rogers was more than a performer; he was a national institution. He straddled every medium—stage, screen, radio, and newspaper—with a lasso in one hand and the pulse of the American people in the other. One might imagine a single figure who combined the warmth of a beloved comedian, the credibility of a trusted commentator, and the ubiquity of a modern media personality. Rogers starred in dozens of films and ranked among the country's leading box-office draws—the Tom Hanks or George Clooney of his age. His syndicated newspaper column, read by millions, offered frank wisdom on politics, the economy, and world affairs. His radio voice—gentle, humorous, and unpretentious—cut across class and geography. When Rogers spoke, presidents and farmers alike leaned closer, believing, perhaps rightly, that he understood them both.

By September 1917, Rogers had not yet reached the summit of his renown, but he was already a principal attraction and unquestionably one of the stars of Murnane Day. Before the game began, he rode a horse onto the field, swinging a broad lasso that spanned some thirty feet in diameter with the easy grace of a man born to it. As he trotted at full speed along the outfield grass, he tried to rope as many players as he could, calling out to the crowd, which roared with delight, with fans even daring him to rope the police officers stationed nearby.

When he passed the reins to Tris Speaker and then to Cobb, spectacle layered upon spectacle. Cowboy met ballplayer. Rival met entertainer. The *Globe* summarized the scene with dry humor: "While they say that the Great Tyrus cannot be beaten, the gent with the rope at least tied him yesterday."[2]

The levity did not trivialize the day. It steadied it. In wartime, laughter served a civic function.

Meanwhile, in the stands was Fanny Brice, rising star of the *Ziegfeld Follies*, who amused herself and those around her by hawking programs to eager fans. Even in that impromptu role, she was impossible to miss—her expressive face and quick wit drawing laughter from anyone within earshot. Brice had already become a sensation on Broadway, famous for the comic songs that mixed humor with heartbreak, like "Second Hand Rose" and "My Man." She embodied a new kind of performer: sharp and self-aware, as willing to parody glamour as to bask in it. To the crowd at Fenway that afternoon, she brought a flash of New York sophistication to the city's working-class exuberance. Years later, her legend would be rekindled through *Funny Girl* and Barbra Streisand's portrayal of her, but in 1917 she needed no revival. Brice was magnetic in her own right, and when she conveniently neglected to return change while selling programs, the proceeds quietly swelled the Murnane Memorial Fund.

John L. Sullivan, the "Boston Strong Boy," strode into the ballpark like a living monument to another age. Once the most feared man in the boxing ring, Sullivan was by 1917 a graying legend, his waistline softened but his presence undiminished. The crowd rose instinctively at the sight of him—his late arrival only heightened the drama—as if welcoming a conquering hero rather than a retired pugilist. For decades, John L. had personified raw American grit: the first heavyweight champion of the gloved era, the man who brought prizefighting out of the saloon and into the national imagination. Now he was back on home soil, cheered by men who had once crowded into smoky halls to hear news of his latest knockout.

His reputation as a fighter had long overshadowed his reputation as a conversationalist, yet contemporaries often noted the latter. "His language is good, and his words well chosen," wrote the *Denver Tribune* decades earlier.[3]

Ironically, boxing had drawn him away from baseball, his earliest passion. His parents had once envisioned the priesthood, and he briefly enrolled at Boston College. The diamond, and later the ring, proved more compelling. Baseball offered modest wages. Boxing offered more. "I have made a great deal of money, and spent a great deal," he concluded at the ripe age of twenty-five.[4]

A curious earlier episode involving Murnane illustrated both Sullivan's temperament and Murnane's reputation. In December 1899, Sullivan received a telephone call from someone claiming to be Tim Murnane and requesting a small loan. The voice sounded uncertain, yet the name inspired trust. Sullivan said he didn't have a lot on him, but if Murnane needed it, he wanted to help. He invited a messenger to come to his hotel room and collect the funds. When the messenger arrived with a handwritten note, purportedly from Murnane, asking for a larger sum, Sullivan complied.

In later telling the story at the hotel bar to a *Globe* reporter, Sullivan displayed the note. The reporter, who knew his colleague's Murnane's handwriting, immediately said it was an obvious forgery, confirming that Murnane was nowhere near the hotel and had not been there for months. The paper described a look of sadness crossing the former champion's face. The impostor had relied upon Murnane's integrity; after all, Murnane was "a good fellow, one of the best" in Sullivan's words. Sullivan admitted the story, embarrassed but unresentful.[5]

The episode revealed as much about character as about deception. Sullivan could not readily imagine someone exploiting Murnane's name. That instinctive trust testified to the writer's standing.

Eighteen years later, Sullivan stood at Fenway coaching

first base in playful fashion. Within months he would succumb to heart disease, his appearance at the game one of his final public moments.

It was a convergence few other spaces in American life could have sustained. The humorist did not diminish the pugilist. The actress did not eclipse the athlete. The politician did not commandeer the stage. Each occupied space within the same frame, distinct yet contained.

The afternoon suggested that baseball's national claim rested not merely on popularity but on permeability. It could absorb theater without dissolving into performance, absorb politics without surrendering to partisanship, absorb spectacle without forfeiting seriousness. Boundaries remained visible even as they flexed.

That permeability was precisely what Murnane had defended for decades. In his columns he treated the game as worthy of literary care yet accessible to dockworker and banker alike. He wrote of ballplayers as craftsmen and as characters. He moved between clubhouse and drawing room without strain. The crowd gathered that September day resembled the world he had long inhabited in print.

To be sure, there was reassurance in that gathering. If figures from such varied domains could sit within a few rows of one another and cheer the same bunt, the same rope trick, the same towering drive, then perhaps the republic itself retained a similar capacity. Baseball offered more than escape; it offered rehearsal. It modeled coexistence within agreed limits.

The irony is that such coexistence depended on conditions easily unsettled. Proximity. Shared ritual. Confidence in the fairness of rules and the integrity of participants. Each would soon face strain. War would thin rosters. Scandal would erode faith. Commerce would reshape intimacy.

Yet on that afternoon the cohesion felt real. The stage and the diamond, the rope and the glove, the champion boxer and the pennant contender, the mayor and the mill worker stood in mutual recognition. Difference was not erased. It was held in equilibrium. And equilibrium, history would soon prove, is harder to preserve than to applaud.

The Participants

The roster reflected comparable range. It featured steady professionals, emerging talents, established champions, and men whose futures would later turn unexpectedly.

George Buck Weaver arrived as a sturdy third baseman for the Chicago White Sox, respected for reliability rather than flamboyance. He approached the game as craft. That he left his club during a pennant race to participate in a benefit exhibition spoke to the priorities of the time.

Ray Chapman, Cleveland's cerebral shortstop, represented a modern, anticipatory style of play. Three years later, he would become the only major leaguer killed by a pitch, struck by Carl Mays. In 1917, that tragedy lay ahead.

Mays himself appeared at Fenway that day. Known for pitching high and inside—Ty Cobb referred to Mays as "that no good son of a bitch" for his headhunting, and even threw his bat at him two years earlier after a beaning—Mays later gained notoriety for the fatal pitch to Chapman.[6] On Murnane Day, he was simply another competitor lending his presence.

Duffy Lewis, though he failed to place among the leaders in the sprint contest, was immortalized in famed cartoonist Wallace Goldsmith's illustration. Bat in hand, flanked by teammates spelling "RUNS," Lewis appeared beneath the caption "Mebby I don't get no [loving] cups for speed, but you notice what happens in a big game or series."[7] Goldsmith's rendering distilled Lewis's reputation for clutch hitting into humor.[8]

Urban Shocker of the St. Louis Browns arrived at Fenway as one of the American League's most formidable pitchers. Born Urbain Jacques Shockcor, he had climbed steadily through perseverance. Pneumonia contracted in wartime service would later threaten his career.

Howard Ehmke, tall and clever, belonged to a newer generation of pitchers attentive to mechanics and preparation. His greatest moment lay years ahead. At Fenway, he was still ascending.

Catchers Wally Schang and Steve O'Neill represented baseball's interior vantage point. They understood the game pitch by pitch. Stuffy McInnis supplied steadiness. Rabbit Maranville—the "cocky, hard-boiled little man" Murnane admired for being "aggressive, smart, quick with his answers, a clown, idolized by the fans, all color and personality"—brought exuberance and the willingness to travel by train overnight after a double-header in Cincinnati to be present.[9]

Connie Mack did not arrive at Fenway so much as *preside* over it with characteristic composure. Tall, impeccably dressed, and unmistakably dignified, Mack embodied baseball's conscience as much as its authority and managed the All-Stars. As manager and part-owner of the Philadelphia Athletics, he believed character equaled talent—which is why he skipped the A's game that day to be in Boston.

Mack and Murnane shared conviction that the game required stewardship and explanation. Mack's attendance signified acknowledgment of Murnane's influence on public understanding. His presence suggested that baseball itself had come to pay respect.

Hughie Jennings, the Tigers manager, offered contrasting energy. Brilliant and emotional, Jennings understood volatile genius. His participation testified to regard for honest chronicling, even when uncomfortable.

Individually, each figure could anchor a narrative. Collectively, they compressed the sport's ecosystem into a single afternoon.

The Motivation

Considered separately, attendance might be attributed to friendship or prestige. Considered together, it reveals a pattern.

Baseball in 1917 operated within overlapping relationships that crossed profession and class. Players knew writers. Writers knew managers. Promoters knew entertainers. Fighters admired infielders. Public life intertwined.

Murnane had spent decades within that network, chronicling without condescension and criticizing without malice. Those assembled recognized the value of that balance.

Beneath the warmth lay fragility. War threatened. The sport's future was unsettled. Some present would soon encounter scandal or sorrow. Others would shepherd baseball through disruption.

For several hours, uncertainty receded. The stars who appeared affirmed a version of baseball grounded in proximity, ritual, and trust. It was a version built on personal relationships rather than bureaucratic safeguards, on reputation rather than regulation.

Such a version could flourish in an afternoon of tribute. It was less certain it could withstand war, commercialization, and scandal. Within a few short years, baseball would confront questions about loyalty, integrity, and authority that no rope trick or reunion could quiet.

On Murnane Day, the game demonstrated what it could be at its most cohesive. History would soon test whether that cohesion could endure.

Fanny Brice, one of America's most beloved entertainers, brought Broadway glamour and comic charm to Fenway Park on Murnane Day, where she sold programs to help raise money for the Murnane family. Her appearance reflected the growing intersection of baseball, celebrity, and popular culture in war-time America.

Heavyweight boxing champion John L. Sullivan sits beside Red Sox manager Jimmy Collins in an earlier Boston baseball scene that captured the close ties between the city's sporting worlds. By the time of Murnane Day in 1917, Sullivan remained a towering local celebrity and delighted the Fenway crowd by coaching first base for the Red Sox during the exhibition.

Tris Speaker combined instinct and calculation in center field, positioning himself with a precision that made the extraordinary seem routine. His prowess at the plate was the stuff of legend; he hit .352 in 1917 and finished his 22-year career a lifetime .345 hitter.

CHESS ON GRASS

September 27, 1917: Bottom of the First, 0-0

The Red Sox jogged into the dugout, the familiar retreat home after retiring the side, eager to get to the plate. The announcer thundered the lineup for the hometown favorites as the Stars took the field, each name met with cheers and hoots. Urban Shocker, the spitballer with a crooked middle finger that gave his ball extra movement, came out to the mound for his warm-ups as his teammates took grounders and warmed their arms. The Fenway faithful were treated to one of the greatest sights baseball has ever produced: an outfield consisting of Tris Speaker, Joe Jackson, and Ty Cobb. The crowd marveled at the moment as the players tipped their caps in appreciation. Rivals though they were, that day they were heroes who received cheers. They rotated the three outfield positions throughout the game, with Speaker initially starting in center.

With Shocker's warm-ups complete, Harry Hooper came to the plate and did his version of digging into his stance. The crowd hummed with anticipation. Shocker aimed and fired, and Hooper popped up to Weaver at third for the first out. Team captain Jack Barry hit a liner to center that was caught by Speaker, which brought the first baseman Doc Hoblitzell to the plate. Shocker launched a fastball that Hoblitzell caught flush, sending it deep to rightfield beyond Cobb's reach. The ball reached the wall as Hoblitzell rounded first, and a favorable carom enabled him to round second before winding up at third for a two-out triple. The crowd roared at the game's first excitement, as Duffy Lewis was announced to hit next.

Shocker bore down on Lewis from the stretch with Hoblitzell leading off third. Lewis choked up on his bat, just looking for contact to drive in the game's first run. But Shocker got Lewis to ground out softly to first base to retire the side. Through one frame, there was no blood. Ruth answered back with zeroes in the top of the second, mowing down the middle of the Stars' order in Jackson (ground out to short), McInnis (fly out to center), and Weaver (another fly out to center).

Walker led off the bottom of the second. Shocker steadied himself on the mound and fired, and Walker's bat made the romantic sound of a solid crack that sent the ball flying deep to left field. The crowd rose as they collectively watched the ball travel, wondering if it might have enough juice in it to clear the towering left-field wall. As the ball soared, and with his characteristic speed, Tris Speaker, now in left, immediately sprinted back toward the wall—but as he traversed the familiar on-field incline of Duffy's Cliff, he tripped, and the ball whizzed just next to his face, missing him maybe by an inch. Walker stood at second comfortably with a double. But Shocker bore down again, and the no-out baserunner on second couldn't be brought home. The third baseman Gardner struck out; "Scoot" Scott grounded out to his fellow shortstop, Maranville; and Agnew flied out to Cobb in center, keeping the game scoreless after two.

In the third inning, with the crowd stirring, the All-Stars came to life. After O'Neill flew out to Hooper in right, Ruth walked Shocker. Lewis made a difficult catch to nab Maranville, but then Ruth walked Chapman. Cobb then hit a soft grounder that drew Hoblitzell off first base. Ruth got to the bag just before Cobb, but Hobby's toss went wide of Ruth, giving Cobb an infield single that some writers thought should have been an error. The second base umpire initially called Cobb out, until he realized that Ruth hadn't caught the ball—and the bases were loaded with two outs.

Speaker came to the plate and Ruth got his old teammate to ground out to Hoblitzell, escaping the inning unscathed.

The Red Sox couldn't muster anything in the bottom of the inning. The crowd roared for Ruth, but he hit a towering ball to second—a reporter wrote the ball was "up in the air a mile"—that Chapman brought in, before Shocker struck out Hooper.[10] *Barry singled to left but Shocker got Hobby to line out to Speaker, then in right field. With a third of the game in the books, there remained no score.*

Red Sox veterans Dick Hoblitzell, Everett Scott, Jack Barry, and Larry Gardner lean along the dugout rail during Boston's championship era. Together, the quartet formed part of the steady infield core that helped make the Red Sox a perennial contender in the years leading up to Murnane Day.

COPPER AND SILVER.

WEATHER FORECAST.

Today, fair. Thursday, fair.

More Butte News in the Standard Than in Any Other Paper

The Anaconda Standard.

THE WORLD'S NEWS.

VOL. XXXII.—No. 26. ANACONDA, MONTANA, WEDNESDAY MORNING, SEPTEMBER 29, 1920. PRICE FIVE CENTS.

CHICAGO BALL PLAYERS CONFESS SELLING OUT GAMES

Montana Entitled to Another Congressman Under Figures Showing Increase in State's Population

CHICAGO WHITE SOX PLAYERS ARE INDICTED BY GRAND JURY

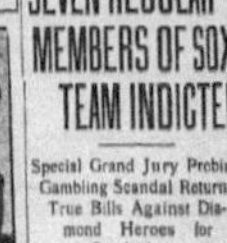

SEVEN REGULAR MEMBERS OF SOX TEAM INDICTED

Special Grand Jury Probing Gambling Scandal Returns True Bills Against Diamond Heroes for Crookedness.

COMISKEY IS HEARTBROKEN

Old Roman Suspends Implicated Players. Cicotte and Jackson Tearfully Admit Accepting Bribes to Lose Series.

NEW YORK, Sept. 28.—A telegram offering to place the entire New York American baseball team at the disposal of Charles A. Comiskey, who today suspended seven of his players indicted in connection with alleged fixing of games, was sent tonight to the White Sox club owner by Jacob Ruppert and T. L. Huston, owners of the Yankee club.

CHICAGO, Sept. 28.—(By the Associated Press.)—Indictments were voted by the Cook county grand jury against eight baseball stars today and confessions obtained from two, when the Old Roman, Charles A. Comiskey, owner of the ofttimes champion Chicago White Sox, smashed his pennant machine to clean up baseball. The confessions told how the Sox threw last year's world's championship to Cincinnati for money paid by gamblers.

CENSUS TOTALS JUSTIFY THIRD HOUSE MEMBER

Present Basis of Representation in Congress Provides for One Member for Every 211,877 Population.

547,593 PERSONS IN STATE

Selection of Additional Representative May Be at Large Unless Legislature Redistricts the Commonwealth.

COX IS HECKLED BY GERMANS IN SOUTH DAKOTA

Democratic Candidate Bombarded With Questions Regarding Prohibition.

Declares "Deutschland Uber Alles" Is Selfish Slogan and Policy Disastrous.

JURY PLACES NO BLAME FOR DEATH OF MILECHEVICH

Witnesses Describe Two Mysterious Strangers Seen With Dead Man.

Testimony Indicates That "Box" Game May Have Played Part in Death.

LIVINGSTON MAN MISSING SEARCHERS FIND NO TRACE

FAST OF NINETY DAYS IS RECORD, SAYS ONE DOCTOR

Physicians of Butte Discuss Case of Mayor MacSwiney, but Differ in Opinions. Fasting Instances Related. One Butte Man Benefited by Going Without Food for Thirty Days.

MRS. BERGDOLL FOUND GUILTY OF CONSPIRACY

U. S. Court Jury at Philadelphia Also Convicts Four Codefendants.

Mother of Notorious Draft Evaders Who Adored Kaiser Bill.

GOVERNMENT REJECTS PROPOSAL OF PACKERS

HELENA GIRL KILLED IN AUTOMOBILE CRASH

GREAT FALLS CONDUCTOR CHARGED WITH MURDER

LEGION CONVENTION STIRRED BY UNION LABOR QUESTION

War Veterans Have Heated Discussion Over Resolution on Stand Between Capital and Organizations.

JAP OWNERSHIP OF CALIFORNIA LANDS SPELLS DOOM OF U. S.

University President Says Educators of Coast Realize Menace of Oriental Plans to Extend Colonization.

Just two years after the Murnane Game, baseball would confront its darkest crisis. Newspaper headlines from the Black Sox scandal revealed a sport suddenly forced to defend its integrity before the American public.

6

TRUST, BETRAYAL & THE BIRTH OF A NEW TRADITION

On September 27, 1917, baseball gathered itself with a confidence that felt unexamined and self-sustaining. The benefit for Tim Murnane unfolded without deliberation about optics or oversight, without the need for league mandates or public-relations choreography. Rival players traveled to Boston in the middle of a season. Owners adjusted schedules. Fans filled the stands knowing precisely why they were there. What took place at Fenway Park that afternoon depended on an assumption so fundamental it rarely required articulation: that the game's participants shared a common understanding of honor. Baseball assumed, almost as a matter of habit, that a contest was a contest. A ballplayer might spit, brawl, or jaw the umpire, but he was not supposed to sell the outcome. The line was simple and absolute: you could play ugly, but you could not play crooked.

That assumption would not survive the decade intact.

By October 1919, Chicago vibrated with anticipation as the White Sox prepared to face the Cincinnati Reds in the World's Series. The Sox were widely considered the superior club. Eddie Cicotte, with a remarkable WAR of 9.7, had won twenty-nine games to lead the league. Claude "Lefty" Williams added twenty-three more. Shoeless Joe Jackson swung with a fluid grace that seemed almost detached from effort, hitting .351. Their infield moved with economy and precision; their outfielders threw out runners with clinical efficiency.

Yet beneath the surface of that confidence lay a more complicated reality. Owner Charles Comiskey's reputation for frugality had long irritated his players. Promised bonuses had been withheld. Contracts felt restrictive. Some players believed they were undervalued, if not exploited outright. That resentment mattered because it converted moral temptation into something that could be rationalized. A fix no longer had to feel like villainy. It could be framed, in the players' own minds, as leverage, as payback, as overdue compensation. In hotel rooms before the Series began, conversations unfolded between ballplayers and gamblers whose networks extended far beyond Chicago. Money was offered. Debts were discussed. Grievances were exploited.

The fix did not arrive as melodrama; it unfolded as quiet coordination. On October 1, in Game 1, Cicotte struck Cincinnati's leadoff hitter with a pitch. Later testimony would suggest that this was the signal that the scheme had begun. In subsequent games, errors surfaced in moments that seemed improbable. Pitches drifted over the plate. Double play opportunities evaporated. The Reds, who had not been expected to win, secured the championship five games to three.

Suspicion took hold slowly. Some reporters noticed oddities but hesitated to accuse. Others dismissed early rumors as bitterness from disappointed bettors. It would take nearly a year before the scandal erupted publicly. In September 1920, a Cook County grand jury investigating gambling in baseball summoned players to testify. Confessions were signed, then misplaced. Statements were retracted. Names circulated in headlines.

When eight White Sox players, including Cicotte, Williams, Jackson, and Buck Weaver, were indicted on charges of conspiracy to defraud the public, the shock extended beyond Chicago.

The betrayal cut so deeply because the game had come to stand for something larger than itself. In cities and towns across the country, baseball functioned as a civic language—a shared ritual that rewarded effort, discipline, and honesty. Children did not merely cheer for players; they modeled themselves after them. The public's bargain with baseball was emotional but also ethical. Fans gave the game their time, their money, their attention. In return, they received something rare in public life: a result that could be trusted because it was earned. When that faith broke, it was not only the sport that suffered. A piece of civic faith that bound fans to the game fractured with it.

Murnane, who had spent decades insisting that the game's beauty rested on fair play and honest competition, would have recognized the danger immediately. His career had been a long campaign to defend baseball's integrity against precisely these temptations and, indeed, his seemingly simple "Murnane's Don'ts" reveal just how much emphasis he placed on virtue as the centerpiece of a national pastime. His words had been a moral compass for the sport. He understood that baseball's democracy depended on an invisible infrastructure: the belief that rules meant what they said, that effort mattered, that no hidden hand tilted the field. Remove that belief, and the game became pageantry without legitimacy.

The "Black Sox" left an indelible stain. Juries might acquit, but the court of public opinion never did. And the scandal itself embedded into the culture, becoming shorthand for moral collapse. F. Scott Fitzgerald even found a way to weave it into *The Great Gatsby*, when Gatsby reveals that Meyer Wolfsheim—modeled on underworld figure Arnold Rothstein—was "the man who fixed the World's Series back in 1919."[1] The line works in Gatsby because Fitzgerald could assume the reader would understand the reference. By the mid-1920s, "1919" had become more than a year. It was a moral shorthand.

The sense of violation thus did not stem solely from the act of gambling; betting on baseball had long been part of its culture. The rupture lay in the intimacy of manipulation to the field itself. The World Series, the sport's most visible stage, had become suspect. And the damage was psychological before it was financial.

A History of Gambling

The shock of the Black Sox scandal did not emerge from nowhere. To see why the betrayal felt so catastrophic, one must see how long the sport had been flirting with its own undoing.

Gambling had trailed professional baseball from its earliest days, following crowds and money wherever the game took root. As early as 1865, just a few months after Lee surrendered to Grant at Appomattox to end the Civil War, two New York teams faced off at the historic Elysian Fields in Hoboken, New Jersey: the Mutuals of New York and the Eckfords of Brooklyn. The game was competitive in the early going, and the Mutuals led 5-4 after four innings, which the *New York Times* observed had been "splendidly played." But things took a turn in the bottom of the fifth. With the Eckfords at bat, the Mutuals "fell off in their play considerably…Over-pitched balls, wild throws, passed balls, and failures to stop them in the field marked the play of the Mutuals to an unusual extent," in which they surrendered eleven runs in one inning."[2]

Thomas Devyr, the Mutuals shortstop, offered a written confession to the club afterward admitting that the game had been thrown by three of the players for the combined sum of $300. All three players were banned at the next meeting of the National Association, which was routinely besieged by betting-related corruption. Wagers were openly placed within ballparks themselves, and everyone understood that part of baseball's entertainment value was the thrill of the gamble.

Baseball did not invent this culture of corruption; it reflected the habits and assumptions of American life itself.

The early ascent of organized baseball unfolded against the backdrop of one of the most corrupt, politically volatile periods in American history. The Civil War had barely ended when the country plunged into the fraught experiment of Reconstruction. It was an era defined by the spoils system, patronage jobs, machine politics, and a federal government increasingly overwhelmed by graft. The Mutuals, as a case in point, were controlled by Boss Tweed—the political boss of Tammany Hall, New York's dominant, and notoriously corrupt, political machine.

In Washington, President Ulysses S. Grant—himself an admirer of the game—presided over an administration riddled with scandals: the Whiskey Ring, the Crédit Mobilier scheme, abuses in the Indian Ring. Newspapers were full of stories of bribes, kickbacks, and cronyism. Public trust in institutions was fragile, sometimes nonexistent.

It was in this climate—this swirling culture of opportunity

and opportunism—that baseball tried to formalize itself into a professional sport. Players jumped contracts for cash under the table. Club owners made deals in smoke-filled back rooms. Gamblers hovered in the shadows, offering payments for outcomes. Standing above all this turbulence was the National Association, founded in 1871 but quickly recognized as unstable, unruly, and lacking enforcement power.

By 1876, the same year that the nation entered the chaos of the Hayes–Tilden presidential election—the closest and most disputed in American history at least until the 2000 election—the National League was formed. It was hardly coincidental. Americans were desperate for order, for rules, for some institution that would not buckle under corruption. The end of Reconstruction—sealed as part of the political bargain that resolved the Hayes–Tilden dispute that tilted the presidency to Hayes—symbolized a nation weary of turmoil and ready to restore a predictable, if deeply flawed, normalcy.

The National League, in its own smaller sphere, was an answer to the same longing. Its founders insisted on structure: fixed schedules, enforceable contracts, and moral discipline. Its creation was part of a broader moment in American life when railroad barons, industrial magnates, and civic reformers were trying to tame the chaos of expansion and corruption through governance and rules. Baseball's leaders were trying to do in sport what reformers were attempting in politics and business: replace informal reputation with enforceable structure. Trust, they believed, could be built by architecture.

As he organized the league, William Hulbert wrote to G.W. Thompson, president of the Philadelphia Athletics, that bookies were ruining baseball and that gambling had to be addressed. In this vein, each club was given broad authority to expel for life any players who engaged in deceitful acts.

Baseball and American history thus did not move in parallel during this period—they were entwined. The sport was being shaped by the same cultural forces that were reshaping the country, mirroring national aspirations and contradictions: yearning for order in a world of opportunity and temptation faith that rules could channel unruly human nature; belief that competition could be fair and honest if the right structures existed; and constant struggle between purity and corruption, idealism and reality.

Yet even with the National League's creation—and with all the dreams its founders sought to inculcate vis-à-vis rules, order, and moral discipline—the young game could not fully escape the forces that had shaped the nation around it. The tension between those very notions of idealism and reality remained ever present. And so, almost immediately, the NL found itself confronting the very same temptations and moral failures it was designed to prevent—a struggle that came into sharp relief in its inaugural season.

In that 1876 campaign, George Bechtel, a member of the Louisville Grays—a charter member of the league to help create geographic balance between East and West—was caught throwing a game and seeking to bribe teammates to throw future games.[3] Recognizing this threat to the fledgling league, Bechtel was promptly banned from the NL for life, and the Grays acquired Bill Craver to replace him as the team's shortstop for the following season.

With a swift handling of the problem, things were looking up for the league and for the Grays in particular as the 1877 season began. As baseball historian Daniel Ginsburg noted, "In addition to Craver, the team had added outfielder George Hall, one of the great early sluggers. During the 1876 season, Hall became the National League's first home run champion, and finished second in the league in batting with an average of .366. With holdovers such as Jim Devlin, rapidly developing into one of the league's best pitchers, and Joseph Gerhardt, one of the best second basemen in the league, Louisville was expected to contend for the 1877 pennant."[4]

The Grays performed as expected and sat in first place late in the season before going on a suspicious nine-game winless streak that cost them the title—including losses to a hapless Cincinnati team that had disbanded and reorganized midseason. The hometown *Louisville Evening News* excoriated the team in no uncertain terms: "The Louisville Grays, alleged baseball players, have returned from their triumphal tour... and will [next] play the Amateurs...It will scarcely be profitable to throw the game to the Amateurs, as the pennant does not depend on it."[5]

In parallel, club president Charles E. Chase received telegrams from strangers claiming that games had been thrown by his players. When Chase confronted his team, Devlin and

Hall confessed to taking money. It soon became apparent that Craver—who repeatedly denied his involvement but refused to let the team look at the inbound telegrams he received through the team—and third baseman Al Nichols were in on the fix too. The club banned all four of them for life from the league, an action ratified by the league after the season. Devlin—who threw every single pitch in every single inning of the entire season for the Grays and was considered perhaps the league's top pitcher, with an effective sinkerball—repeatedly tried to get reinstated but was denied. In one story, Devlin got down on his knees before Hulbert and begged him for a chance at redemption. Hulbert would not budge, knowing the game's integrity was at stake. Having lost some of their best players, the Grays folded before the 1878 season began.

The Louisville affair predated Murnane's journalistic career but took place while he was a player himself, and certainly it helped shape the baseball culture he would soon chronicle. When Murnane later wrote about the game's need for discipline and integrity, he was speaking into a world still defined by these early breakdowns of trust. The Grays scandal became part of the sport's cautionary folklore, a reminder of how fragile the young league had been and how easily corruption could hollow it out.

Murnane absorbed these stories as warnings: examples of what happened when the game's moral spine buckled. His columns in the decades to come carried the weight of that inherited history, urging readers and players alike to protect the purity of the sport. In this sense, he became one of the game's essential interpreters, giving voice to the values that Hulbert and the league's founders had tried to instill at the dawn of professional baseball.*

The Black Sox scandal erupted with a force that dwarfed anything Louisville had faced. This time, the wound was

---

*Baseball in Louisville was not without positive contributions to the game: the defunct Grays were soon replaced by the Louisville Eclipse, which competed in the American Association. The team's best player, Pete "Louisville Slugger" Browning, became the first player to have bats custom-made based on his preferences by a local woodworking shop called J.F. Hillerich. When Hillerich's son, John, took over the family business, he renamed the business "Louisville Slugger," and the company became the leading bat maker in America—used by the likes of Ty Cobb, Babe Ruth, and other stars.

national—front-page news, congressional concern, and a public that felt genuinely betrayed.

Owners recognized that if the public doubted the integrity of outcomes, the foundation of the game would erode. Attendance figures in 1920 reflected unease. Editorial pages demanded reform. What had once been governed by handshake and reputation now required visible authority.

In November 1920, the club owners appointed Kenesaw Mountain Landis as Commissioner of Baseball. Landis was not a baseball man by temperament; he was a federal judge accustomed to commanding silence in a courtroom. His appointment signaled a willingness to cede autonomy in order to preserve legitimacy. He was granted sweeping power to act "in the best interests" of baseball, a phrase broad enough to encompass moral as well as procedural judgment.[6] That vagueness was the point. It authorized the commissioner to protect belief, not just to adjudicate facts. Baseball was legislating for perception because perception was now part of survival.

The indicted players were tried in 1921 and acquitted, but the courtroom verdict did not resolve the deeper crisis of confidence. The following day, Landis banned all eight players for life in a crisp, declarative ruling that left no ambiguity: "Regardless of the verdict of juries, no player that throws a ball game, no player that entertains proposals or promises to throw a game, no player that sits in a conference with a bunch of crooked players and gamblers where the ways and means of throwing games are discussed and does not promptly tell his club about it, will ever again play professional baseball."[7]

The severity of the punishment was intentional. Landis understood that baseball's survival required clarity more than leniency. The commissioner's office thereby became the embodiment of institutional trust, a structure designed to prevent the recurrence of private arrangements that could undermine public faith. Baseball would be governed by certainty.

The sport moved forward, though not unchanged.

A Long Road to Recovery

But strict justice could not by itself mend the rupture

between the sport and the American public. Rules could police behavior; they could not restore enchantment. Fans needed a reason to believe again that the game was clean and, importantly, still worthy of devotion.

In the years that followed, baseball found that belief where Americans often did in moments of disillusionment: in spectacle. No figure embodied that renewal more completely than George Herman Ruth. The Babe did not simply hit home runs; he redefined the boundaries of possibility. Ruth's exuberance felt untethered from scandal. His popularity did not erase the memory of 1919, but it offered something affirmative. Baseball could still astonish. It could still command attention for reasons rooted in skill rather than intrigue. In a sport still nursing suspicion, Ruth offered permission to feel uncomplicated joy again. Wonder became a kind of rehabilitation.

Ruth's statistics illuminate just how transformative he was. From 1919-1929 he led the league in runs scored eight times; in home runs, nine times; in runs batted in, five times; in walks, seven times; in intentional walks, six times; in on-base percentage, seven times; in slugging percentage, ten times; and in batter-fielder wins, nine times.* In his 1923 MVP season, he led the league in nine offensive categories. His *worst* season during this stretch was the 1925 campaign, when he only played ninety-eight games and hit .290 with twenty-five homers—still a fine year. And in 1927 he famously hit sixty home runs. Crowds swelled. Newspapers filled columns. Yankee Stadium truly was the "House That Ruth Built." Baseball, like the Roaring Twenties of America itself, surged back to life—though not without setbacks and controversy.

The 1920s became an era of paradox: centralized authority under Landis, explosive individual stardom under Ruth, proliferating radio broadcasts that carried games into living rooms. The sport regained financial stability. Attendance climbed. Yet the relationship between baseball and the public had shifted. Trust was no longer assumed; it was monitored. And it still required management.

Indeed, other gambling allegations surfaced during this

---

*Batter-fielder wins refers to an older sabermetric statistic measuring a player's value based on their contributions to runs scored and prevented, a precursor to the modern wins-above-replacement.

period involving some of the league's biggest stars, creating a profound crisis for the game. The episode mattered not because it rivaled 1919, but because it proved how little margin for doubt remained. After betrayal, even allegations could wound. Baseball had built an office to police corruption, but it could not police rumor.

On November 3, 1926, coming off a season batting .339, Ty Cobb abruptly announced his retirement from baseball after twenty-two seasons with the Detroit Tigers. Later the same month, and equally suddenly, Tris Speaker announced his retirement from baseball too, having just hit a very strong .304. But there was more to the story. Their retirements were linked to accusations made by former Red Sox and later Tigers pitcher Dutch Leonard that Cobb, Speaker, and Smoky Joe Wood had conspired with him to fix a game near the end of the notorious 1919 season, in a September regular season contest between the Tigers (for whom Cobb was player-manager) and the Indians (for whom Speaker was player-manager).

Leonard's animus toward Cobb was not new: Cobb had accused Leonard of intentionally beaning him some years before, and they were teammates for a few years in Detroit where they didn't get along. The feud reached its zenith in 1924 when Leonard accused Cobb, in Cobb's managerial capacity, of overusing Leonard. As Matthew Stanley surmised, "Seemingly motivated by reprisal, Cobb left the pitcher in for an entire game—which was common in 1924—even though Leonard was being badly beaten and was not throwing well. Leonard was subsequently placed on waiver," but no one claimed him, and his career ended.[8] Leonard thus had a real motive in seeking to discredit Cobb—but he also had evidence.

Leonard started telling people he had something to destroy Cobb around late 1924, including letters written by Cobb and Wood referring to the game fixing. When American League president Ban Johnson learned of the letters, he purportedly authorized an attorney to acquire them from Leonard for a sum of $20,000—essentially a hush money payment. Johnson aptly felt that a new scandal with the game's top stars might permanently stain if not ruin it. Whether the two stars reached the retirement decisions on their own accord in anticipation of public fall-out or were forced into the positions by Johnson as a more dignified exit, it yielded the same outcome: Cobb and

Speaker were done with baseball forever. Hence the surprise November announcements.

But when news of the scandal was passed from Johnson to Commissioner Landis, Landis decided to go public with the allegations, forcing Johnson to take a stand publicly against the players and announcing the situation from league offices in Chicago on December 22, 1926. The following day, an all-caps headline ran on the front page of the *New York Times* that read "PAID FOR LETTERS IN BASEBALL SCANDAL," with three sub-headings: "League Bought the Evidence from Leonard, Who Accuses Cobb and Speaker," followed by "STARS OUT, SAYS JOHNSON," and followed further with "Asserts Neither Cobb Nor Speaker May Ever Return—To Continue War on Gambling."[9]

The *Times* called it "baseball's most astounding scandal." Johnson commented, "I am not over the shock yet," though he also noted he regretted that the story had become public out of concern for the families of Cobb and Speaker. "This thing of betting on ball games was a common practice previous to the world's series of 1919," Johnson said. "Now we have got most of that type of players out of the major leagues and we will not tolerate any wagering again if we know about it."[10]

Wood spoke publicly and denied the allegations. He had not bet on this specific game, he said, but he admitted that he was aware of other instances of players gambling on games—including a game when he pitched against Walter Johnson and "the whole Washington team went broke."[11]

Speaker's supporters claimed that Speaker only resigned to protect his good friend Wood's name. His home telephone rang off the hook as friends and fans called to express their belief in his innocence. Speaker himself asked fans to judge him based on his twenty-year career of "hard, honest effort for the game I have loved"—also noting that Leonard was unwilling to confront him face to face about it.[12]

Detroit similarly stood behind Cobb, and a common storyline among supporters became that the real issue was Landis's decision to make the allegations public. Guy A. Miller, a municipal judge in Detroit, expressed this reflexive view: "I think Judge Landis's act in publishing this story is indefensible and in line with his history of hypocritical sensationalism." Another local judge, E.J. Jefferies, concurred: the commissioner "has fouled his own nest in his desire for sensationalism. He has unnecessarily gone out of his way to destroy two of the greatest idols of the day. The reaction to baseball if this man continues his muckraking will destroy the game."[13]

On the very night that the allegations were made public, the city council of Augusta, Georgia took a stand to defend its favorite son: in a hastily arranged special meeting, the council adopted a resolution labeling the story as a "conspiracy to defame [Cobb's] good name." It went on to assert "complete confidence in the honesty, probity and integrity of Tyrus Raymond Cobb."[14]

Players who participated in the game claimed to remember nothing awry about the outcome or that anything was played inappropriately. But Dickie Kerr, an honest pitcher who won two of his three 1919 World Series starts for the White Sox, said he was "not surprised" by the story.[15]

Though the evidence certainly appeared damning, Landis's investigation yielded an outcome that enabled the game to continue. In January 1927—just a few weeks after the story had been made public, and following significant media coverage of the scandal—Landis ruled that the players were not guilty. "These players," he stated, "have not been, nor are they now, found guilty of fixing a ball game. By no decent system of justice could such finding be made."[16]

Cobb threatened a defamation lawsuit and worked with politicians to investigate the league's handling of the matter. But soon owner-manager of the Athletics, Connie Mack, made a large offer to Cobb to play for his team the following season, and Cobb moved on from the matter. With the not-guilty verdict, Cobb did not need any reinstatement from the league. He went on to hit .357 for the A's that season and .323 the following before hanging up his spikes.

Speaker too came out of retirement. He left Cleveland and joined the Senators, hitting .327 before joining Cobb in Philadelphia for the 1928 season—like Cobb's, his last in the majors.

One wonders how Tim Murnane might have covered the scandal. His writing consistently focused on rules and fair play, the hallmarks of a game that needed this honesty to stay interesting and democratic. He wrote so plainly about the character of the players he observed that there is little doubt he would have pulled no punches had he lived to witness the collapse.

Murnane had long argued that the public invested not merely in the scores but in the character of the men who played the game. Murnane's profiles of Cobb and Speaker often returned to their competitive fire and devotion to craft—traits he believed anchored baseball's universal appeal. A scandal involving stars of their stature would, for him, have represented not just personal failing but a tearing of the bond between player and public. Character was destiny.

Baseball Meets the Great Depression

With the return to baseball of the exonerated stars, and the continued prowess of Ruth, the sport again looked to be on the upswing. But its revival was not immune to the broader tides of history. Mirroring Ruth's rise was the rise of the stock market. The Dow Jones Industrial Average ballooned sixfold between August 1921 and September 1929—leading renowned Yale economist Irving Fisher to foolishly proclaim that a "permanently high plateau" had been reached.[17]

On October 28, 1929, "Black Monday" yielded a drop in the Dow of nearly 13 percent—followed by "Black Tuesday" resulting in the drop of almost another 12 percent—and by mid-November, nearly half the Dow's value had been wiped away.[18]

When the Great Depression struck, it shook the game's foundations as surely as it had shaken factories, banks, and farms. Attendance dwindled everywhere; even the cheapest ticket—once part of the fabric of weekly life—became a luxury many could no longer justify. Ballparks that had roared through the 1920s suddenly echoed with empty seats. Gate-driven finances, the lifeblood of every club, dried to a trickle. Owners slashed payrolls, deferred maintenance, and cut scouting budgets. Broadcast rights were still in their infancy, merchandise sales were minimal, and there was no meaningful revenue stream beyond the turnstile. In this environment, survival depended on austerity.

Nowhere was the crisis more visible than in Philadelphia, where Connie Mack presided over one of the greatest collections of talent baseball had ever seen. His Athletics had stormed through the 1929–31 seasons with an almost regal dominance, winning three straight American League pennants and two World Series behind a core of future Hall of Famers—Lefty Grove, Jimmie Foxx, Mickey Cochrane, and Al Simmons among them. Under ordinary economic conditions, this dynasty might have rivaled the long-term staying power of the Yankees.

But dynasties require stability, and stability requires revenue. When Depression-era unemployment swept Philadelphia and the mills and factories emptied, Shibe Park emptied with them. Crowds shrank to a fraction of their former size, even as the A's continued to win. Mack—unique among major-league owners as a manager who depended almost exclusively on gate money to meet payroll—found himself trapped. Without deep-pocketed partners or diversified business ventures, he had no cushion. Each payday loomed like a crisis.

So began one of the most devastating fire sales in baseball history. Mack sold Cochrane to Detroit, sent Simmons to Chicago, and eventually shipped Grove and Foxx to Boston, not because he wished to rebuild but because he had no alternative. The departures gutted the roster, but they also severed the emotional bond between the city and its championship club. Fans who had watched the A's dominate the league now watched their heroes leave one by one, victims of economic necessity rather than defeat.

The result was a vicious cycle: fewer stars meant fewer wins, fewer wins meant fewer fans, and fewer fans yielded an even more precarious financial position. What had been the sport's most formidable powerhouse just a few years earlier sank rapidly into the cellar. Like many clubs in the early 1930s, the A's clawed for survival, their fortunes tied less to talent and strategy than to the fraying economic fortunes of the nation itself. Even Babe Ruth wasn't immune, forced to take a 30 percent pay cut from 1932 to 1933 and an additional 32 percent pay cut the following year.[19]

As baseball staggered through these lean years, the sport's leaders and promoters searched urgently for ways to reignite public enthusiasm. The Depression had exposed how fragile the game's economic model truly was: without fans in the stands, even dynasties collapsed. What the national pastime needed was a burst of excitement—something bold enough to draw people back through the turnstiles and remind them why the game mattered. It needed a public ritual that could concentrate value in a single afternoon: stars, stakes, and collective attention.

In earlier moments, special exhibitions had briefly filled that role. The 1917 Murnane Game had shown—more vividly than anyone recognized at the time—how powerful a showcase of the game's greatest stars could be. In bringing together rivals and heroes on a single field, united in purpose, it revealed a truth Murnane had articulated for decades: that the game's magic was strongest when its best players stood together, not apart.

Arch Ward, sports editor of the *Chicago Tribune,* read the moment with both anxiety and imagination. As F.C. Lane had proposed years earlier, Ward envisioned a midsummer exhibition featuring the best players from each league, selected in part by fan vote, staged in conjunction with Chicago's Century of Progress Exposition. The proceeds would benefit charity. The spectacle would draw national attention back to baseball at a time when distraction carried its own form of relief.

Owners hesitated. Injuries were a concern. So was precedent. Yet the promise of renewed attendance and civic celebration proved persuasive.

On July 6, 1933, the first Major League All-Star Game took place at Comiskey Park. More than 47,000 fans attended. Babe Ruth, now the sport's towering figure, hit a two-run home run that helped secure a 4–2 victory for the American League. The moment was reported not simply as athletic achievement, but as affirmation. Newspapers emphasized the novelty of seeing rivals share a dugout, of witnessing stars introduced one by one under a unified banner.

The All-Star Game did more than entertain. It ritualized unity.

In 1917, baseball's finest had gathered in Boston under circumstances shaped by grief and generosity. Skill competitions preceded the contest. Trophies were awarded. The crowd leaned forward in recognition that they were part of something larger than standings. That gathering had emerged organically, without mandate, in response to loss.

In 1933, the gathering was planned and promoted. Its origins lay in economic necessity and media savvy. Yet the structural resemblance to 1917 is difficult to ignore. In both instances, excellence was assembled publicly and collectively.

The sport paused its ordinary rivalries to present itself as a whole.

The Black Sox scandal had demonstrated how easily private interests could distort public spectacle. In consequence, the commissioner's office imposed oversight. Later, the All-Star Game supplied ritual. Each July, the sport reintroduced its brightest talents under conditions designed for transparency. Fans participated in selecting players. Introductions were deliberate. The event unfolded under intense scrutiny.

Through repetition, the Mid-Summer Classic became expectation. It offered reassurance that baseball remained capable of gathering openly, its stars standing shoulder to shoulder without suspicion.

The tradition carried forward through war and racial integration, through expansion and television. It adapted to new technologies and commercial realities. Yet at its core it retained a familiar gesture: assemble the best, present them together, invite the public to witness.

Between Fenway in 1917 and Comiskey Park in 1933 lies a narrative of rupture and renewal. The benefit game revealed baseball's instinct for collective action. The scandal exposed the vulnerability of that instinct when left unguarded. The commissioner institutionalized discipline. The All-Star Game institutionalized gathering.

Trust, once broken, required both structure and ceremony. Structure alone could enforce rules; ceremony could rebuild affection. And both had to happen in public. After 1919, baseball learned that trust was no longer something you possessed. It was something you had to demonstrate.

When All-Stars lined up along the baselines each July, they stood within a lineage shaped by both generosity and oversight. The ritual did not erase the memory of betrayal. It answered it, quietly, through visibility and repetition.

Long before the Mid-Summer Classic settled into the national calendar, baseball had already demonstrated that it could gather its finest under shared purpose. It had done so on a September afternoon in Boston, when rivalry gave way to communal affirmation. The years that followed would test that capacity, strain it, and reconfigure it. They did not extinguish it.

The birth of a new tradition in 1933 did not abandon what had been revealed in 1917. Rather, it translated that earlier instinct into form and frequency. It placed the gathering on the calendar and repeated it until it became part of the sport's identity. In that continuity, shaped by both crisis and adaptation, the game rediscovered how to hold trust in public view. What no one in Fenway that afternoon could yet know was that this model—stars setting aside rivalry, spectacle harnessed for care, a single game standing in for a larger civic obligation—would not vanish with the war but lie dormant, waiting for another generation to need it again.

Duffy Lewis mastered the treacherous left field of Fenway Park, playing the steep incline of the "Duffy's Cliff" embankment with fearless familiarity. Known for his clutch hitting, Lewis was a central figure in Boston's championship outfield who thrived in the game's biggest moments.

FIRE & RESOLVE

September 27, 1917: Top of the Fourth, 0-0

Ruth began the fourth by getting Jackson to line out to Duffy Lewis in left. Then McInnis, "for the honor of Gloucester [where he was from] and the Athletics [for whom he played]," in Francis Eaton's words, singled.[20] *Weaver came up and hit a sharp grounder to Gardner at third, who quickly tossed the ball to Barry at second for the first out before Barry relayed the ball to Hoblitzell for what the Globe later called "a lightning double play" that was a "feature of the game."*[21]

In the bottom of the fourth, with Ehmke on the mound, Lewis grounded out to McInnis at first, and Walker grounded out to Chapman at second. Joe Jackson, by this point playing left field, caught Gardner's fly to end the inning.

Ruth had one more inning in him and got O'Neill to fly out to center field to lead off the bottom of the fourth. Ehmke, in his first plate appearance, then flew out to Hooper, before Maranville flew out to Walker.

Ty Cobb had the limelight to himself in the bottom of the inning, catching three successive fly balls from Scott, Agnew, and Ruth. With each fly ball Speaker, revealing his speed, sprinted over to Cobb and positioned himself for any dropped balls—but Cobb had no difficulty with any of them.

0-0 after five.

Rube Foster—in his penultimate professional pitching appearance ever—relieved Ruth in the top of the sixth, and the catcher Thomas relieved Agnew in parallel. Foster walked Chapman but then got Cobb (flew out to right), Speaker (fouled out), and Jackson (flew out to right) to go down in order.

The bottom of the inning was more exciting. After Hooper grounded out to second and Barry flew out to Cobb in left field, Hoblitzell drew a walk. Duffy Lewis hit a hard ground ball that was fumbled by Maranville as he tried to make the force play at second. With Hobby on second and Lewis on first, the Sox were threatening. Walker then slashed a single to center field, and Hoblitzell, a strong baserunner, came barreling around third toward home at top speed. Jackson charged the approaching ball in center and scooped it cleanly, firing a bullet throw to Schang at the plate that mirrored his competition-winning throw: solid but slightly off the plate. The throw forced the catcher Schang to lunge away from the plate to grab the ball, and just as Hobby slid, Schang—ball in mitt—dove across the plate, barely applying the tag to keep the game tied. No blood.

Neither team could produce anything in the seventh, keeping the game scoreless and the fans on the edges of their seats.

Dick Hoblitzell, the dependable Red Sox first baseman, pauses during pregame warmups at Fenway Park. Known for his steady glove and disciplined approach at the plate, Hoblitzell was a respected veteran presence on Boston clubs that remained among baseball's elite through the late 1910s.

The inaugural MLB All-Star Game in 1933 formally matched the American League against the National League. Its spirit echoed the earlier gathering of stars in the 1917 Murnane benefit game at Fenway Park.

7

THE FIRST ALL-STAR GAME

When baseball faced its next great test—this time not war but economic collapse—it reached instinctively for a solution it had already glimpsed once before: the power of its stars, gathered deliberately, to carry the game through crisis. Long before Henry Luce christened the coming era "The American Century" in *Life* magazine in February 1941, Americans sensed that the twentieth century was becoming their moment—an opportunity to claim a leading role in global thought, work, and action.

Against that backdrop, American cities competed to display their vitality, staging world's fairs that advertised the country's industrial muscle, technological ingenuity, cultural optimism, and civic ambition. If the world's fairs displayed American industry and invention, baseball would soon display American excellence in human form. The ballpark, like the exposition hall, offered a curated vision of national strength—disciplined, competitive, forward-looking, and unmistakably public.

In 1904, alongside the Summer Olympics, St. Louis mounted the Louisiana Purchase Exposition to celebrate a century of westward expansion. Fairgoers encountered marvels of the modern age—early X-ray machines, wireless telegraphy, even the debut of the ice-cream cone—and nearly twenty million came to see them.

Other grand fairs followed, including Portland's Lewis and Clark Centennial Exposition, Hampton Roads' Jamestown Exposition, several in New York City, and San Francisco's Panama-Pacific International Exposition celebrating the Panama Canal.

By the late 1920s, with the stock market still roaring, Chicago's leaders planned a grand centennial world's fair to mark the 1833 founding of the Midwest's largest city. They dubbed it "A Century of Progress Exposition"—known to most simply as the Chicago World's Fair.

Central to the project was the *Chicago Tribune*—the self-styled "WORLD'S GREATEST NEWSPAPER," as its masthead boasted each day. The paper's owners, the prominent McCormick family—whose fortune sprang from the revolutionary McCormick reaper—saw the fair as both a public boon and a chance to expand the *Tribune's* influence and profits. When Mayor Ed Kelly proposed adding a major sporting event to anchor the exposition, publisher Robert McCormick seized the idea.

A decorated veteran of the First World War, McCormick had commanded artillery with the U.S. First Division in France and fought at the brutal 1918 Battle of Cantigny, just months after the Murnane benefit game had been played. The memory of that campaign never left him: upon returning home he named his Wheaton, Illinois estate "Cantigny" and used private funds to construct a memorial there to honor the men of his division.

His wartime service had earned him distinction, but it also deepened a skepticism of foreign entanglements. In the years to come, McCormick would devote the editorial pages of the *Tribune* to a fierce isolationism, railing against any future intervention in Europe even as the world slid once again toward conflict. For now, though, he channeled his sense of patriotism and pride into the World's Fair—and into the novel idea of staging a midsummer All-Star baseball game—and he turned to his sports editor, Arch Ward, to make it happen.

The Game of the Century

Ward had begun his career as the first publicity director

for legendary Notre Dame football coach Knute Rockne before moving into journalism and joining the *Tribune* in 1925. Five years later he became sports editor, a post he would hold for the next quarter-century until his death. A devoted sportsman and unabashed White Sox partisan, Ward needed little coaxing when McCormick asked him to dream up a marquee event. His proposal was simple and daring: an All-Star baseball game uniting the era's best players from both leagues—a once-in-a-lifetime "Game of the Century." The proposal felt unprecedented, yet it drew upon an instinct baseball had already shown it possessed. The sport had gathered before its brightest figures under shared purpose. Ward's genius lay not in invention, but in institutionalization.

Most Americans had never seen the stars of both leagues on the same field—unless their hometown club reached the World Series. The sport, moreover, badly needed a lift after the stock-market crash of 1929. Between 1930 and 1933, major-league attendance fell by 40 percent, average salaries dropped by nearly a quarter, and rosters were pared back to cut costs.[1] Clubs tried everything—discounted tickets, giveaways, gimmicks—to lure fans, but the game still desperately needed a spark.

Backed by McCormick and Mayor Kelly, Ward presented his "Game of the Century" to Major League Baseball in April 1933, just weeks before the fair opened. He needed the blessing of Commissioner Landis, both league presidents, and the owners. The plan carried obvious risks: players would leave their clubs mid-season, injuries could alter pennant races, and a rain-out with no makeup date could ruin everything and cost a lot of money. Ward understood—accurately, as historian Lew Freedman observed—that baseball's magnates were "conservative by nature, individually and as a group."[2] But he also knew their hearts were reached through their wallets: show them a profit, and they might listen. What he was really asking, however, was not merely financial assent. He was asking owners to yield a measure of symbolic authority to the press and to the public—to allow fans and newspapers to shape the sport's most visible exhibition. That surrender, however temporary, unsettled men accustomed to control.

To make this case, Ward first sought the support of the league presidents, betting they would grasp the game's potential and help sway the owners. Both men had shaped baseball's growth in the early twentieth century and left distinct fingerprints on the emerging All-Star tradition.

John Heydler, president of the National League, had come a long way from his start as a New York printer's apprentice. At twenty-six he joined the league as an umpire, where he worked for four bruising seasons before becoming private secretary to NL president Harry Pulliam.

Heydler began by compiling league statistics, adding strikeouts and walks to a batter's record, and soon weighed in on rule changes. Among his innovations was the early concept of a designated hitter—meant to "prevent pitchers' battles and close games from being spoiled by taking a pitcher out for a pinch-hitter" while speeding play and boosting offense. The idea outlived him, adopted decades later by the American League.[3]

When Pulliam's health began to fail under the strain of office, Heydler often filled the gap. After Pulliam's death in 1909, Heydler briefly assumed the presidency and then took it officially in 1918. Soon after, he hired Al and Walter Elias—founders of the Elias Sports Bureau—to standardize record-keeping.

By 1933, Heydler's health was failing, but he retained a reputation as a forward-looking executive willing to try new things.

Over in the AL, the president was Will Harridge, who would serve from 1931 to 1959. A lifelong Chicagoan, he caught the eye of Ban Johnson and became his secretary, quickly becoming his right-hand man. He guided the AL through challenges including rivalry with the upstart Federal League, the gambling scandal that rocked Chicago, and the hiring of Commissioner Landis—whose authority soon chafed Johnson. By 1927, the feud boiled over: the owners forced Johnson to take a leave and installed the even-tempered Harridge in his place, who became president after Johnson's successor, Ernest Barnard, died suddenly while visiting spring-training camps.

The owners respected the new president, and his long service made for a smooth, uneventful transition. A stickler for integrity, Harridge once learned of a suspicious remark by a home-plate umpire that hinted at improper dealings; he immediately dismissed the man, who never worked another game.

By spring 1933, Ward saw a chance to showcase baseball on the fair's national stage—but first he needed the approval of Harridge, Heydler, and Landis. He approached Harridge over dinner on April 20 with five selling points: (1) still recovering from the Black Sox scandal, baseball could use a public display of integrity; (2) the Chicago World's Fair was an ideal backdrop; (3) all profits would go to the Association of Professional Baseball Players of America, a fund for retired players in need of medical or burial support; (4) fans nationwide would choose the starting rosters, heightening excitement; and (5) the *Tribune* would guarantee all team expenses if rain forced a cancellation.[4]

Ward found a willing partner in Harridge, but was informed by him that the club owners would be a problem on the basis that "they would be laying themselves open to playing charity games for other papers, too, and there would be no end to the requests."[5] But Harridge agreed to bring Ward's idea to the AL owners. Meanwhile, the following day, Ward got the NL wheels in motion by calling William E. Veeck, president of the Chicago Cubs. Learning that the starting lineups would be chosen by the fans, Veeck said, "That's the greatest idea that has come into baseball in my time."[6] He gave his promise to work with other NL clubs to move the idea forward while Ward also worked on Heydler.

Ward needed to pull an inside straight with the owners. Everyone saw the promise and potential of the game as an individual, one-off contest; it was the fear of endless requests for more games that gave them pause. And so Ward carefully tied the playing of the game back to the World's Fair. It was a once-in-a-lifetime moment, he reasoned—why not play a once-in-a-lifetime game?

By the time the AL club owners gathered at a special meeting in Cleveland held on May 9, 1933, consensus in that league had grown. They marked July 6, 1933, as their preferred date.

Buoyed by the quick approval, Ward awaited word from Heydler's talks with the NL—only to learn that the Giants, Braves, and Cardinals had all balked, each for different reasons. The Cardinals worried the contest would set a precedent and feared injuries to players competing outside regular club duty. The Giants and Braves objected on logistical grounds: they were booked for back-to-back doubleheaders in Boston on July

4th and 5th and doubted their stars could then travel overnight to Chicago for an afternoon game on the 6th.

Ward pressed on creatively. He assured the Cardinals that even if the game set a precedent, future editions could rotate to other cities—becoming potential windfalls for hosts such as St. Louis (which in fact staged the eighth All-Star Game in 1940). The Giants warmed to the plan, but the Braves held out—until Ward, in a bit of brinkmanship, phoned their front office and hinted that the *Tribune* would announce the game was moving forward regardless, or else report that the Braves had just killed it.

"Can you and the National League," he asked, "stand that kind of publicity?" The bluff worked: the Braves capitulated.[7]

With every club on board and no objection from Commissioner Landis, the game was officially on. New questions arose: Where would the game be played? Who would be the "home" team?

Obviously, the contest would be staged in Chicago. Wrigley Field had been the Cubs' home since 1916, and Comiskey Park was the White Sox home since 1910. The fields had different dimensions and seating capacities, and neither league would concede homefield advantage. Finally, they agreed that a coin toss would determine the location and that, on the AL's behalf, Harridge would have the honor of making the call. He called heads, and heads it was—which meant the game would take place at Comiskey. Heydler, revealing just how much the leagues did not like one another, called for a second coin toss to determine which team would bat second, notwithstanding that an AL park was hosting the contest. The AL prevailed in this back-and-forth, but the leagues agreed that the AL official baseball would be used for the first half of the game, whereupon it would be substituted with the NL official baseball for the second half. Even in unity, suspicion lingered. Cooperation required choreography. The leagues would share a stage, but neither would fully yield it.

With the rules and location set, Ward unleashed his promotional flair to make it a hit. Notably, no one had asked any players if they wanted to participate.

Choosing the Rosters

In the *Tribune's* Sunday edition of May 19, 1933, Ward trumpeted with a showman's flair: "This is an announcement of the greatest baseball game ever scheduled. Never has the maximum strength of one major league been pitted against the maximum strength of the other."[8] The boast carried an implicit lineage. While Ward framed the moment as unprecedented, his language echoed—perhaps unknowingly—Murnane Day and its inter-league assembly of stars, if not yet the full "maximum strength" of both leagues.

Ward proposed that fans choose the starting lineups by paper ballot while each league president picked the remaining players. Each roster would consist of fifteen players—a number that would soon expand to eighteen as excitement grew.

Ward and his friends at the *Tribune* determined that they would print up ballots and tabulate the votes cast. As Lew Freedman wryly noted, "Given the long history of Chicago's iffy reputation of handling political elections, not everyone felt this was a great idea."[9] Sports editors nationwide quickly sought a role in the process, both to boost revenue and to rally support for stars from their home cities. Commissioner Landis ultimately opened participation to the broader press, and fifty-five newspapers collectively distributed nearly eight million ballots over the course of a month—ensuring that the fan vote became not just a promotional device, but a genuinely national exercise. For a sport that had recently learned the cost of secrecy, the All-Star Game unfolded in full daylight. Selection was public. Tabulation was announced. Participation was visible. Ritual replaced rumor.

To spur interest, the *Tribune* offered $500 in cash prizes for the best roster predictions. First prize—$250—went to whoever came closest to naming both leagues' full starting lineups, including batting order and the three pitchers in order of appearance. Two $100 prizes rewarded the most accurate AL and NL lineup predictions, and fifty $1 prizes went to fans who correctly named the six pitchers. If multiple fans tied in any category, the earliest postmarked entries claimed the cash.[10]

About half a million ballots were cast, the *Tribune* reported. The results appeared on June 25—just eleven days before the game—and thus many players learned of their selection with little notice, while the managers still had to choose the rest of the rosters. League presidents retained veto power and ensured that every club in each league had at least one player representing it.

Arch Ward himself declared a new king of baseball based on the vote tallies: "Hail to Al Simmons, new monarch of major league baseball! The fans of America have voted him the crown in the greatest test of public sentiment the sport has known." Simmons, of the White Sox, was clearly a hometown favorite who garnered 346,291 votes. Even Ward acknowledged the mixed nature of his achievement: "Chicago [fans] filed the heaviest returns, which was to be expected, for the poll was initiated by The *Tribune* and the game is to be played in a Chicago park."[11] Nonetheless, Ward felt compelled to write that Babe Ruth's failure to beat out Simmons for the highest vote tally "does not necessarily mean" that "the great home run walloper…is losing his popularity," predicting that "no player would receive a warmer welcome than Ruth."[12] Ruth's 320,518 votes were second-highest for an AL outfielder.

Chuck Klein of the Philadelphia Phillies took the voting crown for the National League with 342,283 votes, second overall to Simmons. There is no available breakdown of how many ballots came from each newspaper in each city, so it is impossible to assess how much geography played in the voting outcomes. Many players with recognizable names did not make the popularity cut and also did not get selected by the league presidents to join the rosters, including Mel Ott of the New York Giants and Dizzy Dean of the St. Louis Cardinals. The Cubs' Lon Warneke received the most NL votes among pitchers, despite having lost four consecutive decisions by the day the results were published.

Ward's marketing genius was on full display in the same edition of the newspaper with a short column headlined "I WAS THERE IN '33—BOY, WOTTA GAME!" The gimmicky nature of selling tickets was comical. "Only 50,000 fortunate fans will be able to say, 'I was there at Comiskey park in '33 when the American league stars met the National league's greatest players,'" boasted the article. "If you intend to be there," the article further contended, "you are advised to make your ticket application now. And if you are not there, how are you going to explain it to your grandchildren?" Fans were directed to send paper applications to a new "All-Star Baseball Department" housed at Comiskey Park, including a cashier's check or money order made payable to "All-Star Baseball Game"—with a self-addressed, stamped envelope included alongside such request for those not lucky enough to grab seats.[13]

The abstraction was thus complete. Headlines had been written. Ballots would be counted. Now the idea required embodiment. The promise of "maximum strength" would take human form.

The American League

The American League arrived in Chicago with a roster that reflected baseball's institutional maturity. These were not novelties or local curiosities, but established professionals—men whose authority came from repetition, durability, and command earned over time. The league's stars embodied a version of excellence that prized reliability as much as brilliance, a sensibility well suited to an era when baseball was consolidating its place as a national institution.

Charlie Gehringer, Joe Cronin, and Jimmy Dykes represented the league's steady core—infielders whose value accrued season by season, whose statistics testified less to spectacle than to dependability. Their presence reinforced what the All-Star Game was becoming: not a carnival of surprises, but a sanctioned gathering of proven stewards.

Yet even within this ordered professionalism, there were figures who transcended category, none more so than Lou Gehrig. By 1933, Gehrig was already more than a star; he was a moral presence. His durability had become its own drama, a testament to discipline rather than flair. He did not perform greatness; he inhabited it.

His participation carried particular weight. Gehrig was closing in on Everett Scott's consecutive-games-played record of 1,307. Gehrig was scheduled to break the record the following month, but some worried he wouldn't make it back to the Bronx for the next day's game against the Tigers if the weather was bad in Chicago.

Asked about the risk, Gehrig was unequivocal about attending the special game: "I will go gladly and give up my chance at Scott's mark…I will prize the honor highly, and…you will find me on that train to Chicago."[14] One gets an immediate sense both of Gehrig's character and his humility—the kind Murnane would admire and write about.

Leadership too had its representatives. Connie Mack—another living bridge to the Murnane Game—embodied a managerial ethos of order and restraint. The All-Star Game, viewed through his presence, felt less like innovation than codification: baseball organizing what it had already learned how to celebrate.

The Yankee presence was deep. Lefty Gomez took the mound; Babe Ruth started in right, a fitting bookend to his appearance at Fenway sixteen years earlier; Bill Dickey and Tony Lazzeri were nearby, reminders of "Murderers' Row." Behind the plate stood Rick Ferrell, with Al Simmons roaming the outfield—a hitter as productive as he was combustible, once ejected for making faces at an umpire after a called third strike.

Sam West represented the St. Louis Browns. His auspicious path to the majors began when he was benched by his high school team, leading West to storm into town to watch the semi-professional baseball team play. Their regular right fielder was a no-show for the game, so West volunteered to fill in, played well, and earned a spot on the team.[15]

And then there was Jimmie Foxx, slugging 534 home runs on his way to winning three MVP awards and getting elected to the Hall of Fame. No one was happier to have Foxx as a teammate on this day than Lefty Gomez, who once delayed pitching to Foxx in hopes Foxx might receive a mid-game phone call and need to step away.[16] Decades later, Gomez quipped that when astronaut Neil Armstrong found an unidentifiable white object on the moon, he immediately knew what it was: "That was a home run ball hit off me in 1937 by Jimmie Foxx."[17] Rivalry thus softened into camaraderie, reminding the crowd that beneath the structure remained play—that generosity, humor, and improvisation still had a place within the sport's expanding pageantry.

The roster did not strain for novelty. Its authority lay in recognition: a confirmation of who baseball already knew itself to be. Yet in the day's lighter moments, the league allowed the game to loosen its tie, recalling an older impulse—one that had once animated a benefit game at Fenway Park—where stars gathered not to advance standings but to serve the game itself.

The National League

If the AL represented institutional confidence, the NL—which wore uniforms with the words "NATIONAL LEAGUE" across their chests and hats that said "NL"—carried the weight of memory. Its roster leaned older, freighted with established reputations and familiar heroes. These were not players seeking definition; they were players who had already shaped an era.

The NL team had a strong St. Louis Cardinals presence, including four starters: the pitcher-catcher battery of "Wild Bill" Hallahan and Jimmie Wilson, Frankie Frisch at second base, and Pepper Martin at third.

At third base stood Pie Traynor, the enduring face of Pittsburgh baseball—a craftsman whose steadiness had made him indispensable over nearly two decades. Nearby was Paul Waner, slight in build but immense in consistency, a former MVP whose bat rarely betrayed him. Waner's greatness lay not in spectacle but in accumulation; he played the game as if it were meant to be mastered quietly.

Behind the plate was Gabby Hartnett, long regarded as the National League's premier catcher. His career had already intertwined with baseball legend—behind the plate for Babe Ruth's called shot, guiding pitchers through October pressure, and authoring his own immortal "Homer in the Gloamin'."[18] Hartnett embodied something essential about the All-Star gathering: these were not simply the season's best performers, but custodians of memory.

The pitching staff carried similar gravitas. Lon Warneke, tall and deliberate, had led the league in wins and ERA a year earlier. His presence reflected the era's admiration for endurance and command. Others brought velocity, guile, or reputation—but collectively they projected stability rather than flash. The National League was not here to dazzle; it was here to affirm.

Yet affirmation did not exclude personality. Even among established veterans, there was room for theater. Players who had battled each other for years now shared dugouts, trading stories, comparing grips, and discovering how quickly rivalry could soften into camaraderie when standings were suspended. The All-Star format—like the Murnane Game before it—made space for this duality: competition without consequence, excellence without enmity.

In that sense, the National League's contribution to the afternoon was not merely its talent but its history. The league arrived bearing the accumulated weight of baseball's first half-century. If the American League symbolized professional maturity, the National League symbolized continuity—a reminder that the game's authority rested not only in present brilliance but in remembered greatness.

And as these veterans took the field, the gathering began to resemble something more than an exhibition. It felt, instead, like recognition—of careers, of reputations, of a shared inheritance. What the Murnane Game had done locally in 1917—bringing together the sport's leading figures for a cause larger than standings—the National League now did on a national stage. The difference was scale. The impulse remained the same.

Because no formal precedent existed for selecting a manager, the leagues turned to stature. John McGraw, the imperious former skipper of the New York Giants, came out of retirement to lead the National League. Opposite him stood Connie Mack—three-piece suit immaculate as ever—who had guided the All-Stars at the Murnane Game sixteen years earlier and had managed the Athletics since the American League's infancy. Born during the Civil War, Mack himself was a link between baseball's rough beginnings and its modern ambitions.

The pairing carried history with it. Mack and McGraw were longtime rivals, their relationship reflecting the deeper animus that had simmered between the leagues since the American League's arrival. It was McGraw, after all, who in 1904 had refused to let his Giants face the American League champion Boston Americans in the World's Series, insisting the senior circuit needed no such validation.

The talent assembled beneath them underscored the day's gravity. Eleven of the eighteen starters would eventually enter the Hall of Fame, along with both managers, two of the four umpires, and several reserves. This was not merely a showcase; it was a gathering of a generation.

The Game

On Thursday, July 6, 1933—a beautiful summer day, dry and warm with temperatures in the high eighties—47,595 people filled Comiskey Park. Because the game was played under World Series rules, no fans were permitted on the field, eliminating the standing-room tickets that were still common in that area.

Separately, organizers took deliberate steps to make the game accessible to a broad public. Tickets were sold at regular-season Chicago White Sox prices—$1.65 for box seats, $1.10 for grandstand, and 55 cents for the bleachers—with a maximum ticket purchase of four tickets per buyer. To further maximize attendance, 2,250 bleacher seats were placed on sale just two days before the scheduled game. Despite the grim economy, they sold out within forty-five minutes—as fast as the ticket windows could facilitate the transactions. The players arrived in Chicago the day before, after their regular season games had concluded.

By 1:15pm, the "Game of the Century" began when AL home-plate umpire Bill Dinneen yelled, "Play ball!"

Having won the second coin flip, the AL would bat second. Lefty Gomez retired a quick 1-2-3 to start the game, and Charlie Gehringer of the AL walked and stole second as the only activity in the bottom of the first.

The NL came out swinging in the top of the second, with Chick Hafey hitting an infield single followed by the captain Bill Terry singling to left field. Wally Berger grounded into a double play, after which Dick Bartell struck out to end the team's turn at bat. The AL then struck. With one out in the bottom of the second, Jimmy Dykes and Joe Cronin were each walked by "Wild Bill" Hallahan, who was living up to his nickname. As Harvey Woodruff of the *Chicago Tribune* wrote the following day, "Wild Bill Hallahan...was wild." Rick Ferrell flied out to Chuck Klein in right field, but Gomez helped himself with a single to center that scored Dykes before Gomez got tagged out in a run-down.

Gomez sent the NL down 1-2-3 again in the third, and the game broke open in the bottom of the inning when Gehringer drew a lead-off walk. With Ruth at the plate, Hallahan fired—and the Great Bambino did what he had been doing on exhibition stages for nearly two decades. He lashed a sharp, low liner to deep right field that cleared the fence—the first home run in All-Star Game history.

It was a familiar act: the same theatrical authority he had

displayed during the skill competitions at the Murnane Game sixteen years earlier, when power itself had been part of the spectacle. It was more than a statistic. In a decade shadowed by scandal and depression, the game's most luminous figure had supplied the spectacle the nation craved. The exhibition had found its emblem. Comiskey Park erupted as the American League seized a 3–0 lead, and McGraw quickly summoned Hallahan from the mound.

Wild Bill had walked five in less than three innings pitched, *still* an All-Star Game record for most walks given up by a pitcher in the Mid-Summer Classic. Cubs' ace Lon Warneke—who, the evening before the game, had pledged, "I'll be out there, bearin' down all I can"—relieved Hallahan, and in bearing down indeed, he was able to stop the bleeding.[19]

In the top of the sixth, the NL finally struck back. With one out, the pitcher Warneke tripled to right field. Pepper Martin grounded out to third, and Warneke scored. Then, with the bases clear, Frisch homered to deep right field to bring the game 3-2, still in favor of the AL. But the lead doubled in the bottom of the inning. Cronin led off with a single to center field, Ferrell bunted him over, and Earl Averill—batting for General Crowder—singled to center to bring in Cronin. The NL couldn't muster any more offense, and the AL hung on to win the first official All-Star Game 4-2. Gomez got the win, Hallahan was tagged with the loss, and Lefty Grove earned the save for a three-inning appearance in which he scattered three hits and also struck out three. The whole game took two hours and five minutes to play from start to finish.

Legacy and Tradition

The thrilling game, the roaring crowd, and the unabashed success of that afternoon quickly sparked calls to make the contest an annual tradition. Though the players received no direct payment, they took pride in knowing that ticket revenues would help those who had come before them—former ballplayers who had fallen on hard times. The gate brought in roughly $56,000, with $45,000 set aside for that benevolent fund.

Asked afterward what he thought of the spectacle, Commissioner Landis spoke for nearly everyone watching: "That's a grand show—and it should be continued."[20] Within weeks, baseball's owners agreed. At their next meeting, they resolved to hold another such game the following summer, rotating the host city each year—a vital selling point Arch Ward had devised to get the leagues on board. The 1934 All-Star Game took place at the Polo Grounds, home of the New York Giants. The American League prevailed again, and of the eighteen starters, seventeen would one day enter the Hall of Fame. A tradition had taken root.

The All-Star Game did not invent baseball's capacity for shared meaning; it inherited it. In 1917, the sport had revealed its instinct for collective affirmation. In 1919, it exposed its vulnerability. In 1920, it imposed authority. In 1933, it codified ritual. The Mid-Summer Classic was not a novelty. It was the culmination of a lesson learned in stages. What had once belonged to a city now belonged to a nation. What had once been communal now bore the marks of institution. Yet the impulse remained the same: to gather the game's best not merely to win, but to remind baseball—and the country—what it was for.

Boston owner John I. Taylor helped shape the early Red Sox dynasty—and gave the team the nickname "Red Sox," which soon became one of the most famous in sport. Taylor was a driving force in organizing Murnane Day despite having previously sold the team.

THE GREAT FINISH

September 27, 1917: Top of the Eighth, 0-0

In the top of the eighth Foster retired Walter Johnson, now pitching, and then Maranville. With two outs, Chapman drew his third walk of the day and again stole second. But Cobb couldn't bring him home, as he flew out to Walker in center.

Walter Johnson retired the first two batters he faced in the bottom of the eighth—Foster and Hooper—with the economy that had defined his career. Then Jack Barry singled to left, giving the Red Sox a pulse. Hoblitzell followed with a Baltimore chop grounder that bounded sharply over Johnson's head. Johnson made no play, assuming either Maranville at short or Chapman at second would handle it and flip for the force at second. But the ball skidded too quickly, splitting the infielders and rolling into center.

With two on and two out, reigning World Series hero Duffy Lewis stepped to the plate. He dug in. Johnson bore down. The great Senators pitcher came straight at him, a fastball down Main Street, and Lewis caught it flush—square on the sweet spot—driving it high and deep toward the right and center field bleachers. The crowd erupted. Barry and Hoblitzell scored easily as Lewis cruised into third with a two-run triple. Johnson recovered to retire Walker, but the damage was done. After eight innings, the Red Sox led 2–0, three outs from victory over the All-Star roster.

Foster stayed on for the ninth. The crowd stood throughout, willing each pitch toward its conclusion. Speaker drew a lead-off walk, but after slowly jogging to first base he suddenly burst for second, trying to stretch the walk into a two-bagger. Thomas threw a laser to second, where Everett Scott was waiting to apply the tag, and he nabbed Speaker on the shins. Foster then got Jackson and McInnis, and the game was over—a taut, finely pitched duel decided by a single swing. The contest had taken just under two hours, marked by restraint rather than excess. And then restraint vanished. Fans poured from the grandstand onto the field, flooding the grass in celebration, unconcerned that the result counted for nothing in the standings. This was never about standings. The box score would record the particulars—the hits, the innings, the errors—but no ledger could capture what followed. The Red Sox had won, even if their season had already slipped beyond contention. The pennant race belonged to others now. What lingered instead was the odd inversion the afternoon had produced: champions without a future that season, stars united for a day and then rivals again, and a game that had briefly rearranged baseball's usual hierarchies.

The day was such a success that after the game former Red Sox owner John I. Taylor was asked about the possibility of a city series between the Red Sox and the Braves—a revival of local rivalry not for pennants, but for public enthusiasm—evidence of how readily the afternoon so contemporaneously invited replication.

Everett Scott, the Red Sox shortstop, captured the moment with a grin as he sat in the clubhouse after, unlacing his cleats. "So we are the ex-champs, huh?" he said. "We are the Ex! And they are the stars—well, well!"[21] *The line carried no edge, only recognition. The sting of no pennant chase did not matter.*

The afternoon slipped free of statistics and passed into something rarer: a moment claimed by the crowd, consecrated on the field, and carried forward into memory. One that, as the Boston Journal *noted, Tim Murnane "would have liked."*

The day now belonged to history.

Pitcher George "Rube" Foster warms up for the Boston Red Sox during the club's championship years. A steady right-hander, Foster helped anchor Boston's pitching staff alongside Babe Ruth and Dutch Leonard.

BOSTON Base Ball Club.

PLAYERS.	Pos.	1	2	3	4	5	6	7	8	9	O.	R.	B.
1. G. Wright,	SS												
2. Barnes,	2d												
3. Leonard,	LF												
4. McVey,	C												
5. Spaulding,	P												
6 Gould,	1st												
7. Schafer,	3d												
8. Rogers,	RF												
9. H. Wright,	CF												
Totals.		0	6	1	11	6	0	0	0	0			

6 7 18 24 24 24 24 24

24

Scorer, Umpire,

MANSFIELD Base Ball Club.

PLAYERS.	Pos.	1	2	3	4	5	6	7	8	9	O.	R.	B.
1. Clapp,	C												
2. Bailey,	RF												
3. Bentley,	P												
4. Murnan,	1st												
5. Booth,	2d												
6 Tipper,	3d												
7. O'Rourke,	SS												
8. McCarton,	CF												
9. Fields,	LF												
Totals.		0	0	0	2	0	0	0	1	0			

0 0 2 2 2 2 3 3

3

Scorer, Time of Game, Hrs. Min.

PRINTING of every description executed with Neatness and Dispatch, at THE RICE, GODDARD & CO., Printing Establishment, No. 41 Milk Street, Boston.

This scorecard from Middletown's game against Boston shows Tim Murnane—then spelling his name "Murnan"—playing first base and batting cleanup, while George and Harry Wright led the Red Stockings.

A 19th-century graphic depicting the appearance and atmosphere of baseball during the era when Tim Murnane emerged as one of the game's earliest stewards.

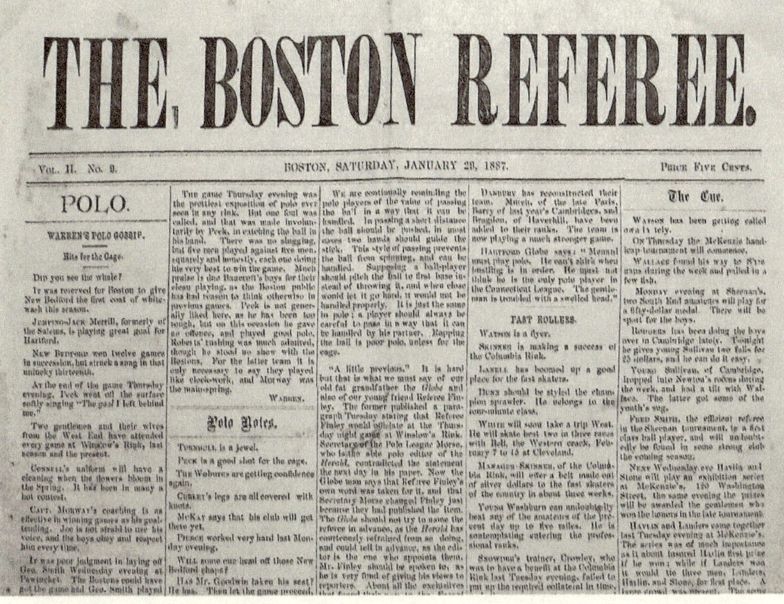

THE BOSTON REFEREE.

VOL. II. No. 9. BOSTON, SATURDAY, JANUARY 29, 1887. PRICE FIVE CENTS.

POLO.

WARREN'S POLO GOSSIP.

Bits for the Cage.

DID you see the whale?

IT was reserved for Boston to give New Bedford the first coat of whitewash this season.

JUMPING-JACK Merrill, formerly of the Salems, is playing great goal for Hartford.

NEW BEDFORD won twelve games in succession, but struck a snag in that unlucky thirteenth.

AT the end of the game Thursday evening, Peck went off the surface softly singing "The *goal* I left behind me."

Two gentlemen and their wives from the West End have attended every game at Winslow's Rink, last season and the present.

CONNELL'S uniform will have a cleaning when the flowers bloom in the Spring. It has been in many a hot contest.

CAPT. MORWAY'S coaching is as effective in winning games as his goal-tending. Joe is not afraid to use his voice, and the boys obey and respect him every time.

IT was poor judgment in laying off Geo. Smith Wednesday evening at Pawtucket. The Bostons could have got the game had Geo. Smith played

THE game Thursday evening was the prettiest exposition of polo ever seen in any rink. But one foul was called, and that was made involuntarily by Peck, in catching the ball in his hand. There was no slugging, but five men played against five men, squarely and honestly, each one doing his very best to win the game. Much praise is due Bancroft's boys for their clean playing, as the Boston public has had reason to think otherwise in previous games. Peck is not generally liked here, as he has been too rough, but on this occasion he gave no offence, and played good polo. Roberts' rushing was much admired, though he stood no show with the Bostons. For the latter team it is only necessary to say they played like clock-work, and Morway was the main-spring.

WARREN.

Polo Notes.

TURNBULL is a jewel.

PECK is a good shot for the cage.

THE Woburns are getting confidence again.

CURLEY'S legs are all covered with knots.

MCKAY says that his club will get there yet.

PIERCE worked very hard last Monday evening.

WILL some one head off those New Bedford chaps?

HAS Mr. Goodwin taken his seat? He has. Then let the game proceed.

WE are continually reminding the polo players of the value of passing the ball in a way that it can be handled. In passing a short distance the ball should be pushed, in most cases two hands should guide the stick. This style of passing prevents the ball from spinning, and can be handled. Supposing a ball-player should pitch the ball to first base instead of throwing it, and when close would let it go hard, it would not be handled properly. It is just the same in polo; a player should always be careful to pass in a way that it can be handled by his partner. Rapping the ball is poor polo, unless for the cage.

"A little previous." It is hard but that is what we must say of our old fat grandfather the *Globe* and also of our young friend Referee Finley. The former published a paragraph Tuesday stating that Referee Finley would officiate at the Thursday night game at Winslow's Rink. Secretary of the Polo League Morse, who is the able polo editor of the *Herald*, contradicted the statement the next day in his paper. Now the Globe man says that Referee Finley's own word was taken for it, and that Secretary Morse changed Finley just because they had published the item. The *Globe* should not try to name the referee in advance, as the *Herald* has courteously refrained from so doing, and could tell in advance, as the editor is the one who appoints them. Mr. Finley should be spoken to, as he is very fond of giving his views to reporters. About all the exclusives

DANBURY has reconstructed their team. Murch, of the late Paris, Barry of last year's Cambridges, and Bragdon, of Haverhill, have been added to their ranks. The team is now playing a much stronger game.

HARTFORD Globe says: "Mennal must play polo. He can't shirk when hustling is in order. He must not think he is the only polo player in the Connecticut League. The gentleman is troubled with a swelled head."

FAST ROLLERS.

WATSON is a flyer.

SKINNER is making a success of the Columbia Rink.

LASELL has boomed up a good place for the fast skaters.

DUNN should be styled the champion sprawler. He belongs to the four-minute class.

WHITE will soon take a trip West. He will skate best two in three races with Bell, the Western crack, February 7 to 15 at Cleveland.

MANAGER SKINNER, of the Columbia Rink, will offer a belt made out of silver dollars to the fast skaters of the country in about three weeks.

YOUNG Washburn can undoubtedly beat any of the amateurs of the present day up to five miles. He is contemplating entering the professional ranks.

SNOWMAN'S trainer, Crowley, who was to have a benefit at the Columbia Rink last Tuesday evening, failed to put up the required collateral in time,

The Cue.

WATSON has been getting called away lately.

ON Thursday the McKenzie handicap tournament will commence.

WALLACE found his way to S[illegible] during the week and pulled in a few fish.

MONDAY evening at Sheenan's, two South End amateurs will play for a fifty-dollar medal. There will be sport for the boys.

RODGERS has been doing the boys over in Cambridge lately. To-night he gives young Sullivan two falls for 25 dollars, and he can do it easy.

YOUNG Sullivan, of Cambridge, dropped into Newton's rooms during the week, and had a tilt with Wallace. The latter got some of the youth's sug.

FRED SMITH, the efficient referee in the Sheenan tournament, is a first class ball player, and will undoubtedly be found in some strong club the coming season.

NEXT Wednesday eve Havlin and Stone will play an exhibition series at McKenzie's, 120 Washington Street, the same evening the prizes will be awarded the gentlemen who won the honors in the late tournament.

HAVLIN and Landers came together last Tuesday evening at McKenzie's. The series was of much importance as it about insured Havlin first prize if he won; while if Landers won it would tie three men, Landers, Havlin, and Stone, for first place. A large crowd was present. The same

Before becoming sports editor of the *Boston Globe,* Tim Murnane founded and ran his own sporting paper, *The Boston Referee.*

JOHN L. "BUNCOED."

Although a Full-Fledged Tenderloiner, He Gave Up $15 Easy—The Trick Cannot be Repeated With Safety.

NEW YORK, Dec 26—John L. Sullivan has been telling recently interesting stories of how he spent, lost, gave away and was robbed of the $1,000,000 he made by earning—and fairly earning—the pugilistic championship.

John L. tells all this as happening several years ago, but he forgets to mention the little 15 spot he lost last week.

The "big fellow" is a full-fledged tenderloiner now, and any one of that class is expected to be "as fly as they make them," and the last ones to be "played," to use John L.'s language.

But, alas! John L. was done, and done brown and rich. He may not, in consequence, like to see the story in print, but it's too good to keep.

A reporter was in John's place the other evening, and the boniface hailed him at once:

"Say, old boy, do you know Tim?"

"Tim? Tim who?" was the reply.

"Tim Murnane," said Sullivan.

"Tim Murnane of Boston, the baseball writer? Of course, I do."

"Well, is this his fist?" John said, holding out a billet doux for inspection.

The note was a "hurry touch" of the rankest kind, and John was told so, and also that Murnane had not been here since the baseball meeting.

"A look of sadness, a flush of shame o'er the face of the ex champion came."

"Bilked again, and running a joint in the tenderloin, too! What do you think of a mug like me? I'll tell you about it. But, here, waiter, the drinks are on me. Give my friend what he wants.

"Well, you see, my telephone rang yesterday afternoon and a mug hollers 'Is that you, John L.?' I says, 'Yes, of course it is. Who do you think it is, Duncan Harrison?'

" 'No,' the mug says; 'I'm Tim.'

" 'Tim who?' says I.

" 'Murnane,' says the mug, in a sort of a muzzled voice, as if he had his head in a bucket of mush.

"Now, I know Murnane, and he's a good fellow; one of the best, and I knew him in Boston.

" 'O, is that you, Tim?' I says, 'Merry Christmas.'

" 'Thanks,' says the mug with a frog in his throat; 'but can you lend me a 10 spot until tomorrow, John? I'm in a little game up here, and I'm broke.'

" 'All right, Tim,' I said. 'I haven't got a block of houses just now, but a tenner won't break me.'

" 'All right,' says the mug; 'I'll send a messenger down for it.'

"Sure enough, in about five minutes a messenger boy came rushing in with a note which read: 'Make it $15 if you can, John,' and I, like a 'sucker,' put another five to the ten.

"Give us another drink, waiter. It's up to me. I'm it. But, just let another bloke ring me up for a tenner over the phony, phone! That's all."

And John glared at a newcomer who had a "touchy" look in his eye.

Boxing champion John L. Sullivan was once "buncoed" into giving money under false pretenses to a swindler posing—of all people—as baseball writer Tim Murnane.

PREFACE

In the last few years base ball has developed in a most remarkable manner, and while the public keep well posted on the doings of the players they know very little about the management of the sport.

With leagues growing up in every quarter of this country and new men coming into the profession, the demand for expert information has increased, until this booklet should be welcome.

T. H. M.

Tim Murnane's writing made him one of the game's leading evangelists. In this preface to *How to Umpire, How to Coach, How to Captain, How to Manage, How to Organize a League,* he sets his sights on making baseball accessible to the masses.

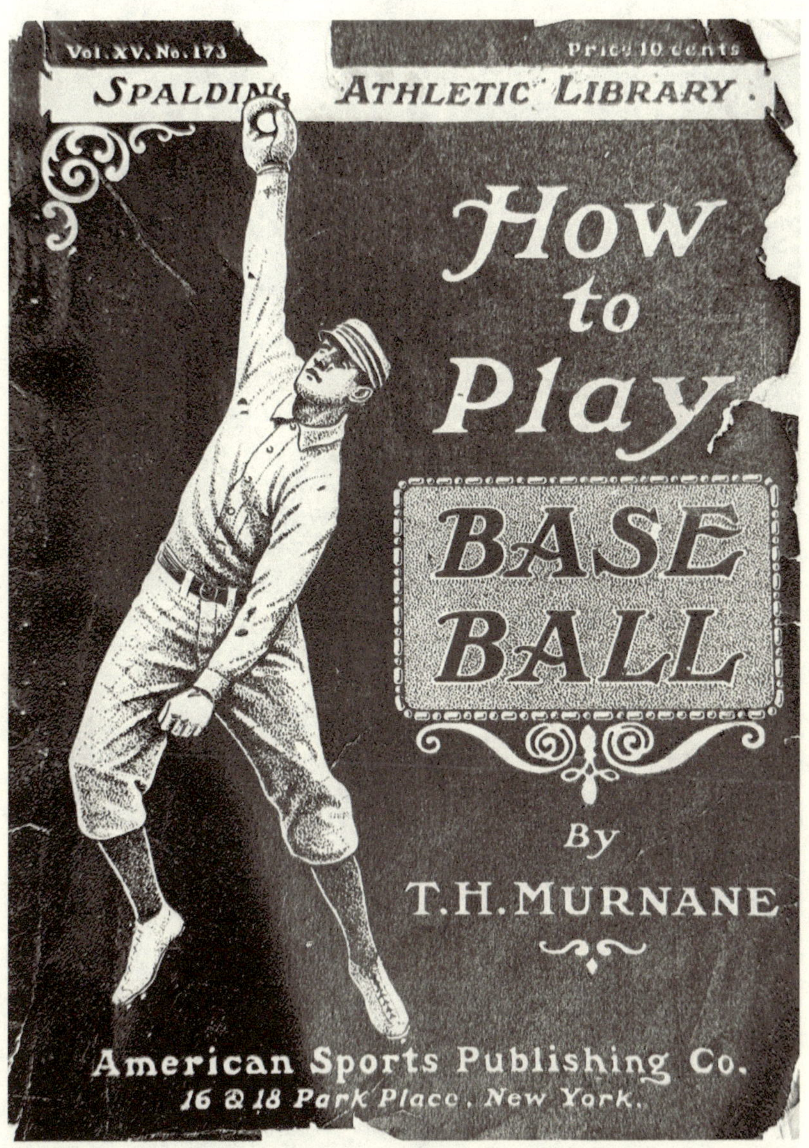

Tim Murnane's *How to Play Base Ball* was one of several books he wrote to help explain and popularize the game.

Cy Young threw the first perfect game in Red Sox history on May 5, 1904, when the club was still known as the Boston Americans, a feat that helped define one of the most remarkable careers the game has ever known.

Red Sox players Babe Ruth, Ernie Shore, Rube Foster, and Del Gainer sit along the edge of the dugout at Fenway Park.

14 THE BOSTON SUNDAY GLOBE—JANUARY 16, 1916

TIM MURNANE VISITS GEORGE FOSTER, WHO IS A REAL FARMER IN OKLAHOMA

BENNY KAUFF, FED STAR WHO HAS BEEN SOLD TO THE YANKEES

PAY $30,000 TO GET KAUFF

Giants Give Big Price for Fed Star.

McGraw and Sinclair Come to Terms After Hour's Talk.

Yanks, Having Leo Magee, Expect to Land Baker.

THIEF'S CALL COSTS BAN JOHNSON $800

Mrs Ban the Chief Loser at Chicago Home.

Her Gown and Sable Cape Are Gone, He Loses Suit and Bag.

BRAVES INTEND TO KEEP EVERS

Quick Checkmate for Tinker Maneuver.

Johnny Under Contract and Boston Needs Him, Too.

"Heinie" Wagner May Get a Job With White Sox.

Tim Murnane distinguished himself as a journalist by visiting players at their offseason homes, offering fans rare glimpses into the private lives of baseball's stars.

Erstwhile allies and rivals, John F. Fitzgerald and James Michael Curley each served as mayor of Boston and as a member of the U.S. Congress. Both were friends of Tim Murnane.

Fenway Park's intimate geometry and famous quirks reflect the character of baseball's oldest ballpark.

In June 1917, gamblers stormed the field at Fenway Park in an attempt to prevent a game from becoming official—an episode illustrator Wallace Goldsmith captured with biting humor.

BIG LEAGUE STARS PLAY HERE ON "TIM MURNANE DAY," SEPT 27

Red Sox Will Meet Some of Johnson's and Tener's Best in Memorial Game

Thursday, Sept 27, will be "Tim Murnane Day" at Fenway Park.

That afternoon, which is an open date for the world's champion Red Sox, Manager Barry's team will play an all-star nine of American and National League players, and, besides the ball game, the big leaguers will have a field competition in fungo hitting, throwing and running.

The ball game and the competitions have been arranged as a part of a memorial to Timothy H. Murnane, who for so many years wrote baseball for the Globe and was so closely identified with the game as advisor to its officers and magnates and as its champion as the greatest of all the Nation's sports. It is believed that a very substantial memorial fund will be raised, as all proceeds from the game will be placed in trust as an educational fund for Mr Murnane's children.

Sept 27 the American League baseball clubs will be in the East and Boston has an open date between series with the Indians and the Browns. Stars from all the other American League Clubs and from the National League teams, then in the West, will be selected by a committee of newspaper men, and club owners everywhere have agreed to have the players on hand.

Pres Johnson of the American League and Pres Tener of the National have started the subscription with checks for $100 for their boxes, and major and minor league club owners from all parts of the country are getting together to show their appreciation of Mr Murnane and all he accomplished for baseball.

The list of big league players who will come here to play against the World's Champions on "Tim Murnane Day" has not been completed, but the team selected will be an interesting one to see together, not only in the ball game, but in the competition of running around the bases, getting down to first, fungo hitting, accurate throwing and throwing for distance. Cups will be awarded in each event.

The following committee will have the memorial in charge: Col Harry E. Russell, chairman; John F. Morrill, treasurer; John I. Taylor, secretary; Harry H. Frazee, president of the Red Sox; Percy D. Haughton, president of the Braves; A. C. Wise, treasurer of the Braves; Mayor James M. Curley, Congressman James A. Gallivan, Postmaster William F. Murray, Joseph J. Lannin, Dist Atty Joseph C. Pelletier, Joseph Santosuosso, A. Shuman, William F. Garcelon, John Dooley, W. S. Barnes Jr, John Campbell, Daniel O'Neill, president of the Eastern League; A. Paul Keith, George V. Brown, Patrick J. Donovan, Hugh Duffy, Alfred S. Codman, Jacob C. Morse and Louis M. Jacobs.

On September 27, 1917, Fenway Park was the place to be as Boston celebrated "Tim Murnane Day."

"Duffy's Cliff," the steep embankment that once rose in left field at Fenway Park, turned routine fly balls into adventures for visiting outfielders.

A young Joe Jackson proudly holds the loving cup he won for the longest throw on Murnane Day, an early token of his remarkable natural talent in both his and the game's more innocent days.

Years later, Jackson still kept the loving cup—one of the treasured reminders of the game that had once embraced him.

Military services held at Fenway Park during World War I reminded Boston that baseball and the wider world were deeply intertwined.

American League

FIRST BASE.

Gehrig, New York........312,680
Foxx, Philadelphia........127,104
Kuhel, Washington....... 4,836
Alexander, Boston......... 3,556
Davis, Detroit............. 1,451

SECOND BASE.

Gehringer, Detroit........239,756
Lazzeri, New York........164,830
Melillo, St. Louis.......... 32,457
Hodapp, Boston........... 32,194
Cissell, Cleveland......... 15,826
Bishop, Philadelphia...... 11,617
Myer, Washington........ 8,003
Hayes, Chicago........... 4,935
Foxx, Philadelphia........ 891

THIRD BASE.

Dykes, Chicago...........207,992
Foxx, Philadelphia........142,418
Kamm, Cleveland......... 67,295
J. Sewell, New York....... 41,232
McManus, Boston......... 11,521
Higgins, Philadelphia..... 2,604

SHORTSTOP.

Cronin, Washington.......337,766
Crosetti, New York........ 34,289
Appling, Chicago.......... 27,755
Kress, Chicago............ 2,883
Burnett, Cleveland........ 2,661
Rogell, Detroit............ 1,740
Levey, St. Louis.......... 1,643

CATCHERS.

Dickey, New York.........297,382
Cochrane, Philadelphia....174,530
R. Ferrell, Boston......... 29,431
Hayworth, Detroit........ 7,034
L. Sewell, Washington.... 3,096
Spencer, Cleveland........ 1,845
Berry, Chicago............ 981
Grube, Chicago........... 923

OUTFIELDERS.

Simmons, Chicago.........346,291
Ruth, New York...........320,518
Averill, Cleveland.........246,913
Chapman, New York......108,645
West, St. Louis........... 59,670
Goslin, Washington....... 40,950
Combs, New York......... 32,890
Schulte, Washington...... 30,674
Manush, Washington..... 24,179
Haas, Chicago............ 7,135
Vosmik, Cleveland......... 7,132
Stone, Detroit............. 4,312
Swanson, Chicago......... 3,770
Cramer, Philadelphia...... 3,144
Porter, Cleveland.......... 3,114
Reynolds, St. Louis....... 2,416
G. Walker, Detroit........ 2,240
Roy Johnson, Boston..... 2,237
Oliver, Boston............ 2,094
Foxx, Philadelphia........ 1,095
Fox, Detroit 1,062
Coleman, Philadelphia..... 964
White, Detroit........... 702
Rice, Washington......... 580

PITCHERS.

Grove, Philadelphia.......327,242
Gomez, New York.........253,000
W. Ferrell, Cleveland.....193,120
Hildebrand, Cleveland..... 86,232
Lyons, Chicago........... 49,956
Crowder, Washington..... 31,605
Bridges, Detroit........... 26,195
Ruffing, New York....... 19,563
Marberry, Detroit......... 6,163
Earnshaw, Philadelphia... 4,857
Allen, New York.......... 4,526
Blaeholder, St. Louis...... 2,694
Rowe, Detroit............. 1,626
Pipgras, Boston........... 1,575
Weaver, Washington..... 1,537
Whitehill, Washington.... 1,283
Hadley, St. Louis......... 864
Brennan, New York...... 472
Jones, Chicago............ 443

The first official Major League Baseball All-Star Game took place in Chicago in 1933, when fans voted to select the teams and began a tradition that continues today.

National League

FIRST BASE.

Terry, New York.........278,545
Bottomley, Cincinnati..... 81,525
Grimm, Chicago........... 37,094
Hurst, Philadelphia....... 29,832
Suhr, Pittsburgh.......... 24,697
Leslie, Brooklyn.......... 19,355
Collins, St. Louis.......... 7,599
Jordan, Boston........... 1,688

SECOND BASE.

Frisch, St. Louis..........276,802
W. Herman, Chicago...... 71,184
Critz, New York.......... 47,524
Piet, Pittsburgh........... 29,842
Maranville, Boston........ 25,636
Cuccinello, Brooklyn...... 12,555
Grantham, Cincinnati..... 6,658
Hornsby, St. Louis........ 5,022

THIRD BASE.

Traynor, Pittsburgh.......304,101
Martin, St. Louis......... 88,462
English, Chicago.......... 67,335
Whitney, Boston.......... 33,719
Vergez, New York........ 11,465
Stripp, Brooklyn.......... 6,932
Adams, Cincinnati........ 4,404

SHORTSTOP.

Bartell, Philadelphia......231,639
Vaughan, Pittsburgh......104,607
Durocher, St. Louis....... 31,789
Jurges, Chicago........... 22,224
Koenig, Chicago........... 10,952
Jackson, New York....... 8,305
Wright, Brooklyn......... 5,661

CATCHERS.

Hartnett, Chicago.........338,653
J. Wilson, St. Louis.......137,927
Grace, Pittsburgh......... 47,834
Davis, Philadelphia....... 15,318
Mancuso, New York....... 14,222
Lombardi, Cincinnati...... 11,901
Lopez, Brooklyn.......... 6,820
Hogan, Boston............ 2,464

OUTFIELDERS.

Klein, Philadelphia........342,283
P. Waner, Pittsburgh.....269,291
O'Doul, New York.........230,058
Berger, Boston............136,856
Lindstrom, Pittsburgh.... 85,695
L. Waner, Pittsburgh..... 81,617
Hafey, Cincinnati......... 52,549
Ott, New York............ 40,791
Frederick, Brooklyn....... 24,974
Cuyler, Chicago........... 12,316
Martin, St. Louis......... 11,929
Stephenson, Chicago...... 9,003
F. Herman, Chicago....... 7,610
L. Wilson, Brooklyn...... 2,194
Taylor, Brooklyn.......... 1,654
Douthit, Chicago.......... 1,319
Watkins, St. Louis........ 1,074

PITCHERS.

Warneke, Chicago........312,960
Hubbell, New York.......299,099
Lucas, Cincinnati.........142,669
Hallahan, St. Louis....... 82,583
Dean, St. Louis........... 35,050
Brandt, Boston............ 34,744
Silas Johnson, Cincinnati. 31,942
Meine, Pittsburgh 24,284
Swift, Pittsburgh.......... 15,395
French, Pittsburgh........ 13,613
Swetonic, Pittsburgh..... 12,601
Carleton, St. Louis........ 10,164
Schumacher, New York... 4,417
Clark, Brooklyn........... 4,064
Bush, Chicago............ 2,235
Carroll, Brooklyn......... 1,447
Fitzsimmons, New York... 1,324

The 1933 All-Star tallies read like a who's who of the era's brightest stars.

ALL FENCES ON LEAGUE CIRCUIT LOOK ALIKE TO BIG BABE RUTH

Babe has hit a home run out of every ball park in the American league.

In the seventh article of the series telling the story of his life, the Home Run King today tells of some of the longest hits he has made.

BY BABE RUTH

CHAPTER VII.

There is no telling the exact length of the longest hit made in baseball. Out in St. Louis they still tell of a drive Cap Anson made with his Chicago White Stockings about 20 years ago, which not only cleared the outer fence of the park, but sailed across the street and through the window of a German saloon, where the ball was kept back of the bar for years as a curio.

I don't know whether any of my drives have beaten this one or not, because, as I say, you can't put a foot rule on the flight of a ball. But they gave me a silver cup on the day of the benefit for Tim Murnane's family, Sept. 27, 1917, at Fenway Park, Boston. The Red Sox, with whom I was then playing, went up against a team of American league stars, supposed to have been the greatest ball club ever assembled. We had a fungo contest as a side attraction, and Carl Mays, Duffy Lewis and I went in to see how far we could knock the ball.

THE GREAT THRILL

When my turn came I tossed up a nice new ball and took a long swinging smack at it. Oh, the feel of that club as it met the horsehide square on the nose. I tell you, the ball sang on its way. The distance was measured as accurately as those things can be measured at 435 feet. Remember, I didn't have a pitcher against me to help with the speed of the ball. The ball was practically motionless in the air when I swung into it. It was a dead ball, starting from scratch, with no bounce except what I gave it.

This was quite some ball game, by the way. Ty Cobb, Tris Speaker and Joe Jackson were the outfield, and each one played all the positions in the big outer pasture. In the five innings I pitched the All-Stars got only three hits, but they had their eye on it, all right, for I got only one strikeout. Anyway, the Red Sox won, 2 to 0, scoring those two runs by bunching some hits in the eighth inning.

THE LONGEST HIT

There is one hit of mine which will not stay in the official records, but which I believe to be the longest clout ever made off a major league pitcher. At least, some of the veteran sport writers told me they never saw such a wallop. The Yanks were playing an exhibition game with the Brooklyn Nationals at Jacksonville, Fla., in April, 1920. Al Mamaux was pitching for Brooklyn. In the first inning the first ball he sent me was a nice fast one, a little lower than my waist, straight across the heart of the plate. It was the kind I murder, and I swung to kill it. The last time we saw the ball it was swinging its way over the ten-foot outfield fence of Southside Park and going like a shot. That ball cleared the fence by at least 75 feet. Let's say the total distance travelled was 500 feet; the fence was 429 feet from the plate. If such a hit had been made at the Polo Grounds, I guess the ball would have come pretty close to the top of the green screen in the centre-field bleachers.

There was another blow this year, and the blow almost killed the White Sox. I think Dick Kerr was on the mound for Kid Gleason's olio. Anyway, the pitcher served me one with a home-run ticket on it, and I punched the ticket for a round trip. I knew by the ballyhoo that I had put it over the fence somewhere, but I was pretty close to second base before I got my eye on the ball again—in time to see it drop over the wall close to the dividing line between centre field and right. They say it landed on a soccer field and broke up a run or something.

The 1919 season was a short one, you know. The schedule called for 140 games, of which I played only 130. Normally, the schedule reads 154 games, so you see I got my 29 official home runs and my 31 actual ones on short rations. I felt sure I'd be able to beat that record this season, and now I have proved it, with a long time to go. I don't make any promises, but at the rate I'm going now I think I see something hanging up that looks mighty like a 45—if the pitchers behave.

MADE THE CIRCUIT

And now while we're buzzing about records, I don't remember that any other player has ever made a home run on every park in the circuit in one season. Fenway Park is said to be the most difficult in the league in which to make a home run, and some of the heaviest hitters in the game have always fallen short of the

Years later, Babe Ruth was still talking about Murnane Day, recalling in this piece the fungo distance contest he won that afternoon.

"I WAS THERE IN '33—BOY, WOTTA GAME!"

The Game of the Century! A Century of Progress!

As long as you remember one you will recall the other. But only 50,000 fortunate fans will be able to say, "I was there at Comiskey park in '33 when the American league stars met the National league's greatest players."

"Yep, I saw that game—the greatest game ever played!"

If you intend to be there, you are advised to make your ticket application now. And if you are not there, how are you going to explain it to your grandchildren?

You can still purchase grand stand seats. The cost per ticket is $1.10, the regular daily big league admission in Chicago. Send your application to the All-Star Baseball Department, Comiskey Park, Chicago, with a cashier's check or money order made payable to All-Star Baseball Game. Self-addressed, stamped envelope should accompany each request.

Arch Ward, mastermind of the *Chicago Tribune's* campaign to stage an All-Star Game, wrote this dramatic advertisement that appeared in the paper.

Ticket stubs from the inaugural 1933 All-Star Game evoke a bygone era, when fans carried away small souvenirs from baseball's biggest events.

Babe Ruth, Lou Gehrig, Al Simmons, and a young fan named Edwin Diamond pose at the 1933 All-Star Game at Comiskey Park.

On July 6, 1933, Comiskey Park in Chicago hosted the first official Major League Baseball All-Star Game, echoing Murnane Day's enduring premise: baseball is part of the fabric of American life.

Tim Murnane's grave is marked by a monument paid for by the proceeds of the 1917 benefit game at Fenway Park—a quiet reminder that the game he chronicled for decades ultimately helped memorialize him.

8

AFTER THE APPLAUSE

On Friday morning, September 28, 1917, Boston woke to ordinary light, the kind that arrived without ceremony and asked nothing in return. The harbor smelled of coal smoke and salt, a briny haze drifting inland as tugs nudged freighters toward their berths. Milk carts rattled along brick streets still damp from an overnight rinse, while shopkeepers lifted metal grates and swept yesterday's grit into the gutter with the practiced efficiency of people who knew the hour mattered more than the moment. At South Station, steam rose beneath the arched ceiling as trains arrived and departed in close succession, swallowing and releasing men whose destinations were printed neatly on paper slips tucked into their pockets. Uniforms were everywhere—not as symbols, just as facts of daily life. The city did not pause to ask what it had just taken in.

On stoops and in vestibules newspapers lay folded, their ink still fresh. The benefit game appeared on the front pages, though not at the top. Headlines competed with war dispatches, shipping updates, speeches from Washington—news that asserted its urgency by repetition rather than surprise. The game had been extraordinary, but it had not displaced the world. It had entered it briefly, made its case, and then yielded space again.

In a modest Boston home, the Murnane family faced a different kind of morning, one less concerned with headlines than with continuity. Breakfast still had to be made. Children still had to be dressed and sent out into the world, their routines intact even as the ground beneath them had shifted. Letters arrived—many from people who had never met Tim Murnane but felt, somehow, that they knew him all the same. Alongside them were the quieter obligations, unavoidable and unsentimental: bills to pay, winter approaching, time suddenly measured in new and unfamiliar ways.

The money raised by the game would matter. It bought time, stability, a margin against the abruptness of loss. But money was not the only thing the afternoon had produced. It had converted reputation into protection, admiration into something functional—into leverage against uncertainty. The proceeds were not abstract. They paid for a gravestone where there had been none, marking a life that had until then been left to memory alone. They helped ensure that Murnane's children could remain in school, their days governed by schedules and lessons rather than by the disruptions of loss. These were not gestures of sentiment but of continuity—quiet uses of money that did not promise futures so much as preserve the possibility of them.

Murnane's name, printed for decades at the top of a sports column, now carried weight in rooms he would never enter again. That weight could not guarantee outcomes, but it could open doors. In an era before pensions, before safety nets, before the language of institutional care, that distinction mattered more than sentiment ever could.

Across the city—and across the league—the players dispersed, returning to pennant races that had been briefly interrupted and now resumed as if interruption itself were an inconvenience rather than an event. Schedules reasserted themselves, indifferent to emotion. Ty Cobb traveled to Philadelphia to rejoin the Tigers, where he went 2-for-4, drove in two runs, stole his fifty-fifth base of the season, and was caught stealing twice as well. Connie Mack, who had coached Cobb the day before, now stood in the opposite dugout, focused again on his own struggling Athletics. Tris Speaker, Ray Chapman, and Walter Johnson headed south to Washington, D.C., where the Indians squared off with the Senators. Joe Jackson and Buck Weaver made their way to New York for a series with the Yankees. The geography of the game reassembled itself, line by line.

At Fenway Park, the gates opened again—not for ceremony or remembrance, but because the schedule required them to. Only 356 people passed through, one of the smallest crowds the park would ever record. The St. Louis Browns defeated the Red Sox, 2–1, in a game that seemed almost eager to disappear. It lasted less than ninety minutes, and all three runs were unearned. Five errors interrupted whatever rhythm the afternoon attempted to establish, as if the game itself were shrugging off the burden of significance.

There were no heroics, no sustained rallies, no sense that anything of consequence had just occurred—or that anything needed to. The ballpark, so recently a gathering place for meaning larger than the game itself, felt ordinary again, nearly anonymous. Baseball had returned to its most familiar register: present, unsentimental, unbothered by what had come before.

This too was the game's truth. Baseball did not linger in moments of elevation, nor did it pause to take stock of what it had briefly represented. It moved forward, day by day, inning by inning, carrying its meaning lightly and leaving most of it behind. Whatever sense of unity or purpose had filled the stands the day before was not carried forward in any formal way—or any visible one. It was entrusted, quietly, to memory.

And yet ordinariness did not mean stasis. The very next afternoon the same teams met again at Fenway Park, and the tone shifted without announcement. Babe Ruth took the ball. The Red Sox scored eleven runs. The Browns were shut out. What had felt flat and forgettable a day earlier now unfolded as something emphatic and complete—not as a correction, but as a reminder of how quickly the game could change its posture. Baseball, returning to routine, demonstrated that routine did not mean lifelessness; it simply meant that significance often arrived unmarked.

The season continued. The war did too. Life resumed its uneven rhythm, punctuated less by grand conclusions than by quiet transitions back to the everyday. What lingered from the extraordinary was more residue than spectacle—the knowledge that even as the world moved on, something had briefly been held in common, and then released.

By evening, Fenway Park was locked again. The gates were shut. Jersey Street returned to its narrow routines. Trolleys passed without slowing. The park waited, as it always did, for the next demand.

What remained was not an institution or a formal tradition but a memory—durable enough to survive without tending, flexible enough to be recalled when circumstances required it.

Sixteen years later, in the depths of economic collapse, baseball would remember. Not the names, and not even the score, but the shape of the solution: the knowledge that when the ground gave way beneath the game, it had once steadied itself by gathering its best, placing them before the public, and allowing excellence to stand in for reassurance.

That future lay beyond September 1917, still unimagined. For now, the city moved on. The players did as well. The Murnane household settled into a quieter rhythm. Fenway Park slept. And somewhere between the echo of cheers and the silence that followed, baseball carried forward a lesson it had not yet learned how to name—but would not forget.

As the crowds drifted away from Fenway Park, Boston resumed the rhythms of wartime city life—streetcars rattling, pedestrians filling the avenues, and the State House watching over a city balancing duty, uncertainty, and moments of shared escape. Though photographed in 1918, scenes like this reflected the Boston players and fans returned to after Murnane Day.

FEATURES OF THE RED SOX-ALL STARS CLASH FOR BENEFIT OF MURNANE MEMORIAL FUND

Illustrator Wallace Goldsmith captured baseball's characters with wit and exaggeration, turning the sport's heroes into figures of humor as well as admiration. This is his *Boston Globe* recap of Murnane Day's key moments.

TWILIGHT AT FENWAY

September 27, 1917: Postgame

By the time twilight reached Fenway, the park had already begun to let go.

The late light entered from the west, catching first on the upper deck before descending toward the field. Shadows lengthened across the grass. The stands were empty now. The last voices had dissolved into something gentler than silence—a kind of settled air.

The grounds crew worked without hurry. Dirt around home plate was smoothed. Basepaths were raked. The infield was dragged until the surface bore no sign of the afternoon's urgency. The game receded into the soil. That, too, was part of the ritual.

From the concourse, the park felt smaller at this hour. Grandeur yielded to particulars: scuffed paint along a railing, the worn lip of a step, the faint scent of cut grass lingering in the cool. Fenway did not declare itself. It endured.

Twilight collapses distances. In this light, decades feel adjacent. Different crowds. Different uniforms. The same field receiving them all. Fenway does not divide its history into neat compartments; it layers them.

Beneath a seat in the lower grandstand, a program remained where it had been tucked away. Its cover bent, its edges beginning to curl. Objects rarely demand significance. They simply wait to be found—or not.

Beyond the outfield wall, Boston resumed its rhythm. Windows brightened. Streetcars hummed. Fenway was never the center of the city. Its gravity came from something quieter: its capacity to hold what passed through it.

Along the aisle near the lower grandstand, Mrs. Murnane gathered her children and thanked team owner Henry Frazee for his generosity. Near her, one child clutched a program folded thin by nervous hands. Another paused halfway down the steps and looked back at the field that had carried so many familiar names. A player approached briefly, cap tipped, voice low. She nodded. There was nothing theatrical in the exchange. Only recognition.

Outside the gates, streetlamps flickered awake. Carriages rolled by in steady cadence. The family stepped into the current of evening, absorbed gradually into its movement.

In the clubhouse, wool uniforms hung cooling on their hooks. Cleats rested side by side. A towel lay where it had been dropped. Duffy Lewis tried not to dance on his way to the shower, that's how happy he was and how perfect the day had been. Not even the large sum of $500 would have "bought back from him that hit," Francis Eaton would write.[1]

Earlier laughter soon thinned into practical departure. Some men would board trains before midnight. Others would disappear into boardinghouses or quiet streets.

Up near the press box, a reporter lingered over his copy. Ink settled onto paper. Names were checked carefully. By morning, the account would be fixed in type, even as the field below dissolved into shadow.

When full dark arrived, Fenway became shape more than detail—the geometry of a diamond held against night.

The gates closed without fanfare. A lock turned. A chain slipped into place.

The infield lay restored. The grass breathed in the cool air. Above it, the sky deepened.

Tomorrow the chalk would be drawn again.

But for now, Fenway rested—not empty, but prepared.

Harry Frazee, the theatrical producer turned owner of the Boston Red Sox, presided over one of baseball's most successful clubs of the 1910s. He would later become infamous for selling Babe Ruth to the New York Yankees after the 1919 season—a transaction that altered the course of baseball history and helped fuel the legend of the "Curse of the Bambino."

Tim Murnane spent his life recording baseball's story. Here his downward gaze suggests a quiet sentinel, one of the game's earliest guardians still watching over the field he loved.

9

THE MEMORY WE CARRY

When the afternoon ended in 1917, Fenway did what it had always done after a game: it returned to itself.

Vendors packed up their trays. Programs were folded beneath seats or tucked into coat pockets, already beginning their slow transformation into keepsakes. The field looked the same as it had that morning, and yet it did not. It had been witnessed. Something had passed across it that would not be entirely erased, even after the dirt was smoothed and the chalk renewed.

There is something revealing about a ballpark once it empties. Without the noise and motion, its scale changes. The distance from home plate to the outfield fence feels longer. The stands feel steeper. Time seems to loosen its grip. Fenway, more than most places, carried its past this way—layered rather than preserved, accumulated rather than curated. It did not announce its history. It allowed it to linger, unevenly, in corners and shadows, in the grains of the wood and the worn edges of concrete steps.

On the afternoon in 1917, the crowd did not leave knowing it had participated in something that would endure. Those who attended came for familiar reasons: to see great players compete, to raise money for a fallen writer's family, to spend a few hours together inside the rhythms of the game. When it ended, they gathered their coats, said their goodbyes, and moved on. The day felt complete. Whatever meaning it would come to hold was not visible in the moment. Then again, meaning rarely is. It accumulates slowly, acquiring weight only as it is carried forward.

At first, the story lived in voices.

The men who played that day told it themselves. They remembered the sun on the grass, the casual confidence of stepping onto a field they knew by heart, the chatter between contests. They remembered jokes exchanged, rivalries teased, moments that felt small at the time and later grew in the telling. But there were plenty of details the players would not recall. Memory is selective, even when it is sincere.

As years passed, others took up the task. Writers retold the afternoon in sporadic columns and reminiscences. Fans repeated the stories as they had heard them, sometimes embellishing, sometimes compressing, always shaping the past to fit the present moment. The story migrated—from clubhouse to newspaper, from newspaper to scrapbook, from scrapbook to family lore. Each telling altered it slightly, not out of carelessness but necessity. Memory does not survive by standing still.

Eventually, even the voices faded.

The players grew old. Then they were gone. Those who had been there, who could answer questions with authority and ease, were no longer available. What remained were fragments: a photograph with faces only partially identified, a program browned at the edges, a box score clipped and saved for reasons no one fully recalled. These objects did not explain themselves. They waited.

This is the moment when memory becomes a responsibility—when preservation ceases to be passive and becomes deliberate.

Objects do not remember on their own. They require a keeper. Someone who pauses before throwing something away. Someone who wonders who held it first, and why. A program is only paper until it is opened and read. A photograph is only an image until someone tries to name the figures inside it, even imperfectly. What survives is not the event in its entirety, but the decision to return to it—to refuse to let it dissolve into anonymity. Left unattended, even significant days recede into trivia.

Fenway, like baseball itself, has always depended on this kind of inheritance. The park did not impose meaning. It absorbed it. Each generation arrived with its own reasons for caring, its own version of the story, and left something behind—an echo, a habit, a way of watching the game. The sounds faded but the impression remained, pressed lightly into the place itself.

To walk through the park on a quiet day, one could feel it: the sense that time had stacked rather than passed. That what happened there once had not disappeared but settled. Fenway did not hold memory the way a museum does, sealed behind glass. It held it the way a house does, shaped by the people who had lived inside it—some things not known to the eye but to the heart.

This is why places matter. It is why stories matter.

Not because they freeze the past, but because they allow it to remain accessible. Fenway has never demanded reverence. It has asked only for attention. It invited the present to brush up against what came before and decide what to carry forward.

For many, that decision began early. A first game. A question asked from the edge of a seat. Why is that wall so close? Who played here before? Why does this place feel different? The answers were often partial, sometimes improvised, but they were offered nonetheless. This is how meaning travels—not through institutions alone, but through relationships. From parent to child. From fan to fan. From storyteller to listener, who in turn becomes another storyteller.

What was passed along was rarely the full story. It was a gesture, an orientation, a sense that something there was worth paying attention to. That the game once asked something of the people who played it and the people who watched. That it offered, in return, a feeling of belonging that extended beyond the final score. And that if the story lingered, it did so for a reason.

The afternoon in 1917 survived this way. Not as a fixed moment, but as a touchstone. It reappeared whenever the game briefly recaptured that sense of shared purpose, whenever competition gave way to something more communal. It reminded those who knew it that baseball had once made room—deliberately and publicly—for generosity, for remembrance, for gathering in the face of loss.

And so we must ask: when the last cheers drifted out of Fenway and the grandstand's echo finally settled into quiet, what actually remained? Not the applause. Not the box score. Something quieter—and more durable.

The benefit game had revealed the depth of affection the baseball world felt for Tim Murnane. The memorial fund would support his family and secure a monument at his grave in Old Calvary Cemetery, calling him a "pioneer of baseball," a "champion of its integrity," and a "gifted and fearless writer." Yet affection alone does not guarantee memory. Memory must be renewed.

It was renewed almost immediately. In April 1919, the *Worcester Telegram* published a column mourning the absence of Murnane's voice. "Old boys of baseball miss the authoritative writings of that good, gray philosopher of the game," it read, recalling his "kindly, courteous pen" and "time-tempered philosophy."[1] What left a vacuum, the writer insisted, was not merely his prose but his perspective—his lived knowledge of the game from its earliest days as a national sport. Writers might come and go, but Murnane's accounts, stripped of frills, would remain a standard.

The players remembered him as well. Writing in 1920, Babe Ruth revisited the fungo contest of that September afternoon. He had just picked up a brand new ball and took a "long, swinging smack at it," as Ruth uniquely could. "Oh, the feel of that club as it met the horsehide square on the nose," he wrote. "I tell you, the ball sang on its way." He misremembered the distance of his drive—recalling 435 feet rather than the measured nearly 403—but what endured was the sensation. He noted that Cap Anson had once hit a ball so far over the Fenway fence that it entered the window of a saloon across the street from the outfield; he wasn't sure if his fungo ball had gone as far, but it made him wonder. He remembered the silver trophy he received and described the opposing lineup as "the greatest ball club ever assembled," specifically recalling the outfield of Speaker, Jackson, and Cobb.[2] The game had entered folklore.

The Red Sox institutionalized that remembrance. After the 1939 season, Ted Williams—still a rookie—was awarded the

Tim Murnane Award as the club's most valuable player, having hit .327 and led the team with 145 RBIs.[3] In doing so, the club tethered its emerging greatness to its inherited conscience—linking new brilliance to remembered integrity.

The *Boston Globe* continued to revisit Murnane's legendary influence decades after his death. In 1945, the writer Jerry Nason penned a column titled, "Duffy's Hall of Fame Excursion Starts and Finishes in The Globe," highlighting his keen eye for talent. It was Murnane, Nason emphasized, who had first spotted future Hall of Famer Hugh Duffy—who once batted .440 for the Boston Beaneaters—and helped set him on the path to Cooperstown. "On the strength of Tim Murnane's judgment," wrote Nason, "young Duffy got his chance with Chicago Colts," and the rest was history.[4] The following year, Murnane's name appeared on a memorial Roll of Honor at the Baseball Hall of Fame.

In 1966, nearly half a century after the benefit game, a seventy-seven-year-old Red Sox fan wrote to the *Boston Globe* seeking confirmation that what he remembered had truly happened. Had there really been a Tim Murnane Day featuring Cobb, Speaker, Walter Johnson, John L. Sullivan, Will Rogers, and even a horse in the outfield? "I assure you," the fan wrote, "it was no nightmare. Here is where you [the Globe] enter the picture: If you can come up with an account of the event and the date, I'm off the hook, otherwise my friends will think I'm flakey."[5]

The *Globe* assured him that he was indeed off the hook. The game had been real and had "always been something of a classic," the paper wrote, "though most of us had forgotten about Will Rogers' participation in the proceedings." Duffy Lewis, it added, had always considered his game-winning triple the high point of his distinguished career—even though it had come in what was technically only an exhibition game.[6]

Lewis himself had explained why.

Years earlier, in an interview about his relationship with the old Red Sox owner John I. Taylor—the man credited with discovering him—Lewis returned not to a pennant race or a championship, but to the Murnane game. "I'll always remember John I. in connection with the Tim Murnane game," he said. When the contest ended, the crowd spilled onto the field and surrounded the players in a friendly crush. Taylor, though no longer owner of the club, was the first out of his box, running straight toward Lewis and shouting, "Duffy, you're still my boy!" He seized Lewis' hand, shook it hard—and when he finally let go, Lewis found a $100 bill folded in his palm.[7]

It was not the size of the gift that endured so much as the gesture. The money would be spent; the moment would be carried. The affection was visible. The bonds were immediate. In that instant, remembrance was not archival or institutional. It was human.

In 1979, more than sixty years after his death, the Baseball Writers' Association of America posthumously awarded Murnane the J.G. Taylor Spink Award for meritorious contributions to baseball writing. In honoring him, the association remembered a man who had been player, manager, league president, editor, discoverer of talent, and tireless advocate for the sport—a man who, in their words, had been "one of the game's best friends."[8]

And yet memory can thin.

History survives in such references and reminiscences. In a son's letter to Cooperstown recalling his father's final night at the Shubert Theatre; in a columnist's quiet tribute decades later; in Bob Ryan's 2004 assertion—just before the first inter-league game between the Red Sox and the Dodgers since the 1916 World Series—that none of the modern scribes, from Gordon Edes to Bob Hohler to Peter Gammons, were worthy to stand in Murnane's journalistic presence.[9] Remembrance persists—but in pieces.

The day did not disappear. It receded. It resurfaced. It lingered in print and in memory, in trophies and in correspondence. It entered baseball's bloodstream.

Looking back at September 27, 1917, what stands out is not innocence so much as proximity. The distance between player and writer, between star and fan, was shorter—and so was the distance between loss and response. The bonds were visible. When Murnane died, the response was not outsourced or abstract. It was enacted on the field.

That afternoon did not halt the war. It did not resolve the tensions of its age. It did not prevent the coming scandals that would shake the sport two years later. What it did was demonstrate, in practical terms, that a game could momentarily transcend its own boundaries. That competition and compassion need not preclude one another. That a public institution could acknowledge private loss.

The memory of that day invites neither nostalgia nor lament. It invites care.

Care enough to notice how traditions evolve. Care enough to ask what is preserved and what is quietly set aside. Care enough to recognize that memory is not automatic. It requires attention, effort, and sometimes recovery.

Baseball has always depended on people willing to carry its stories forward. On writers who believed the box score was not the whole account. On fans who saved programs and told their children why a particular afternoon mattered. On players who understood that their work unfolded within a lineage larger than themselves.

The afternoon in 1917 belongs to that lineage. It does not demand grand commemoration. It asks only to be remembered generously, as one instance among many when the sport revealed what it could be at its best.

What we owe the past is not necessarily awe or reverence, but stewardship—a willingness to tend what we did not create but have nonetheless inherited. Stewardship of stories. Stewardship of places. Stewardship of the idea that games can do more than entertain—that they can bind, console, and occasionally instruct.

When later generations gather to celebrate baseball's finest, when All-Stars assemble under brighter lights and before larger audiences, they do so within a tradition shaped in part by that earlier gathering. The form has changed, but the impulse endures.

The memory we carry is not perfect, and it is not complete. But it remains available. It waits in archives and attics, in columns and recollections, in the quiet decision to ask again what happened there and why.

That is how the afternoon in 1917 continues—not as spectacle, but as inheritance. Not as a frozen scene but as a story chosen, again and again, to be told. What endures is more than the crowd and even the contest: it is the decision to remember.

Autographs from the Murnane Game on a single ball read today like a roll call of baseball immortals: Ruth, Cobb, Jackson, Johnson, and others whose names continue to echo across generations.

AFTERMATH

September 28, 1917: The Globe

Just about the only thing missing from the game was Tim Murnane himself. It is tempting to imagine how he would have set it down for the Globe. Perhaps it would have read like this:

The Boston Globe: September 28, 1917
The Game and Its Guardians
By T. H. Murnane

Yesterday's contest at Fenway Park was played under no ordinary circumstances, yet it unfolded in a manner so free of strain and so full of honest endeavor that one might almost have mistaken it for a midsummer afternoon in calmer times.

The names upon the scorecard were enough to command attention. Veterans whose deeds have long occupied the sporting page took the field once more, not in pursuit of pennants or private distinction but in tribute to the game itself. The crowd, large and attentive, required no urging. It came in the right spirit and remained in it.

There are occasions when baseball, like a capable orator, speaks plainly without raising its voice. This was one of them.

The terms were simple, as they have always been: three outs to an inning, nine innings to a contest, and the umpire's word final. No special allowances were sought, no liberties taken because the afternoon carried sentiment. The old framework held. That is the quiet genius of the sport. Within those fixed boundaries—the ninety feet between bases, the chalked lines that define fair from foul—endless variation and invention may occur, yet the foundation does not shift.

No bitterness crept into the play. There was no wrangling over decisions, no indulgence of temper, no exhibition designed to draw applause at the expense of propriety. The umpire ruled and the players abided. Runners were retired in due order; innings yielded their allotted chances; advantage changed hands, as it must when men of skill contend. The competition was wholesome and direct. Those upon the field conducted themselves as craftsmen mindful that their craft depends upon discipline.

For those of us who recall the game's more turbulent youth—when arguments outnumbered innings and order was sometimes an afterthought—there was quiet satisfaction in observing such composure. I have seen contests in which the noise from the stands exceeded the discipline upon the field, and seasons when distrust traveled faster than the ball itself. To see the sport comport itself yesterday with steadiness and mutual regard was to recognize how far it has journeyed.

Baseball has grown in scale, in spectacle, and in enterprise. But its true advancement lies elsewhere. It lies in the acceptance that rules are not hindrance but safeguard; that three outs mean precisely three; that nine innings are sufficient; that an umpire's judgment, once rendered, must stand if the game is to stand with it.

That understanding was visible yesterday.

The public, weary of dispatches from distant fronts and the relentless pace of modern cares, found again the simple pleasure of a well-conducted afternoon. There is relief in watching a contest governed by known terms and honored obligations. A cleanly played ballgame is not a trivial thing; it is evidence that ordered competition remains possible in a restless age.

When the players departed the field to sustained applause, the sound carried less clamor than gratitude. The sport they have preserved through long seasons of labor stands as more than diversion. It reflects, in modest compass, the habits a republic requires: restraint, fairness, steadiness under pressure, and respect for lawful authority.

If baseball is to remain worthy of the affection it commands, it must continue to exhibit these qualities—in triumph and in trial alike.

Yesterday, it answered to its highest self.

The Boston Daily Globe EXTRA

VOL. XCII—NO. 90 BOSTON, FRIDAY MORNING, SEPTEMBER 28, 1917—SIXTEEN PAGES PRICE TWO CENTS

AGREE ON WAR TAX OF $2,700,000,000

Three-Cent Postage and Tax on Bank Checks Restored

Conferees Retain Senate Levy on Excess Profits and Incomes

BRITISH AIRMEN ROUT ARTILLERY

Disperse German Infantry in Flanders Battle

Says Wilson Pledged U. S. To Last Man and Last Dollar

DETAILS OF NEW LIBERTY LOAN OUT

Total Three Billions and Half Over-Subscription

Rate 4 Percent—Bonds Will Be Delivered Promptly

17,000 OUT TO HONOR MURNANE

Red Sox Win Memorial Day Game, 2 to 0

More Than $13,000 Contributed to Fund by Admiring Fans

THE WEATHER

CLOUDY

FOUR IN AUTO BADLY INJURED

Car Turns Over Several Times in Cliftondale

DEMAND CONGRESS EXPEL LA FOLLETTE

Wisconsin League of Municipalities Adopt Resolve---American Bankers Cheer Same Stand by Dr Butler

ROBERT M. LA FOLLETTE, United States Senator From Wisconsin

TAKE OVER ALL SHIPS OCT 15

Board Announces Big Cut in Charter Rates

Many Vessels to Be Returned to Owners for Operation

SOME SCHOOLS MAY BE CLOSED

Possibility, If Very Cold, Committee Says

Answers Teachers' Plea for Heat With Appeal to Patriotism

Heflin Calls For Wide Probe Of Congressmen's Acts

Names La Follette, Britten, Mason and Baer

CALLS ON SENATE TO EXPEL LA FOLLETTE

HEFLIN BITTER IN DEMANDING PROBE

Wisconsin League Calls on Senate to Expel La Follette

TODAY'S GLOBE CONTENTS

THE GLOBE WILL DO IT

Sell Your Autos

USE THE MEDIUM THAT MAKES SALES ADVERTISE YOUR

Used Autos
Accessories
Motorcycles

COMING TO BOSTON HOTEL HOLLIS

SAVINGS DEPT.

4%

United States Trust Co.

BELL-ANS Absolutely Removes Indigestion. One package proves it. 25c at all druggists.

WE TEACH SPANISH

BURDETT NIGHT SCHOOL

NEW STUDENTS ADMITTED EVERY MONDAY

Enroll Now for Oct. 1

Only $15,000 Raised in 4 Days
$35,000 STILL TO GO
ONLY TWO DAYS LEFT

Unless YOU give to the CAMP LIBRARY FUND Boston will be Shamed

SEND A CHECK TODAY TO
WILLIAM A. GASTON, Treasurer
NATIONAL SHAWMUT BANK, BOSTON

Savings Deposits

COSMOPOLITAN TRUST CO.

SAVING IS PATRIOTIC

Boylston National Bank

We Are Paying 4%

GLOBE ADVERTISEMENTS PAY BEST TRY ONE AND SEE

The front page of the *Boston Daily Globe* on September 28, 1917 reflected a nation consumed by war, politics, and uncertainty even as Boston paused the day before for baseball and remembrance. Nestled among headlines about Liberty Loans, war taxes, and Congress was coverage of the Murnane Day benefit game, a reminder of how deeply baseball remained woven into the civic life of wartime America.

Now the score is known. What began as a simple baseball has become a relic of a singular day when the game paused to honor one of its own.

EPILOGUE: THAT INNOCENT PROMISE

There is one movie scene that makes my eyes water every time I watch it. If you're reading this book, you know the scene. It's dusk on a magical cornfield in Iowa. A man in a faded wool Chicago White Sox jersey, like ones worn on Murnane Day, is fresh off a pick-up game of old-timers, packing up his catcher's gear. He begins to walk toward the stalks beyond the baseball diamond, his daily return to Heaven before the newness of a bright, beautiful day will bring him back.

What has been whispered but never said aloud through the story now becomes clear: the man in the gear is John Kinsella, long gone from the living world, summoned by his estranged son's impossible dream. The music swells. Kevin Costner's character, Ray, turns to him, unsure, almost afraid, and says the most tender, even vulnerable words he can offer, "Hey…Dad… you wanna have a catch?" John pauses, then smiles, his voice breaking as he replies, "I'd like that."

The camera pulls back, revealing the simplest, most American of images: a father and son playing catch as the sun sets. No dialogue is needed. Only the steady rhythm of ball hitting glove, the unspoken promise of the next throw. In that exchange, life feels simple, it feels right, even whole again. The pain has been eased. The tradition endures.

Field of Dreams can make anyone fall in love with baseball. It did for me. The movie came out when I was six, and though I can't remember the first time I saw it, I've returned to it more times than I can count. It contains everything: triumph and heartbreak, the tensions of family, the lure of chasing a dream, even Fenway Park and a vision of the eternal. And then, of course, James Earl Jones, in that unforgettable baritone, reminding us at the end of the film that money is common but peace is rare; that people return to the baselines where they once sat as children, dipping themselves in magic waters as they cheer on their heroes; that America may change but baseball endures; that this game "reminds us of all that once was good, and it could be again."

At its heart, that is what baseball gives us: tradition. Fathers and sons, mothers and daughters, grandparents and grandkids, brothers and sisters, friends across generations. We pass along the game like a gift because it connects us to those we love, to those we've lost, and to the best of who we hope to be. I felt that spirit most clearly right after buying my first house, when the very first thing I wanted to do was not unpack a box or paint a wall, but to step onto my new lawn with my dad, mitts in hand, to have a catch. I claimed a tradition, in my space, with him—returning, if only for a moment, to my childhood and to his, back whence we came, as if somehow recapturing our own ghosts and the people in our lives we miss.

In that way, the game has always been less about wins and losses than about the memories it carries forward. The sun has long since set over the Fenway of 1917, but the glow of that special afternoon remains. It lingers not in scorebooks or highlight reels, but in the quiet memory of a nation that once paused for a ballgame played for something finer than fame.

In the century that followed, baseball would change in every way imaginable. The parks would grow larger, the owners and players richer, the game quicker, louder, more commercial. It would be broadcast across continents and consumed in real time. It would weather strikes, scandals, wars, and reckonings. And yet something essential remains—something ineffable and enduring, passed down in the language of innings and averages, in the smell of a glove or the echo of a cheer.

What happened that afternoon at Fenway was more than a benefit. It was a blueprint. The All-Stars gathered that day did more than honor a fallen comrade; they modeled a version of the sport, and the country, driven by unity, generosity, and principle. In the middle of a fractured world, they showed what could still hold.

For a few blessed hours, something pure indeed held firm in the American soul. There were no endorsement deals, no television breaks, no algorithms or agents. Just a ballgame, a cause, a crowd, and a shared sense that this—*this*—was what mattered.

What they built that day was a tradition, even if they didn't know it. The All-Star Game that would become an annual fixture in American life began with no fanfare, no league decree. It was just with a group of players who said yes. *Yes* to stepping aside from rivalry. *Yes* to stepping up for someone else. *Yes* to the idea that sport, like country, was stronger when joined in common cause.

We remember them now not only for their talent but for their gesture. For what they chose to do with a single autumn afternoon. And how that choice echoes still.

This was the promise of that day: that beneath the spectacle and the statistics, beneath the grandstands and the legends, baseball could still be what it was at its best—a communion. A reminder. A hope. A nation, still young and uncertain, caught a glimpse of its better self on a sunlit field in Boston.

And though the world has grown noisier, harder, and more cynical, that promise remains—innocent, enduring, and waiting still at the edge of every freshly chalked line.

Even now, to walk into a ballpark is to feel something timeless. It's one of the last truly democratic spaces in American life, where the banker and the busboy, the nurse and the novelist, sit side by side and cheer for the same outcome. It doesn't matter what you do for a living or where you live or how you pray. There's a universal faith enshrined in our hearts that still finds expression in a seventh-inning stretch. It's still about family and friendship, ritual and tradition. A day at the ballpark is a bond shared between generations, stitched with scorecards and soft pretzels, memories and moments. It's where the dreams of the past are handed off to new fans, and where we collectively remember what it means to root for something, to believe in something, even to feel the familiar ache of hope deferred.

And if we keep this sense of play in our lives—if we retain that youthful, participatory love of the game—then, as MLB historian John Thorn says in Ken Burns' *Baseball* documentary, "It's like Peter Pan. We remain boys forever, we don't die."[1] And if we don't die then our memories don't die, which means those with whom we have shared our most cherished ballpark moments don't die either.

In an era too often filled with darkness and despair, baseball can illuminate the eternal truths that bring us together. Collectively, we may watch this game for different reasons. We may cheer for different teams. We may argue over trades, strategy, records, rule changes, or historic moments. But in the end, baseball is much more than a game. It is about love and remembrance, perpetually returning us to the better angels of our youth, to times of smaller concerns and bigger dreams, and times when we were the younger generation looking up to fresh heroes who inspired us and shaped our worldview. In this, we find more than nostalgia. We find a path back to the simple grace of playing catch at dusk with someone we love.

May this forever be true. It was certainly true one day in September.

Tim Murnane

Full name Timothy Hayes Murnane
Born June 4, 1850, Lisfornane, Ireland
Died February 7, 1917, Boston, Massachusetts
Buried at Mount Calvary Cemetery, Roslindale, Massachusetts
First Game: April 26, 1872; Final Game: October 19, 1884
Managed First Game: April 17, 1884; Managed Final Game: October 19, 1884
Umpired First Game: October 16, 1873; Umpired Final Game: September 21, 1886
Bat: Left Throw: Right Height: 5' 9.5" Weight: 172

Batting Record

Year	Team		G	AB	R	H	2B	3B	HR	RBI
1872	Middletown Mansfields (NA)		23	114	28	41	1	1	0	16
1873	Philadelphia Athletics (NA)		41	176	53	39	2	1	1	10
1874	Philadelphia Athletics (NA)		21	82	11	17	2	0	0	11
1875	Philadelphia White Stockings (NA)		69	313	71	85	5	0	1	30
1876	Boston Nationals (NL)		69	308	60	87	4	3	2	34
1877	Boston Nationals (NL)		35	140	23	39	7	1	1	15
1878	Providence Grays (NL)		49	188	35	45	6	1	0	14
1884	Boston Unions (UA)		76	311	55	73	5	2	0	
Total	NA	(4 Years)	154	685	163	182	10	2	2	67
Total	NL	(3 Years)	153	636	118	171	17	5	3	63
Total	UA	(1 Year)	76	311	55	73	5	2	0	
Total		(8 Years)	383	1632	336	426	32	9	5	130i

i: Incomplete
NA: National Association
NL: National League
UA: Union Association

Managerial Record

Year	Team	G	W	L	PCT	RS	RA	START
1884	Boston Unions (UA)	111	58	51	.532	636	559	

Umpiring Record

Year		G	HP	1B	2B	3B	LF	RF
1873		1	1	0	0	0	0	0
1874		1	1	0	0	0	0	0
1875		4	4	0	0	0	0	0
1886		1	1	0	0	0	0	0
Total	(4 Years)	7	7	0	0	0	0	0

BB	SO	HBP	SH	GDP	SB	CS	AVG	OBP	SLG	*BFW
0	0	0	0	0	1	2	.360	.360	.386	0.1
8	13			1	8	2	.222	.255	261	-1.0
1	3	0	0	0	0	1	.207	.217	0.232	-0.7
7	7			0	30	9	.272	.288	.297	0.3
8	12						.282	.031	.334	-0.4
6	7						.279	.308	.364	0.0
8	12						.239	.270	.282	-0.5
22							.235	.285	.264	-2.7
16	23	0i	0i	1	36	14	.226	.282	.295	-1.3
22	31						.269	.293	.325	-0.9
22							.235	.285	.264	-2.7
60	54i	0i	0i	1i	39i	14i	.261	.287	.307	-4.9

*BFW: Batter-fielder wins refers to an older sabermetric statistic measuring a player's value based on their contributions to runs scored and prevented, a precursor to the modern wins-above-replacement.

END STANDING
4

Altogether, it was a great occasion, and a grand day's sport. The score:

RED SOX	ab	bh	po	a
Hooper rf	4	0	5	1
Barry 2b	4	2	1	0
Hoblitzel 1b	3	2	5	1
Lewis rf	4	1	4	1
Walker cf	4	2	5	0
Gardner 3b	3	0	0	2
Agnew c	2	0	2	0
Thomas c	1	0	2	1
Ruth p	2	0	0	0
Foster p	1	0	1	0
Totals	31	7	27	6

ALL-STARS	ab	bh	po	a
Maranville ss	4	0	0	1
Chapman 2b	1	1	1	2
Cobb l c r f	4	1	5	0
Sp'ker r c l f	3	0	2	0
Jack'n r c l f	4	0	5	1
McInnis 1b	4	1	8	0
O'Neil c	2	0	1	0
Schaug c	1	0	1	0
Shocker p	0	0	0	1
Ehmke p	1	0	0	0
Johnson p	1	0	0	1
Totals	28	3	24	7

Innings	1	2	3	4	5	6	7	8	9
Red Sox	0	0	0	0	0	0	0	2	X

Runs made, by Barry, Hoblitzel. Error made, by Maranville. Two-base hit, Walker. Three-base hits, Hoblitzel, Lewis. Hits off Shocker, 2 in 2 innings; off Ehmke, 1 in 3 innings; off Johnson, 3 in 3 innings; off Ruth, 3 in 5 innings; off Foster, 0 in 4 innings. Stolen base, Chapman. Base on balls, by Ehmke, by Ruth 2, by Foster 3. Struck out, by Ruth, by Shocker. Double play, Gardner, Barry and Hoblitzel. Time, 1h 55m. Umpire-in-chief, Connolly. Umpire on bases, Nallin. Attendance, 17,119.

This is the box score that appeared in the *Boston Globe* on September 28, 1917.

MURNANE DAY WAS GREAT

The Tim Murnane Memorial game yesterday was an unqualified success. There were more than 17,000 people at the ball park, nad the Memorial Fund will amount to nearly if not quite $14,000, when all accounts are in. The ball game was a dandy, Duffy Lewis breaking it up with a triple against Walter Johnson in the eighth and with two men on bases, the final score being 2 to 0.

The visiting ball players as well as the Red Sox enjoyed the day hugely. Never have they been made to feel more at home by the fans. The temper of the crowd was shown also when some thoughtless fan attempted to start a "boo" for Buck Weaver, one of the guests of the day. The "booer" stopped his chatter so suddenly that something must have happened.

Men like Cobb and Weaver, who sometimes have felt they were unduly criticised by the Boston fans, must have gone back to their team with a very different feeling regarding Boston's fairness. It's certain that both, as well as all the other boys who helped make the day so wonderfully successful, made also hosts of friends by their willingness to help. It was a great day not only for the Murnane memorial, the fans and the players, but for the National game itself. The late Tim Murnane was a man who never would allow that "sentiment" in baseball was a dead issue. Yesterday's Memorial was a splendid argument for the "Silver King's" point of view.

The *Boston Globe's* evening edition hailed Murnane Day as "a splendid argument" for the idea that baseball could still embody sentiment, fellowship, and civic purpose.

FINAL MLB STANDINGS 1917

AMERICAN LEAGUE	W	L	PCT	GB	L10	STRK
Chicago White Sox y	100	54	.649	-	5-5	L1
Boston Red Sox	90	62	.592	9.0	5-5	L2
Cleveland Indians	88	66	.571	12.0	7-3	W1
Detroit Tigers	78	75	.510	21.5	7-3	L2
Washington Senators	74	79	.484	25.5	6-4	W2
New York Yankees	71	82	.464	28.5	4-6	W1
St. Louis Browns	57	97	.370	43.0	5-5	L2
Philadelphia Athletics	55	98	.359	44.5	5-5	L1

NATIONAL LEAGUE	W	L	PCT	GB	L10	STRK
New York Giants y	98	56	.636	-	5-5	w2
Philadelphia Phillies	87	65	.572	10.0	5-5	l2
St. Louis Cardinals	82	70	.539	15.0	5-4	l2
Cincinnati Reds	78	76	.506	20.0	4-4	W2
Chicago Cubs	74	80	.481	24.0	2-8	L2
Boston Braves	72	81	.471	25.5	6-4	W1
Brooklyn Robins	70	81	.464	26.5	5-5	L1
Pittsburgh Pirates	51	103	.331	47.0	4-6	W1

y CLINCH INDICATORS

W = Wins L = Losses

PCT = Winning percentage

GB = Games back from first place

L10 = Record in final ten games of season

STRK = Streak of wins or losses

RS = Runs scored RA = Runs against

DIFF = Difference between runs scored and runs against

HOME = A team's record at home

AWAY = A team's record on the road

>.500 = A team's record against teams with a PCT above 50%.

RS	RA	DIFF	HOME	AWAY	>.500
655	463	+192	56-21	44-33	42-24
555	455	+100	45-33	45-29	29-36
584	543	+41	44-34	44-32	32-34
639	577	+62	34-41	44-34	28-37
544	566	-22	42-35	32-44	38-50
524	558	-34	35-40	36-42	35-53
810	687	-177	31-46	26-51	27-61
529	691	-162	29-47	26-51	26-61

RS	RA	DIFF	HOME	AWAY	>.500
635	457	+178	50-28	48-28	39-27
578	500	+78	46-29	41-36	35-31
531	567	-36	38-38	44-32	30-36
601	611	-10	39-38	39-38	28-38
552	567	-15	35-42	39-38	31-57
536	552	-16	35-42	37-39	34-53
511	559	-48	36-38	34-43	38-47
464	595	-131	25-53	26-50	32-56

Murnane's Don'ts

Don't overlook the fact that the winners are the heroes.

Don't fail to appreciate the kind words in the newspapers.

Don't use cheap talk to your opponents on the field.

Don't forget that Hans Wagner, Larry Lajoie, James Collins and Hal Chase have no superiors as a hard-hitting, wonderful fielding infield.

Don't think you can't do with practice what others have done.

Don't practice throwing a ball high in the air.

Don't pay attention to the spectators.

Don't blame others for the fruits of your blunders, but take your medicine cheerfully.

Don't fail to keep your spikes in good working order.

Don't mechanically overrun first base after hitting the ball, but be on the alert to take advantage of any opening to make the next base.

Don't blame the bats or balls when your batting average is dwindling.

Don't try to get the crowd after the umpire—it's poor sportsmanship.

Don't bunt the ball when basemen are playing close up.

Don't think that the game cannot be improved by some new plays.

Don't quit when your opponent is ahead, as you can never tell when luck will change.

Don't slide into third when the coacher is sending you home with the wave of the hands.

Don't be in too much of a hurry at the plate, especially when facing a pitcher for the first time.

Don't pay any attention to your base hits or errors—simply hustle from start to finish.

Don't depend on one set of signals.

Don't eat hearty food for lunch the day of the game.

46 SPALDING'S OFFICIAL MINOR LEAGUE GUIDE.

Don't read small print by artificial light, or print of any kind while traveling on the cars.

Don't depend wholly on the manager or captain, but do a little thinking of your own. In other words, don't be a machine.

Don't talk with outsiders during the progress of a ball game.

Don't be the last one to reach the park, nor the first to get away.

Don't fail to notice the direction of the wind, if strong, and play accordingly.

Don't wait for a bounding ball to come to you in the outfield—simply rush in and get it on the short or long bound.

Don't continually kick at your luck in drawing an upper berth in a sleeping car.

Don't be superstitious and turn pale at the sight of a load of empty barrels or a funeral going the same way.

Don't take it easy going to first, for you never can tell when the ball will be thrown wild or muffed.

Don't take it for granted that you are out—wait for the umpire's ruling.

Inaugural All-Star Game Box Score: July 6, 1933

Thursday, July 6, 1933
Attendance: 47,595
Venue: Comiskey Park I
Game Duration: 2:05

	1	2	3	4	5	6	7	8	9	R	H	E
NL All-Star	0	0	0	0	0	2	0	0	0	2	8	0
AL All-Star	0	1	2	0	0	1	0	0	X	4	9	1

WP: Lefty Gomez (1-0) • LP: Bill Hallahan (0-1) • SV: Lefty Grove (1)

NL ALL-STARS Starting Lineup (#)		AB	R	H	RBI	BB	SO
1 Pepper Martin	3B	4	0	0	1	0	1
2 Frankie Frisch	2B	4	1	2	1	0	0
3 Chuck Klein	RF	4	0	1	0	0	0
4 Chick Hafey	LF	4	0	1	0	0	0
5 Bill Terry	1B	4	0	2	0	0	0
6 Wally Berger	CF	4	0	0	0	0	0
7 Dick Bartell	SS	2	0	0	0	0	1
8 Jimmie Wilson	CF	1	0	0	0	0	0
9 Bill Hallahan	P	1	0	0	0	0	0
Manager							
John McGraw							
Reserves							
Paul Waner	RF	0	0	0	0	0	0
Pie Traynor	PH	1	0	1	0	0	0
Carl Hubbell	P	0	0	0	0	0	0
Tony Cuccinello	PH	1	0	0	0	0	1
Lefty O'Doul	PH	1	0	0	0	0	0
Gabby Harnett	C	1	0	0	0	0	1
Lon Warneke	P	1	1	1	0	0	0
Woody English	PH-SS	1	0	0	0	0	0
Tony Cuccinello	2B						
Hal Schumacher	P						

	AL ALL-STARS Starting Lineup (#)		AB	R	H	RBI	BB	SO
1	Ben Chapman	LF-RF	5	0	1	0	0	1
2	Charlie Gehringer	2B	3	1	0	0	2	0
3	Babe Ruth	RF	4	1	2	2	0	2
4	Lou Gehrig	1B	2	0	0	0	2	1
5	Al Simmins	CF-LF	4	0	1	0	0	0
6	Jimmy Dykes	3B	3	1	2	0	1	0
7	Joe Cronin	SS	3	1	1	0	1	0
8	Rick Ferrell	C	3	0	0	0	0	0
9	Lefty Gomez	P	1	0	1	1	0	0
	Manager							
	Connie Mack							
	Reserves							
	Sam West	CF	0	0	0	0	0	0
	General Crowder	P	1	0	0	0	0	0
	Earl Averill	PH	1	0	1	1	0	0
	Lefty Grove	P	1	0	0	0	0	0
	Bill Dickey	C						
	Jimmie Foxx	1B						
	Tony Lazzeri	2B						
	Wes Ferrell	P						
	Oral Hildebrand	P						

NOTES

PROLOGUE

1. Francis Eaton, "Red Sox Win Brilliant Game From All-Stars," *Boston Journal*, September 28, 1917, front page; continued on p. 8.
2. *The Boston Globe*, September 18, 1887, 4.
3. Ronan C. Lyons et al. "The Price of Housing in the United States, 1890-2006," *National Bureau of Economic Research*, p. 7.
4. Woodrow Wilson, *Address to Congress Requesting a Declaration of War Against Germany*, April 2, 1917, National Archives, https://www.archives.gov/milestone-documents/address-to-congress-declaration-of-war-against-germany.

---

1 THE RISE OF MURNANE'S GAME
ARRIVAL AT FENWAY

1. *Harper's Weekly*, "The National Game. Three 'Outs' and One 'Run,'" September 15, 1860. https://ushistoryscene.com/article/baseball-and-the-civil-war/.
2. George B. Kirsch, "Hurry Up and Wait and Play Ball!" *New York Times*, October 24, 2012. https://archive.nytimes.com/opinionator.blogs.nytimes.com/2012/10/24/hurry-up-and-wait-and-play-ball/
3. Tom Goldman, "How Sports Met 'The Star-Spangled Banner.'" *NPR*. September 6, 2018. https://www.npr.org/2018/09/06/644991357/how-sports-met-the-star-spangled-banner.
4. Harold Seymour and Dorothy Seymour Mills, *Baseball: The Early Years* (New York: Oxford University Press, 1989), 13.
5. *Boston Globe*, "Popularity of Tim Murnane, The Globe's Base Ball Writer," August 12, 1888, 6.
6. Bill James, *The New Bill James Historical Baseball Abstract* (New York: Simon & Schuster 2003), 52-53.
7. James, *The New Bill James Historical Baseball Abstract*, 52.
8. James, *The New Bill James Historical Baseball Abstract*, 53.
9. Tim Murnane, "Tim Murnane's Views on Managing a Team," *Boston Globe*, August 20, 1888, 8.
10. Tim Murnane, "Better for the Batter: Probably Change in Next Year's Pitching Rules," *Boston Globe*, August 27, 1888.
11. *Boston Globe*, "'Sporty' Barker, An Old-Time Baseball Umpire, Has Gone 'Gof.,' Evidently," August 21, 1930, 16.
12. Barbara W. Tuchman, *The Guns of August* (New York: Macmillan, 1962), 1.
13. *National Army Museum*. "Battle of the Somme," accessed August 5, 2025. https://www.nam.ac.uk/explore/battle-somme.
14. "Battle of the Somme." *History*. November 12, 2009. https://www.history.com/articles/battle-of-the-somme.
15. Arthur Duffey, "Arthur Duffey's Comment on Sports," *Boston Post*, September 24, 1916, 14, accessed via *newspapers.com*, https://www.newspapers.com/image-view/74642492/?match=1&terms=Tim%20Murnane.
16. *Duffey*, "Arthur Duffey's Comment on Sports."
17. Eaton, "Red Sox Win Brilliant Game From All-Stars," front page, continued on page 8.
18. National Archives and Records Administration, *Joint Address to Congress*

Leading to a Declaration of War Against Germany, April 2, 1917, National Archives Milestone Documents, accessed December 20, 2025, https://www.archives.gov/milestone-documents/address-to-congress-declaration-of-war-against-germany.

19. As America crept toward war, many wondered: should baseball stop—should the national pastime take a pause amid the horrors of global conflict? Some believed it should. Elected officials argued that leisure was unseemly in wartime, that all able-bodied men should serve at the front or in the factories. The idea culminated in the "Work or Fight" order issued by the U.S. Secretary of War, which would later shorten the 1918 baseball season. Players enlisted, giving up their roster spots. Owners worried who would attend games.

But others saw in baseball a vital source of national morale. Woodrow Wilson certainly did. An avid fan and a former collegiate player at Davidson College, where he led the school's baseball association, Wilson carried the game with him long after he traded the diamond for academia and politics. He had been a capable player, but his "only trouble," as his former teammate (and future North Carolina governor) Robert Glenn teased, "was that he cared more for history than for Spalding's rules."

That lifelong concern for history, and for the role he might play in it, made Wilson unusually attuned to the importance of unity and brotherhood in an era of strain. In 1913, when he had learned that a semi-centenary commemoration at Gettysburg would bring together veterans "both blue and grey [sic]," he abandoned plans for a quiet Independence Day and insisted on traveling to attend the ceremonies. He felt compelled to be present for a moment that symbolized reconciliation.

Two years later, in 1915, he became the first sitting president to attend a World Series, and he would go on to throw multiple ceremonial first pitches for the local Washington Senators. Wilson grasped instinctively that baseball was too deeply woven into the national fabric to be set aside. Even if he never articulated it explicitly, the Southern preacher's son had never heard "The Star-Spangled Banner" until he went north to Princeton, yet ultimately made his political home in New Jersey. He understood the game's quiet power. Baseball had become part of the postbellum cultural peace between North and South, a shared ritual that smoothed regional wounds much as fighting shoulder-to-shoulder in World War I soon would. To halt the sport, he believed, would feel like a kind of national backsliding, a retreat from the fragile sense of brotherhood Americans were struggling to sustain. And so the games went on, even as the public watched with divided hearts.

---

2 THE SILVER KING OF BASEBALL
THE WARM-UP

1. Statue of Liberty–Ellis Island Foundation, *Passenger Record for Bridget Murnan, Ellen Austin*, arrived January 1, 1857, accessed December 20, 2025, https://heritage.statueofliberty.org/passenger-details/czoxMzoiOTAxMjAwNzgzMTc5NyI7/czo4OiJtYW5pZmVzdCI7. Later obituaries incorrectly labeled Murnane's birthplace as the United States. But as Charlie Bevis noted, in responses to two federal censuses, Tim's mother reported that he had been born in Ireland—which aptly squares with the family's 1857 arrival in New York Harbor. Confusion existed because in 1874, seeking a passport to participate in a European baseball tour—and perhaps concerned how his origin might impact his ability to travel given passport requirements—Murnane declared to a government official that he had been born in Connecticut. Though less likely, it is also possible that he did not actually know his place of birth. Note: the passenger logs refer to the Ellen Austin arriving at Ellis Island. But Ellis Island did not function as an immigration

station until 1892. Some digitized immigration databases label all New York arrivals under the umbrella term "Ellis Island," even for ships that predate the island's operation. It's a metadata simplification, not a historical claim about the physical site.

2. The Cincinnati club had been formed by Harry Wright, a former player from the Knickerbocker club, and his roster played against any team willing to face them, anywhere in the country. During the 1869 "season"—referred to loosely since it was a series of one-off games against amateur clubs—the Red Stockings went 65-0, including a 32-10 victory over the Atlantics. The recent completion of the Transcontinental Railroad made such dominance portable, allowing Wright's club to barnstorm across the nation and spread the game with missionary zeal.

The Red Stockings began their 1870 campaign in the South before returning to Cincinnati to play several local clubs—"area nines," they were called—where the club continued to win. The tour took them north to upstate New York and to Massachusetts, the two areas where baseball had initially taken hold most vibrantly. Wright wrote to the sports journalist Henry Chadwick—Murnane's Homeric predecessor, if there was one—that his 1870 team was even better than his roster from the season before. His players were "all members of the gymnasium… and exercise daily…when we go East this season we will be able to play a game or games of ball that will keep our reputation." Chadwick, who became a writer for the New York Clipper, is credited with creation of the box score and player statistics.

In New York, Cincinnati first played the Mutuals, one of the top clubs in the city, cruising to an easy 16-3 victory, and local newspapers predicted a similar outcome for the upcoming game against the Atlantics the following day. By the time they faced off against the Atlantics, Wright's boys were riding a winning streak of between 65-80 games—the exact number depended on whether all of the exhibition games they played should count.

3. John Thorn, "George Wright – June 14, 1870," *Our Game, April 21, 2025,* https://ourgame.mlblogs.com/george-wright-june-14-1870-9a3ce11cbc48.

4. Society for American Baseball Research, *Games Project,* "June 14, 1870: The Atlantic Storm: Red Stockings Suffer First Defeat," accessed December 20, 2025, https://sabr.org/gamesproj/game/june-14-1870-the-atlantic-storm-red-stockings-suffer-first-defeat/.w

5. Thorn, "George Wright — June 14, 1870," Wright had learned this trick playing for an amateur team called the Washington Nationals three years prior.

6. *Edmonton Journal,* "Player Who Couldn't Bat By Accident Discovered The Bunt in Early Days," January 12, 1924, 31.

7. John F. Morrill, "Funniest Play I Ever Saw," *Boston Globe,* January 30, 1913.

8. Abe Kemp, "Los Angeles Downs Seals, 4 to 3 in 15th," *San Francisco Chronicle,* June 9, 1934.

9. The Mansfields were named after Civil War hero General Joseph Mansfield, who was mortally wounded at the bloody battle of Antietam, a reminder of the entwined nature of baseball, history, and how generational legacies live on in myriad ways.

10. A motivating factor for the European barnstorming trip was to lay claim to America's pastime. Although baseball is widely regarded as America's game, the familiar claim that Abner Doubleday invented the game in Cooperstown, New York, in 1839 is a myth. The origins of the sport are more complex and transatlantic. As Harold Seymour and Dorothy Seymour Mills document in *Baseball: The Early Years,* references to "base-ball" appear in John Newbery's 1744 publication *A Little Pretty Pocket-Book,* and variants of the game were played in both England and colonial America throughout the eighteenth century. A Revolutionary War soldier recorded playing "base" at Valley Forge in 1778; a

Princeton student referenced "baste ball" in 1786; and Thurlow Weed organized a baseball club in Rochester, New York, in 1825. The British game of rounders closely resembled early baseball, as described in *The Boy's Own Book* (London, 1829).

The Doubleday origin story took institutional form with the Mills Commission of 1905, established after a banquet honoring Albert Spalding's global barnstorming tour. Seeking to affirm baseball as a distinctly American creation, the commission credited Doubleday—despite the absence of supporting evidence and despite the fact that Doubleday himself never claimed the invention. He was not even in Cooperstown in 1839. The commission's conclusion rested largely on the recollection of an elderly local resident recalling events from decades earlier.

As Seymour and Mills note, many baseball leaders "found it increasingly difficult to swallow the idea that their favorite pastime was of foreign origin. Pride and patriotism required that the game be native." The resulting myth reflected broader national impulses at a moment when the United States was asserting cultural as well as political identity. The debates over baseball's lineage underscore how quickly the sport became entwined with questions of ownership, memory, and national story.

11. *Boston Globe*, "Murnane Drops Dead in Theatre," February 8, 1917, 7.
12. *Boston Globe*, "Murnane Drops Dead in Theatre," February 8, 1917, 7.
13. Tim Murnane, "Tim Murnane on Hanlon," *Boston Globe*, March 13, 1904.
14. Tim Murnane, "Base Ball Matters: Tim Murnane's Gratuitous Counsel," *Boston Globe*, July 30, 1888, 8.
15. Seymour and Mills, *Baseball: The Early Years*, 299.
16. Seymour and Mills, *Baseball: The Early Years*, 299.
17. Murnane, "Base Ball Matters: Tim Murnane's Gratuitous Counsel," 8.
18. *Boston Post*, "About the Boston Globe: A Rash Post Man's New Year's Call on 'the Sheet Across the Way,'" January 7, 1894, 9.
19. Tim Murnane, "Back We Go," *Boston Globe*, August 24, 1888, 5.
20. Tim Murnane, "Never Give Up: Timely Suggestions by Tim Murnane" *Boston Globe*, July 23, 1888, 8.
21. *Buffalo News*, "Tim Murnane, the Veteran Base Ball Writer and Player," May 20, 1889, 3.
22. Tim Murnane, "Tim Murnane Visits George Foster, Who Is a Real Farmer in Oklahoma," *Boston Globe*, January 16, 1916, 14.
23. Aljercluis [pseud.], "Globe Features I've Enjoyed Reading," *Boston Globe*, November 20, 1931, 35.
24. Sault Star, "What's What in Sport," February 15, 1933, 9. Also, *Springfield Press*, "Father of Scouts," March 20, 1933, 4.
25. *Boston Globe*, "Popularity of Tim Murnane," 6.
26. *Buffalo News*, "Tim Murnane, the Veteran Base Ball Writer and Player," May 20, 1889, 3.
27. *Tacoma Daily Ledger*, "Billy Sunday Comes Back at Tim Murnane," August 16, 1908, 29.
28. *Boston Globe*, "Billy Sunday Was All Wrong; Picked Philadelphia to Beat Red Sox; Likes Murnane's Baseball, for 'He Gives Good Stuff,'" October 14, 1915, 8.
29. *Boston Globe*, Tim Murnane, "Base Ball Players," July 8, 1888, 6.
30. *The Pittsburgh Press*, "Tim Murnane's Awful Break," November 4, 1901, 8.
31. T.H. Murnane, *Wright & Ditson Guide to Baseball*, (Boston: Wright & Ditson, 1911), 32.
32. *Baseball History Daily*, "Anger Management," December 27, 2012, https://baseballhistorydaily.com/2012/12/27/anger-management/.
33. *Pittsburgh Press*, "Tim Murnane Roasts Valentine—Morris Poorly Supported," September 23, 1888, 15.

34. Ed McGrath, "Dodgers Blank the Braves 5 to 0: Notes of Braves' Game," *Boston Post*, September 10, 1916, 14.
35. *Boston Globe*, "Miss Murnane Dies: Daughter of Tim," June 12, 1931, 15.
36. *Wright & Ditson's Base Ball Guide* (Boston: Wright & Ditson, 1884).
For the reader wondering why the Union Association may be unfamiliar, it is because it lasted that one single season in 1884. Murnane's Reds finished the season above .500, but despite the volatility it aimed to eliminate, one-third of the 12-team league folded at some point midseason, with new teams replacing them, and the Chicago franchise moved to Pittsburgh literally during the season. Derisively known as the "Onion League," the Union Association crowned the St. Louis Maroons as champions, only to watch them immediately decamp for the National League—an exit that both validated the NL's supremacy and effectively sealed the Union's fate. At a January 15, 1885 meeting in Milwaukee to discuss the league's future, only two clubs showed up, and the owners of Milwaukee and Kansas City unanimously approved a disbanding of the league. See *Baseball Library*, "1885 Chronology," archived January 1, 2008, https://web.archive.org/web/20080101103130/http://www.baseballlibrary.com/chronology/byyear.php?year=1885.
37. *Wright & Ditson's Base Ball Guide.*
38. Murnane, *Wright & Ditson Guide to Baseball*, introduction.
39. T. H. Murnane, *Spalding's Guide to Baseball* (New York: Spalding, 1915), 45–46.
40. "Bob Quinn Believes American Boy and Baseball Go Together: Says Game is Not Slipping," *Boston Globe*, May 14, 1932, 6.

---

3 BOSTON, FENWAY & THE RISE OF THE RED SOX
A PAGEANT OF SKILL

1. *Cincinnati Magazine*, "Nothing But the Facts," April 1982, 111.
2. *Cincinnati Magazine*, "Nothing But the Facts."
3. *Toronto Star Weekly*, "How Majority of Major League Clubs Were Named," November 4, 1933, 16. See also Al Mitchell, "Out of the Pressbox," Mason City Globe-Gazette, March 22, 1934, 15.
4. *Baseball Library*, "1884 Chronology," , archived March 24, 2007, https://web.archive.org/web/20070324223117/http://www.baseballlibrary.com/chronology/byyear.php?year=1884&previous=yes.
5. General Charles Taylor was a leading Bostonian who had served in the Civil War at age 16, began his career as a printer at 18, served in the Massachusetts State House, and subsequently became what the *New York Times* dubbed in his obituary "a prophet of a new generation of journalists and a new era in journalism." Despite being a private secretary in a non-military capacity on the staff of former Massachusetts Governor William E. Russell, Taylor was given the rank of Brigadier General as part of the state militia. Boston society accepted his desire to be known as "General Taylor" for the remainder of his life. Notably, he was an innovator in the ten-cent magazine field, founding the periodical *American Homes* that reached a circulation of 40,000 readers only to lose everything in a single hour in 1872 during the great Boston fire of that year, leaving him flat broke. His success there made him an appealing candidate for the struggling Globe, which he transformed by adding Sunday and evening editions of the paper while cutting prices from three cents per copy to two, which drove readership. He also aimed to convert the paper "from a man's paper to a family paper, one that pleased every member of the household." This meant including new content such as an expanded sports news section, more pictures, and even fictional stories for kids. Within three weeks

of the new strategy, the money-losing Globe became a financial juggernaut, and circulation of the paper leaped from 8,000 to 30,000. In a speech in New York on the centennial anniversary of American commerce, he poignantly said: "Where it fulfills its highest mission [journalism] carries just as little sorrow or trouble among the people as possible and it endeavors to scatter rays of sunshine and inspire feelings of hope in the homes of the toiling millions, to encourage them and their families in the great battle of life." *The New York Times*, "Charles H. Taylor, Boston Editor, Dies," June 23, 1921. https://timesmachine.nytimes.com/timesmachine/1921/06/23/109809151.pdf.

6. Bob Ryan, "Perfect Time When Game Was Young," *Boston Globe*, May 5, 1998, 69.

7. *Baseball Reference*, "1912 Boston Red Sox Statistics," accessed December 20, 2025, https://www.baseball-reference.com/teams/BOS/1912.shtml.

8. Glenn Stout, *Fenway 1912* (Boston: Houghton Mifflin Harcourt, 2012), 201.

9. Thomas J. Whalen, *When the Red Sox Ruled: Baseball's First Dynasty, 1912-1918*, p. 45.

10. George R. Holmes, "Boston Outfield Best of All Time," *Pittsburgh Press*, October 14, 1915, 21.

11. *Pittsburgh Press*, "Harry Hooper Was Real Redsox Hero," December 13, 1912, 32.

12. Lawrence S. Ritter, *The Glory of Their Times* (New York: Macmillan, 1966), 165.

13. *Reading Eagle*, "Harry Hooper Dies at 87," December 18, 1974, 60.

14. Mark Bushnell, "Then Again: Larry Gardner, from Enosburg Falls to Red Sox Fame," *VTDigger*, June 16, 2024, https://vtdigger.org/2024/06/16/then-again-larry-gardner-from-enosburg-falls-to-red-sox-fame/.

15. Tris Speaker, "Hurlers Work Was Wellnigh Perfect," *Pittsburgh Press*, October 14, 1915, 21.

16. Thomas J. Whelan, *When the Red Sox Ruled: Baseball's First Dynasty 1912-1918*, p. 78.

17. The upstart Federal League emerged in 1913, operating as a "third major league." The league nixed the so-called "reserve clause" that had spurred player discontent for years in forcing players to remain with the clubs who had initially contracted with them. In consequence, competition for top players was driven largely by compensation, causing players' salaries to skyrocket in bidding wars. The Brooklyn Feds offered Tris Speaker $18,000 to play for them in 1915, prompting panic in Boston over the prospect of losing their star player. To retain his top players, Red Sox owner Joseph Lannin signed Speaker and Wood to exorbitant contracts. To keep Speaker, Lannin gave the outfielder a two-year contract of $15,000 per year, plus a bonus of $5,000, making him one of the highest paid players in the game.

Despite its attempt to compete with the AL and NL, a variety of factors (including interference from the AL and NL) led the Federal League to fold after the 1915 season. The disgruntled Federal leadership initiated what became a momentous federal lawsuit ultimately decided by the United States Supreme Court. In *Federal Baseball Club v. National League*, the Court ruled that the Sherman Antitrust Act, which promoted free market competition and prohibited unfair monopolies, did *not* apply to MLB. Justice Oliver Wendell Holmes' opinion for the Court got to the heart of the issue in a brief writing, in which he essentially stated that baseball did not qualify as interstate commerce. "The business is giving exhibitions of baseball, which are purely state affairs," he wrote. "It is true that, in order to attain for these exhibitions the great popularity that they have achieved, competitions must be arranged between clubs from different cities and states. But the fact that, in order to give the exhibitions, the Leagues must induce free persons to cross state lines and must arrange and pay for their doing so is not enough to change the character of the business…the transport is a mere incident, not the essential thing."

With the Federal League gone after 1915, Lannin sought to right-size the compensation of his star players. Smoky Joe Wood was offered a sizable contract reduction, which so infuriated him that he chose to retire at the ripe old age of 26 rather than play for so much less money. Lannin offered Speaker $8,000 a year, a stark reduction from what he had just earned while delivering customary all-star numbers. Speaker, recognizing the changed marketplace, demanded $12,000 as a compromise. As spring training began in 1916, Speaker did not have a contract but played in exhibition games for the Red Sox in good faith on the basis that Lannin told him they had a deal. But behind closed doors, Lannin met privately with J.C. Dunn and P.S. McCarthy, Chicago contractors who had bought the Cleveland Indians for $500,000, and cut a deal to ship his star outfielder to the Indians for two unproven prospects and $55,000 of cash.

In learning the news that he had been traded to Cleveland, Speaker traveled from New York to Boston on April 9, 1916. Speaker complained to the press that the transfer had been a complete surprise to him: "As I understood it," he said, "Mr. Lannin and I had practically agreed upon terms [for him to return to the Red Sox]. I shall see Mr. Lannin tomorrow forenoon and look for an explanation. I have not signed any contract with the Cleveland Club yet…Whether I shall go to Cleveland remains to be seen. Everything depends upon my interview with Mr. Lannin."

The next day, Speaker and Lannin met briefly, but the deal with the Indians had already been made. "I leave for Cleveland tonight at 11:15," Speaker subsequently told the press, saying that he planned to discuss contract terms with them upon his arrival. "If I am a hold-up or a holdout [like Wood] as things are now, I don't know it." Asked if he was upset about being traded to Cleveland, Speaker, dejected, replied: "Of course I am. One does not like to leave a team such as the Red Sox to go to the Cleveland team." The transaction was seen as a big gain for the Indians, though Speaker presciently noted: "Don't worry about these Red Sox…[they] have a chance to repeat this year."

Angry that Lannin was pocketing cash off the trade, Speaker arrived in Cleveland and promptly demanded a $5,000 bonus out of the cash proceeds that Cleveland had paid as a condition for signing a contract with the team. When he met with Dunn, the Cleveland owner, Dunn explained to Speaker that the two deal points were unrelated—and besides: it was Lannin, of course, who had received those funds, not Dunn. Dunn tried to reach Lannin by phone that night but did not connect. Ultimately, Cleveland was able to sign Speaker, and after sitting out the full 1916 season, Wood joined his pal Speaker there where he spent the rest of his career, ultimately retiring after the 1922 season with a career pitching record of 117-57 and a 2.03 ERA. They won the World's Series there together in 1920, with Speaker as player-manager.

With Wood and Speaker out, and a combination of new prospects in the fold, the Red Sox went 91-63 that 1916 season on their way to a second consecutive championship, while Cleveland went 77-77. Ruth started 40 games on the mound and went 23-12 with a 1.75 ERA while Leonard went 18-12 with a 2.36 ERA. Third baseman Larry Gardner, a left-handed hitting veteran of the Sox since 1908, led the team in batting with a .308 average, Harry Hooper stole 27 bases, and second baseman Jack Barry, a Shrewsbury, Massachusetts native who had joined the team in time for the 1915 championship season, managed to get hit by a pitch a league-leading 17 times.

18. Jacob Pomrenke, "1917 Fenway Park Gamblers' Riot," *Jacob Pomrenke*, accessed December 20, 2025, https://jacobpomrenke.com/black-sox/1917-fenway-park-gamblers-riot/.

19. Pomrenke, "1917 Fenway Park Gamblers' Riot."

20. Samantha Burkett, "Babe Ruth Made History with Help from Ernie Shore," *Baseball Hall of Fame,* accessed December 21, 2025, https://baseballhall.org/discover/babe-ruth-made-history-with-help-from-ernie-shore.
21. *Retrosheet,* "Box Score: Boston at Washington Senators, June 23, 1917," accessed December 20, 2025, https://www.retrosheet.org/boxesetc/1917/B06231BOS1917.htm.
22. *Extreme Weather Watch,* "Boston Weather in 1917," accessed December 20, 2025, https://www.extremeweatherwatch.com/cities/boston/year-1917#september.
23. Francis Eaton, "Red Sox Win Brilliant Game From All-Stars," *Boston Journal,* September 28, 1917, front page; continued on p. 8.
24. *Boston Globe,* "Live Tips and Topics," by "Sportsman," September 28, 1917, 7.

---

4 THE ROAD TO MURNANE DAY
OPENING SALVOS

1. *Sentinel-Record,* "Boston Party of Players Here," March 12, 1912, 1.
2. *Boston Globe,* "Murnane Drops Dead in Theatre."
3. *Boston Globe,* "Murnane Drops Dead in Theatre."
4. *Boston Globe,* "Murnane Drops Dead in Theatre."
5. *Boston Globe,* "Murnane Drops Dead in Theatre."
6. *Boston Globe,* "Mayor Curley's Tribute," February 8, 1917, 8.
7. Woodrow Wilson, *Address to Joint Session of Congress Requesting Declaration of War Against Germany,* April 2, 1917, National Archives and Records Administration, accessed December 20, 2025, https://www.archives.gov/milestone-documents/address-to-congress-declaration-of-war-against-germany.
8. F. C. Lane, "An All-Star Baseball Contest for a Greater Championship: Where the Present World's Series Falls Short of the Ideal—How a Greater Series, the Real Grand Opera of Baseball, Might Be Staged," *Baseball Magazine,* November 1915, 57–64.
9. *Boston Globe,* "Big League Stars Play Here On 'Tim Murnane Day,' Sept. 27," September 2, 1917, 12.
10. *Boston Globe,* "Big League Stars Play Here On 'Tim Murnane Day,' Sept. 27," September 2, 1917, 12.
11. *Boston Globe,* "Murnane Day Plans," September 5, 1917, 7.
12. Society for American Baseball Research, *SABR BioProject,* "Benny Kauff's," January 4, 2012, https://sabr.org/bioproj/person/benny-kauff/. When he arrived on the Giants in 1916, the 26-year-old had told reporters, "I'll make them all forget that a guy named Ty Cobb ever pulled on a baseball shoe." He was, in David Jones' words, "the most heralded young player of his generation." But this was before he was suspended from baseball in 1921 amid multiple allegations: one including his purported participation in facilitating the throwing of the 1919 World's Series, and the other an indictment on auto-theft charges. Though he was cleared of criminal charges, Commissioner Landis decided to ban him for life. The trial, Landis said, "disclosed a state of affairs that more than seriously compromises your character and reputation. The reasonable and necessary result of this is that your mere presence in the lineup would inevitably burden patrons of the game with grave apprehension to its integrity." New York courts, responding to Kauff's appeal, determined they had no authority over the matter.
13. Society for American Baseball Research, *SABR BioProject,* "Pete Alexander," January 4, 2012, https://sabr.org/bioproj/person/pete-alexander/. Grover Cleveland "Pete" Alexander went 30-13 that 1917 season with a 1.83 earned run average while leading the league in games pitched, complete games, shutouts,

innings pitched, strikeouts, and wins. Thinking Alexander would be drafted into the army, the Phillies' front office shipped him and a teammate off to the Chicago Cubs for $55,000. He began the 1918 season before indeed being drafted, and as Jan Finkel noted, he was destroyed by the Great War. His seven weeks on the front line left him deaf in one ear and with permanent muscle damage in his right arm from operating cannons, and he was never the same.

14. *Boston Globe*, "Speaker Again Hurt, In Trying to Steal Home," September 2, 1917, 12.

15. Washington owner Clark Griffith had created a fund with which to purchase baseballs, bats, and other baseball equipment for American troops stationed in Europe. Three team presidents prospectively pledged that if their team made the championship series, they would each contribute one percent of the club's share of gross receipts across the whole series. Players would also be given the opportunity to make contributions.

16. *Boston Globe*, "Live Tips and Topics," by "Sportsman," August 15, 1914, 7.

17. Francis Eaton, "Red Sox Win Brilliant Game From All-Stars," *Boston Journal*, September 28, 1917, front page; continued on p. 8.

---

5 THE STARS WHO CAME
CHESS ON GRASS

1. *Boston Globe*, "17,000 Out to Honor Murnane," September 28, 1917.
2. *Boston Globe*, "17,000 Out to Honor Murnane," September 28, 1917.
3. *The Inter Ocean*, "The Champion Slugger: John L. Sullivan Tells the Story of His Life to a Denver Reporter," January 1, 1884, 16, via *Newspapers.com*, https://www.newspapers.com/image/32570392/?clipping_id=7228862&fcfToken=eyJhbGciOiJIUzI1NiIsInR5cCI6IkpXVCJ9.eyJmcmVlLXZpZXctaWQiOjMyNTcwMzkyLCJpYXQiOjE3NjIxMDczNzEsImV4cCI6MTc2MjE5Mzc3MX0.4E6ldC2Jjd5ffiKElB1L-Oe8-LMX1S638mAA7WL5bMk.
4. *The Inter Ocean*, "The Champion Slugger: John L. Sullivan Tells the Story of His Life to a Denver Reporter."
5. *Boston Globe*, "John L. 'Buncoed': Although a Ful'-Fledged Tenderloiner, He Gave Up $15 Easy—The Trick Cannot Be Repeated with Safety," December 27, 1899, 5.
6. *The Deadball Era*, "Prelude to Disaster," accessed January 12, 2026, https://www.thedeadballera.com/prelude.html. The fastball Mays delivered struck Chapman in the head with such force that Mays initially believed the ball had hit Chapman's bat; he even fielded the carom and threw to first, thinking it was a ground-out. Hitters did not wear helmets back then, and the blow caused a 3.5-inch depressed skull fracture in Chapman's head. Chapman tried to stand, muttered a few words—including that he was okay, that Mays should not worry about him—and then collapsed with blood coming from his head. Rushed to St. Lawrence Hospital, he underwent emergency surgery, but he died within twelve hours—still the only major leaguer ever killed by a pitch. The New York District Attorney declined to press charges, ruling the tragedy a terrible accident. The calamity spurred MLB to require umpires to replace dirty or scuffed balls, which pitchers had long manipulated to make them harder to see. Even so, batting helmets would not arrive for decades. A modicum of solace came just weeks later when Chapman's Indians—with Smoky Joe Wood and Tris Speaker on the roster—won the World Series.
7. Wallace Goldsmith, "Features of the Red Sox–All Stars Clash for Benefit of Murnane Memorial Fund," *Boston Globe*, September 28, 1917, 7.

8. Wallace Goldsmith was a Cleveland native who had made Boston his adopted home, was as much a part of the city's sports culture as any player he drew. Trained as a book illustrator, he had provided artwork for writers such as Oscar Wilde, Barry Pain, and John Townsend Trowbridge, but his true passion lay elsewhere. What he loved most was capturing the rhythms and personalities of baseball in the days before newsreels or television brought the games to life, and he was the lead cartoonist covering the Red Sox and Braves. Goldsmith had a knack for distilling an athlete's essence into a single, humorous image—a kind of visual column that could make fans smile the morning after a game. "Because the scenes depicted were entirely of his choosing," one historian wrote, "he created an interpretation of the game that resulted in a summary more like that of a fan than reporter." Like Murnane, Goldsmith traveled with the Red Sox to their various spring training destinations in Arkansas and California to gain access to the players and help fans picture what lay in store for the season ahead.

9. Walter McMullen, "The Sport Trail: Peer of Them All," *The Hamilton Spectator*, May 28, 1930, 22.

10. Francis Eaton, "Red Sox Win Brilliant Game From All-Stars," *Boston Journal*, September 28, 1917, front page; continued on p. 8.

---

6 TRUST, BETRAYAL & THE BIRTH OF A NEW TRADITION
FIRE & RESOLVE

1. F. Scott Fitzgerald, *The Great Gatsby* (New York: Scribner, 2004), 73.
2. *New York Times*, "Out-Door Sports: The National Game," September 29, 1865, 8.
3. Society for American Baseball Research, *SABR Journal*, "The 1877 Louisville Grays Scandal," accessed December 20, 2025, https://sabr.org/journal/article/the-1877-louisville-grays-scandal/.
4. *SABR Journal*, "The 1877 Louisville Grays Scandal."
5. J. E. Findling, "The Louisville Grays' Scandal of 1877," *Journal of Sport History* (2017): 176–187.
6. Ted Curtis, "In the Best Interests of the Game: The Authority of the Commissioner of Major League Baseball," *Seton Hall Journal of Sport Law* 5 (1995): 7.
7. Society for American Baseball Research, *SABR Research*, "Judge Landis and Baseball's Ban Hammer," accessed December 20, 2025, https://sabr.org/research/article/judge-landis-and-baseballs-ban-hammer/
8. Matthew E. Stanley, "Ty Cobb and Tris Speaker Are Accused of Fixing Baseball Games," *EBSCO Research Starters*, 2022, accessed December 20, 2025, https://www.ebsco.com/research-starters/history/ty-cobb-and-tris-speaker-are-accused-fixing-baseball-games.
9. *New York Times*, "Paid for Letters in Baseball Scandal," December 23, 1926, 1, 16.
10. *New York Times*, "Paid for Letters in Baseball Scandal."
11. *New York Times*, "Paid for Letters in Baseball Scandal."
12. *New York Times*, "Paid for Letters in Baseball Scandal."
13. *New York Times*, "Paid for Letters in Baseball Scandal."
14. *New York Times*, "Paid for Letters in Baseball Scandal."
15. *New York Times*, "Paid for Letters in Baseball Scandal."
16. "Cobb and Speaker Cleared by Landis: Verdict Exonerating Stars of Baseball Scandal," *New York Times*, January 28, 1927, 11, https://www.nytimes.com/1927/01/28/archives/cobb-and-speaker-cleared-by-landis-verdict-exonerating-stars-of.html.

17. Gary Richardson, Alejandro Komai, Michael Gou, and Daniel Park, "Stock Market Crash of 1929," *Federal Reserve History*, accessed December 20, 2025, https://www.federalreservehistory.org/essays/stock-market-crash-of-1929.
18. *Federal Reserve History*, "Stock Market Crash of 1929."
19. Michael Haupert, "The Business of Being the Babe," *Baseball Research Journal* 50, no. 1 (Spring 2021): 7–15, https://sabr.org/journal/article/the-business-of-being-the-babe/.
20. Francis Eaton, "Red Sox Win Brilliant Game From All-Stars," *Boston Journal*, September 28, 1917, front page; continued on p. 8.
21. *Boston Globe*, "17,000 Out to Honor Murnane," September 28, 1917.

---

7 THE FIRST ALL-STAR GAME
THE GREAT FINISH

1. Deb Seymour, *BallNine*, "The Game of the Century," July 20, 2022.
2. Freedman, *The Day All the Stars Came Out*, 17.
3. *Courier-News*, "Suggest Ten Man Team for Baseball; Player to Bat for Pitcher," December 12, 1928, 20.
4. David Vincent, Lyle Spatz, and David W. Smith, *The Midsummer Classic: The Complete History of Baseball's All-Star Game* (Lincoln: University of Nebraska Press, 2001), xi.
5. Freedman, *The Day All the Stars Came Out*, 53.
6. Vincent, Spatz, and Smith, *The Midsummer Classic*, xi.
7. Freedman, *The Day All the Stars Came Out*, 21.
8. Kori Rumore and Marianne Mather, "Vintage Chicago Tribune: We Started Baseball's First All-Star Game — 90 Years Ago," *Chicago Tribune*, July 6, 2023, accessed December 20, 2025, https://www.chicagotribune.com/2023/07/06/vintage-chicago-tribune-we-started-baseballs-first-all-star-game-90-years-ago/?clearUserState=true.
9. Freedman, *The Day All the Stars Came Out*, 22.
10. *Chicago Tribune*, "Final Returns in All-Star Baseball Poll," June 25, 1933, 1.
11. *Chicago Tribune*, "Al Leads Ruth, Klein in Total For Star Game," June 25, 1933, 1.
12. *Chicago Tribune*, "Al Leads Ruth, Klein in Total For Star Game."
13. *Chicago Tribune*, "Al Leads Ruth, Klein in Total For Star Game."
14. Vincent, Spatz, and Smith, *The Midsummer Classic*, 4.
15. Gary Sarnoff, "Sam West," *SABR BioProject*, January 4, 2012, https://sabr.org/bioproj/person/Sam-West/.
16. Freedman, *The Day All the Stars Came Out*, 64.
17. Freedman, *The Day All the Stars Came Out*, 64-65.
18. *SABR Games Project*, "September 28, 1938: Hartnett hits Homer in the Gloamin'." In 1938, the Pittsburgh Pirates stood atop the NL with four weeks left in the season, seven games in the lead. The Pirates were already selling World Series tickets and undertook a renovation of Forbes Field to accommodate a larger-than-usual press corps that would descend on the ballpark for the championship series. But the Cubs got hot in September and inched their way right behind the Pirates, just in time for a final weekend series with each other at Wrigley Field with the Cubs only 1.5 games back. The Cubs won the first game, and with the next game tied in the ninth inning, darkness threatened the game's continuation. The umpires agreed to go one more half-inning, and with two outs in the bottom of the ninth, Hartnett hit a hanging curveball over the fence—which many in the ballpark struggled to see given the darkness—to win the game and send the Cubs up half a game in the standings. Hartnett was mobbed at the plate, and though

there was one more game to play, the Pirates were so down from the walk-off homer that they just couldn't muster a victory, and the once-certain World Series berth alluded them. An Associated Press writer dubbed Hartnett's hit "The Homer in the Gloamin," referring to the fleeting period of dim light after the sun goes down.

19. *Chicago Tribune*, "American Stars Win Game of Century," July 7, 1933, 1.

20. Scott Pitoniak, "MLB All-Star Game Created a Blueprint For Other Leagues to Follow," *Baseball Hall of Fame and Museum*, accessed March 7, 2026, https://baseballhall.org/discover/mlb-all-star-game-created-blueprint-for-other-leagues-to-follow.

21. Francis Eaton, "Red Sox Win Brilliant Game From All-Stars," *Boston Journal*, September 28, 1917, front page; continued on p. 8.

---

8 AFTER THE APPLAUSE *TWILIGHT AT FENWAY*

1. Francis Eaton, "Red Sox Win Brilliant Game From All-Stars," *Boston Journal*, September 28, 1917, front page; continued on p. 8.

---

9 THE MEMORY WE CARRY *AFTERMATH*

1. Sportsman, "Live Tips and Topics," *Boston Globe*, April 29, 1919, 11.
2. Babe Ruth, "The Story of His Life" [Chapter VII], *Boston Post*, August 15, 1920, 15.
3. *Boston Globe*, "Williams Gets Tim Murnane Honor Plaque," December 21, 1939, 20.
4. Jerry Nason, "Duffy's Hall of Fame Excursion Starts and Finishes in the *Globe*," *Boston Globe*, April 28, 1945, 4.
5. Victor O. Jones, "Notes from the Back of an Envelope: Will Rogers Galloped in the Outfield," *Boston Globe*, August 12, 1966, 11.
6. Victor O. Jones, "Notes from the Back of an Envelope: Will Rogers Galloped in the Outfield," *Boston Globe*, August 12, 1966, 11.
7. Jones, "Notes from the Back of an Envelope," *Boston Globe*, August 12, 1966.
8. The specific award text of the recognition for Murnane read: *"Professional ballplayer for 15 years; toured Europe with 1874 Athletics. Managed Boston club in Union Association. Discovered many of game's early stars. Organized Boston Unions and Blues. Was President of New England League for 24 years, President of Eastern League, member of Arbitration Board and first Vice President of National Association. Published Boston Referee, edited Minor League Guide, and was Baseball Editor of Boston Globe for 30 years. Delightful wit and Irish brogue made him popular after-dinner speaker. Tireless and enthusiastic worker. Authority on Baseball and one of game's best friends."* J.G. Taylor Spink Award presented by Baseball Writers' Association of America at Cooperstown, New York, August 5, 1979, accessed from Baseball Hall of Fame.
9. Bob Ryan, "Time to Stop Dodging Us," *Boston Globe*, June 11, 2004, E7. Note: The team that played the Red Sox in 1916 was known as the Brooklyn Robins, a predecessor to the Brooklyn Dodgers.

EPILOGUE: THAT INNOCENT PROMISE

1. Ken Burns, dir, *Baseball*, episode 1, originally aired September 18, 1994, PBS.

IMAGE SOURCES

Every effort has been made to identify and credit the sources of images included in this book. In some cases, despite diligent research, complete attribution information could not be determined. The publisher and author welcome any additional information and will make appropriate corrections in future editions.

---

1 THE RISE OF MURNANE'S GAME
ARRIVAL AT FENWAY

PAGE 6

Top Image: "The national game. Three 'outs' and one 'run.'" Published by Currier & Ives, c. 1860. Sourced from: Library of Congress Prints and Photographs Division, Washington, D.C. 20540. According to the Library of Congress: "A pro-Lincoln satire, deposited for copyright weeks before the 1860 presidential election. The contest is portrayed as a baseball game in which Lincoln has defeated (left to right) John Bell, Stephen A. Douglas, and John C. Breckinridge. Lincoln (right) stands with his foot on "Home Base," advising the others, "Gentlemen, if any of you should ever take a hand in another match at this game, remember that you must have a 'good bat' and strike a 'fair ball' to make a 'clean score' & a 'home run.'" His "good bat" is actually a wooden rail labeled "Equal Rights and Free Territory." Lincoln wears a belt inscribed "Wide Awake Club." A skunk stands near the other candidates, signifying that they have been "skunk'd." Breckinridge (center), a Southern Democrat, holds his nose, saying, "I guess I'd better leave for Kentucky, for I smell something strong around here, and begin to think, that we are completely skunk'd.'" His bat is labeled "Slavery Extension" and his belt "Disunion Club." At far left John Bell of the Constitutional Union party observes, "It appears to me very singular that we three should strike foul' and be put out' while old Abe made such a good lick.' Bell's belt says "Union Club," and his bat "Fusion." Regular Democratic nominee Douglas replies, "That's because he had that confounded rail, to strike with, I thought our fusion would be a short stop' to his career." He grasps a bat labeled "Non Intervention.'" https://www.loc.gov/pictures/item/2003674584/

Middle Image: Otto Boetticher. *Union Prisoners at Salisbury, North Carolina.* Lithograph. New York: Sarony, Major & Knapp, 1863. Prints and Photographs Division, Library of Congress (013.00.00). https://www.loc.gov/exhibitions/baseball-americana/about-this-exhibition/origins-and-early-days/baseball-as-the-national-game/civil-war-prisoners-at-play/.

Bottom Image: The 48th New York Regiment poses in 1863 at Fort Pulaski in Savannah, Georgia. National Baseball Hall of Fame and Museum.

PAGE 20

Top Image: Hand-colored map of the City of Boston, Plate 33, Fenway Park Site, from the 1902 Atlas of the City of Boston, Massachusetts, Boston Proper and Back Bay by G. W. Bromley and Company.

Bottom Image: Front entry façade of Fenway Park in 1912. Photographer unknown.

PAGE 23

Walter Johnson. Date, location, and photographer unknown.

---

2 THE SILVER KING OF BASEBALL
THE WARM-UP

PAGE 24

Baseball card of Tim Murnane as a member of the Philadelphia Athletics c. 1874.

PAGE 46

Ty Cobb and Joe Jackson stand during warm-ups on Murnane Day, September 27, 1917, at Fenway Park in Boston. Photographer unknown.

PAGE 49

Ray Chapman and Walter "Rabbit" Maranville stand during warm-ups on Murnane Day, September 27, 1917, at Fenway Park in Boston. Photographer unknown.

---

3 BOSTON, FENWAY & THE RISE OF THE RED SOX
A PAGEANT OF SKILL

PAGE 50

Harry Hooper, Tris Speaker, and Duffy Lewis—Boston's "Golden Outfield"—c. 1915. Photographer unknown.

PAGE 64

Will Rogers on horseback on Murnane Day, September 27, 1917, at Fenway Park in Boston. Published by *Boston Globe*, September 28, 1917. Photographer unknown.

---

4 THE ROAD TO MURNANE DAY
OPENING SALVOS

PAGE 70

Murnane Day game advertisement, published by *Boston Globe* on September 26, 1917.

PAGE 80

Babe Ruth at Fenway Park, c. 1917. Photographer unknown.

---

5 THE STARS WHO CAME
CHESS ON GRASS

PAGE 84

Top image: All-Star team on Murnane Day, September 27, 1917, at Fenway Park in Boston. Published by *Boston Globe*, September 28, 1917. Photographer unknown.

Bottom image: Boston Red Sox team photo c. 1916, at Fenway Park in Boston. Photographer unknown.

Page 95

Top image: Fanny Brice poses. Date, location, and photographer unknown.

Bottom image: John L. Sullivan sits in the Red Sox dugout at Fenway Park in Boston with manager Jimmy Collins c. 1905-1908. Photographer unknown.

PAGE 96

Tris Speaker c. 1915. Photographer unknown.

PAGE 99

Dick Hoblitzell, Everett Scott, Jack Barry, and Larry Gardner stand together at Fenway Park in Boston c. 1915. Title and date based on research by the Pictorial History Committee, Society for American Baseball Research, 2006. Originally published by Bain News Service. Courtesy of Library of Congress.

6 TRUST, BETRAYAL & THE BIRTH OF A NEW TRADITION
FIRE & RESOLVE

PAGE 100

Cover image of *The Anaconda Standard*, September 29, 1920.

PAGE 118

Duffy Lewis c. 1915-1918, at Fenway Park in Boston. Photographer unknown.

---

7 THE FIRST ALL-STAR GAME
THE GREAT FINISH

PAGE 121

Dick Hoblitzell squats during warm-ups at Fenway Park in Boston. Date and photographer unknown.

PAGE 122

Top image: July 6, 1933 MLB All-Star Game at Comiskey Park in Chicago, National League All-Stars. Photographer unknown.

Bottom image: July 6, 1933 MLB All-Star Game at Comiskey Park in Chicago, American League All-Stars. Photographer unknown.

PAGE 138

Boston Red Sox owner John I. Taylor. Date, location, and photographer unknown.

PAGE 141

George "Rube" Foster warms up at Fenway Park in Boston. Date and photographer unknown.

PAGE 142

Scorecard of Middletown Mansfields game against the Boston Red Stockings on June 15, 1872.

PAGE 143

Top image: Artistic graphic of a baseball game attributed to artist Henry Sandham, *Base Ball* (aquarelle print by L. Prang & Co.), c. 1887. Attribution determined by the Boston Public Library, which has a copy of the print with the artist's name on it.

Bottom image: Cover page of Tim Murnane's *The Boston Referee*, January 29, 1887.

PAGE 144

Top image: "John L. 'Buncoed.'" Article appeared in the *Boston Globe* on December 27, 1899.

Bottom image: Preface to *How to Umpire, How to Coach, How to Captain, How to Manage, How to Organize a League*, in *Spalding's Athletic Library* (New York: American Sports Publishing Co., 1905), edited by Tim Murnane.

PAGE 145

Cover image of *How to Play Base Ball*, by T.H. Murnane, published in 1903 by American Sports Publishing Co., 16 & 18 Park Place, New York.

PAGE 146

Top image: Photograph of Cy Young c. 1904. Photographer unknown.

Bottom image: Photograph of Babe Ruth, Ernie Shore, Rube Foster, and Del Gainer at Fenway Park c. 1916-1917. Photographer unknown.

PAGE 147

Top image: "Tim Murnane Visits George Foster, Who is a Real Farmer in Oklahoma" article appeared in the *Boston Globe* on January 16, 1916.

Bottom image: Photograph of John F. Fitzgerald and James Michael Curley. Date and photographer unknown.

PAGE 148

Top image: Interior overhead image of Fenway Park c. 1916-1917. Photographer unknown.

Bottom image: Illustration by Wallace Goldsmith, published by the *Boston Globe,* June 17, 1917.

PAGE 149

Top image: "Big League Stars Play Here On 'Tim Murnane Day,' Sept 27" article appeared in the *Boston Globe* on September 2, 1917.

Bottom image: Interior photograph of left field in Fenway Park depicting "Duffy's Cliff" c. 1910s. Photographer unknown.

PAGE 150

Photograph of Joe Jackson posing with the loving cup he won at Murnane Day. Date and photographer unknown.

PAGE 151

Top image: Photograph of Joe Jackson posing in old age with the loving cup he won at Murnane Day. Date and photographer unknown.

Bottom image: Military services at Fenway Park c. 1918. Photographer unknown.

PAGE 152 - 153

American League and National League all-star ballot vote tallies published by the *Chicago Tribune* on June 25, 1933.

PAGE 154

"All Fences on League Circuit Look Alike to Big Babe Ruth" article appeared in the *Boston Post* on August 15, 1920.

PAGE 155

Top image: "I Was There in '33—Boy, Wotta Game!" article appeared in the *Chicago Tribune* on June 25, 1933.

PAGE 156

Top image: Ticket stubs from the July 6, 1933 inaugural All-Star Game. Photographer unknown.

Bottom image: Photograph of Babe Ruth, Lou Gehrig, Al Simmons, and Edwin Diamond on July 6, 1933 at Comiskey Park. Photographer unknown.

PAGE 157

Photograph taken July 6, 1933. Photographer unknown.

---

8 AFTER THE APPLAUSE *TWILIGHT AT FENWAY*

PAGE 158

Photograph of Tim Murnane gravesite. Date and photographer unknown.

PAGE 163

Boston Common c. 1918, showing Tremont and Park Streets. Title and date provided by the Boston Public Library.

PAGE 164

Illustration by Wallace Goldsmith, published by the *Boston Globe*, September 28, 1917.

PAGE 167

Boston Red Sox owner Harry Frazee. Date, location, and photographer unknown.

---

9 THE MEMORY WE CARRY *AFTERMATH*

PAGE 168

Photograph of Tim Murnane. Date and photographer unknown.

PAGE 176

Images of autographed baseball from Murnane Game. Published by Heritage Auctions in connection with a sale that occurred on February 20, 2016. https://sports.ha.com/itm/baseball-collectibles/balls/1917-tim-murnane-benefit-game-signed-baseball-with-shoeless-joe-jackson-babe-ruth-ty-cobb/a/7155-80018.s.

PAGE 179

Cover image of the *Boston Globe*, September 28, 1917.

EPILOGUE: THAT INNOCENT PROMISE

PAGE 180

Image of game ball from Murnane Game. Published by RR Auction in connection with a sale that occurred on October 11, 2017. https://www.rrauction.com/auctions/lot-detail/33813540510757-boston-red-sox-vs-all-stars-1917-game-used-baseball-from-the-1917-tim-murnane-benefitplayed-in-by-babe-ruth-ty-cobb-walter-johnson-and-shoeless-joe-jackson

PAGE 189

"Murnane Day Was Great." Article appeared in the *Boston Globe* evening edition on September 28, 1917.

BIBLIOGRAPHY

Aljercluis [pseud.]. "Globe Features I've Enjoyed Reading." *Boston Globe*. November 20, 1931.

Allardice, Bruce. "Judge Landis and Baseball's Ban Hammer." *SABR Research*. Accessed December 20, 2025. https://sabr.org/research/article/judge-landis-and-baseballs-ban-hammer/.

Anson, Adrian C. *A Ball Player's Career.* 1900. Reprint, Whitefish, MT: Kessinger Publishing, 2008. https://atlas.cs.brown.edu/data/gutenberg/1/9/6/5/19652/19652.txt.

Armour, Mark. "Will Harridge." *SABR BioProject*. January 29, 2012. Accessed December 20, 2025. https://sabr.org/bioproj/person/Will-Harridge/.

Baseball Almanac. "Addie Joss All-Star Game." Accessed October 11, 2025. https://www.baseball-almanac.com/tsn/addie_joss_benefit_game.shtml.

Baseball History Daily. "Anger Management." December 27, 2012. https://baseballhistorydaily.com/2012/12/27/anger-management/.

Baseball Library. "1884 Chronology." Archived March 24, 2007. Accessed December 20, 2025. https://web.archive.org/web/20070324223117/http://www.baseballlibrary.com/chronology/byyear.php?year=1884&previous=yes.

Baseball Library. "1885 Chronology." Archived January 1, 2008. Accessed December 20, 2025. https://web.archive.org/web/20080101103130/http://www.baseballlibrary.com/chronology/byyear.php?year=1885.

Baseball Reference. "1912 Boston Red Sox Statistics." Accessed December 20, 2025. https://www.baseball-reference.com/teams/BOS/1912.shtml.

Baseball Reference. "Career Leaders & Records for Double Plays Turned as CF." Accessed December 20, 2025. https://www.baseball-reference.com/leaders/DP_cf_career.shtml.

Baseball Reference. "Career Leaders & Records for Double Plays Turned as LF." Accessed December 20, 2025. https://www.baseball-reference.com/leaders/DP_lf_career.shtml.

Baseball Reference. "Career Leaders & Records for Double Plays Turned as RF," accessed December 20, 2025, https://www.baseball-reference.com/leaders/DP_rf_career.shtml.

Baseball Reference. "Tris Speaker Stats." Accessed December 20, 2025. https://www.baseball-reference.com/players/s/speaktr01.shtml.

Baseball Writers' Association of America. *J.G. Taylor Spink Award.* Presented August 5, 1979, Cooperstown, NY. Baseball Hall of Fame.

Berg, A. Scott. *Wilson*. New York: G. P. Putnam's Sons, 2013.

Bevis, Charlie. "Tim Murnane." *SABR Baseball Biography Project.* Society for American Baseball Research. September 17, 2012. https://sabr.org/bioproj/person/tim-murnane/.

Boston Daily Advertiser. "17,000 See Red Sox Defeat All-Stars." September 28, 1917.

Boston Globe. "Rad Does Well." September 18, 1887.

Boston Globe. "17,000 Out to Honor Murnane." September 28, 1917.

Boston Globe. "Baseball Men Did Not Forget Tribute to 'Tim.'" December 12, 1917.

Boston Globe. "Big League Stars Play Here On 'Tim Murnane Day,' Sept. 27." September 2, 1917.

Boston Globe. "Billy Sunday Was All Wrong; Picked Philadelphia to Beat Red Sox; Likes Murnane's Baseball, for 'He Gives Good Stuff.'" (Boston, MA). October 14, 1915.

Boston Globe. "Bob Quinn Believes American Boy and Baseball Go Together: Says Game is Not Slipping." May 14, 1932.

Boston Globe. "Fine Floral Tributes at Murnane Funeral." February 8, 1917.

Boston Globe. "John L. 'Buncoed': Although a Ful'-Fledged Tenderloiner, He Gave Up $15 Easy—The Trick Cannot Be Repeated with Safety. December 27, 1899.

Boston Globe. "How to Play Baseball." July 14, 1907.

Boston Globe. "Late Justice Moody Real Baseball Fan: New England League Named Him First President." July 8, 1917.

Boston Globe. "Mayor Curley's Tribute." February 8, 1917.

Boston Globe. "Miss Murnane Dies: Daughter of Tim." June 12, 1931.

Boston Globe. "Murnane Day Plans." September 5, 1917.

Boston Globe. "Murnane Drops Dead in Theatre." February 8, 1917.

Boston Globe. "Popularity of Tim Murnane, The Globe's Base Ball Writer." August 12, 1888.

Boston Globe. "Speaker Again Hurt, In Trying to Steal Home." September 2, 1917.

Boston Globe. "'Sporty' Barker, An Old-Time Baseball Umpire, Has Gone 'Gof.,' Evidently." August 21, 1930.

Boston Globe. "Umpires Enforce Balk Rule Now: American League Is Attempting Now To Give Base Runner Even Break." April 21, 1930.

Boston Globe. "Williams Gets Tim Murnane Honor Plaque." December 21, 1939.

Boston Post. "About the Boston Globe: A Rash Post Man's New Year's Call on 'the Sheet Across the Way.'" January 7, 1894.

Boston Post. "Arthur Duffey's Comment on Sports." September 24, 1916.

Boston Post. "Ball Players on Trip Today: Several of Red Sox Going to N.H. Camp." October 16, 1916.

Buffalo News. "Tim Murnane, the Veteran Base Ball Writer and Player." May 20, 1889.

Burkett, Samantha. "Babe Ruth Made History with Help from Ernie Shore." *Baseball Hall of Fame.* Accessed December 21, 2025. https://baseballhall.org/discover/babe-ruth-made-history-with-help-from-ernie-shore.

Burns, Ken, dir. *Baseball.* Episode 1. PBS, 1994.

Bushnell, Mark. "Then Again: Larry Gardner, from Enosburg Falls to Red Sox Fame." *VTDigger*. June 16, 2024. https://vtdigger.org/2024/06/16/then-again-larry-gardner-from-enosburg-falls-to-red-sox-fame/.

Chicago Examiner. "Baseball Loses Great Star." April 15, 1911,17. https://www.newspapers.com/article/chicago-examiner-baseball-loses-great-st/78141289/.

Chicago Tribune. "Al Leads Ruth, Klein in Total For Star Game." June 25, 1933.

Chicago Tribune. "American Stars Win Game of Century." July 7, 1933.

Chicago Tribune. "Final Returns in All-Star Baseball Poll." June 25, 1933.

Chicago Tribune. "Peters Beats 2 Congressman in Race for Mayor." December 19, 1917.

Cincinnati Enquirer. "Big Sum Realized." September 28, 1917.

Cincinnati Magazine. "Nothing But the Facts." April 1982.

Courier-News. "Suggest Ten Man Team for Baseball; Player to Bat for Pitcher." December 12, 1928.

Curtis, Ted. "In the Best Interests of the Game: The Authority of the Commissioner of Major League Baseball." *Seton Hall Journal of Sport Law 5* (1995).

Eaton, Francis. "Red Sox Win Brilliant Game From All-Stars." *Boston Journal.* September 28, 1917, front page; continued on p. 8.

Edmonton Journal. "Player Who Couldn't Bat By Accident Discovered the Bunt in Early Days," January 12, 1924.

Extreme Weather Watch. "Boston Weather in 1917." Accessed December 20, 2025. https://www.extremeweatherwatch.com/cities/boston/year-1917#september.

Federal Baseball Club v. National League. 259 U.S. 200 (1922).

Findling, J. E. "The Louisville Grays' Scandal of 1877." *Journal of Sport History* (2017): 176–187.

Finkel, Jan. "Pete Alexander." *SABR BioProject.* January 4, 2012. Accessed December 20, 2025. https://sabr.org/bioproj/person/pete-alexander/.

Fitzgerald, F. Scott. *The Great Gatsby.* New York: Scribner, 2004.

Forr, James. "September 28, 1938: Hartnett hits Homer in the Gloamin'." *SABR Games Project.* Accessed December 20, 2025. https://sabr.org/gamesproj/game/september-28-1938-hartnett-hits-homer-in-the-gloamin/.

Francis, Bill. "Polo Grounds Pass Tells Story of Woodrow Wilson's Love of Baseball." *Baseball Hall of Fame.* December 23, 2019. Accessed December 20, 2025. https://baseballhall.org/discover/polo-grounds-pass-tells-story-of-woodrow-wilson.

Freedman, Lew. *The Day All the Stars Came Out: Baseball's First All-Star Game,* 1933. Lincoln: University of Nebraska Press, 2013.

Ginsburg, Daniel. "The 1877 Louisville Grays Scandal." *SABR Journal.* Accessed December 20, 2025. https://sabr.org/journal/article/the-1877-louisville-grays-scandal/.

Goldsmith, Wallace. "Features of the Red Sox–All Stars Clash for Benefit of Murnane Memorial Fund." *Boston Globe.* September 28, 1917.

Goldstein, Warren. *Playing for Keeps: A History of Early Baseball.* 20th anniversary ed. Ithaca, NY: Cornell University Press, 2009. (Originally published 1989.)

Hamilton Spectator. "Paid Tribute to Late Tim Murnane." September 28, 1917.

Haupert, Michael. "The Business of Being the Babe." *Baseball Research Journal* 50, no. 1 (Spring 2021): 7–15. https://sabr.org/journal/article/the-business-of-being-the-babe/.

Hickey, David, Raymond Sinibaldi, and Kerry Keene. *Images of America: Fenway Park.* Charleston, SC: Arcadia Publishing, 2012.

History. "Battle of the Somme," November 12, 2009, https://www.history.com/articles/battle-of-the-somme.

Hoffman, Christopher. "The Pro Baseball Team That Called Middletown Home." *Connecticut Magazine,* March 28, 2022. https://www.ctinsider.com/connecticutmagazine/article/The-pro-baseball-team-that-called-Middletown-home-17046891.php.

Holmes, George R. "Boston Outfield Best of All Time." *Pittsburgh Press.* October 14, 1915.

Hutchinson News. "Benefit for Tim Murnane." September 27, 1917.

Ivor-Campbell, Frederick, Robert L. Tiemann, and Mark Rucker, eds. *Baseball's First Stars.* Cleveland: Society for American Baseball Research, 1996.

James, Bill. *The New Bill James Historical Baseball Abstract.* New York: Simon & Schuster, 2003.

Johnson, Bill. "Gabby Hartnett." *SABR BioProject.* January 4, 2012. Accessed December 20, 2025. https://sabr.org/bioproj/person/Gabby-Hartnett/.

Jones, David. "Benny Kauff." *SABR BioProject.* January 4, 2012. Accessed December 20, 2025. https://sabr.org/bioproj/person/benny-kauff/.

Jones, Victor O. "Notes from the Back of an Envelope: Will Rogers Galloped in the Outfield." *Boston Globe.* August 12, 1966.

Kemp, Abe. "Los Angeles Downs Seals, 4 to 3 in 15th." *San Francisco Chronicle.* June 9, 1934.

King, Norm. "Pepper Martin." *SABR BioProject.* January 4, 2012. Accessed December 20, 2025. https://sabr.org/bioproj/person/Pepper-Martin/.

Lane, F. C. "An All-Star Baseball Contest for a Greater Championship: Where the Present World's Series Falls Short of the Ideal—How a Greater Series, the Real Grand Opera of Baseball, Might Be Staged." *Baseball Magazine,* November 1915.

Lyons, Ronan C., Allison Shertzer, Rowena Gray, and David N. Agorastos. *The Price of Housing in the United States, 1890–2006.* NBER Working Paper no. 32593. Cambridge, MA: National Bureau of Economic Research, 2024.

McCoid, Eugene C. Letter to Lee Allen. July 2, 1962. Baseball Hall of Fame, Cooperstown, NY.

McGrath, Ed. "Dodgers Blank the Braves 5 to 0: Notes of Braves' Game." *Boston Post.* September 10, 1916.

McKenna, Brian. "Lefty O'Doul." *SABR BioProject.* January 4, 2012. Accessed December 20, 2025. https://sabr.org/bioproj/person/Lefty-ODoul/.

McMullen, Walter. "The Sport Trail: Peer of Them All." *The Hamilton Spectator,* May 28, 1930.

Melin, Roger. "Hal Schumacher." *SABR BioProject.* January 4, 2012. Accessed December 20, 2025. https://sabr.org/bioproj/person/Hal-Schumacher/.

Mitchell, Al. "Out of the Pressbox." *Mason City Globe-Gazette.* March 22, 1934.

Murnane, T. H. *How to Play Base Ball.* Boston: Wright & Ditson, 1884.

Murnane, T. H. How to Umpire; *How to Captain a Team; How to Manage a Team; How to Coach; How to Organize a League.* New York: American Sports Publishing Company, 1905.

Murnane, T. H. *Spalding's Guide to Baseball.* New York: Spalding, 1915.

Murnane, T. H. *Wright & Ditson Guide to Baseball.* Boston: Wright & Ditson, 1910.

Murnane, T. H. *Wright & Ditson Guide to Baseball.* Boston: Wright & Ditson, 1911.

Murnane, Tim. "Back We Go." *Boston Globe,* August 24, 1888, 5.

Murnane, Tim. "Base Ball Matters: Tim Murnane's Gratuitous Counsel." *Boston Globe,* July 30, 1888, 8.

Murnane, Tim. "Base Ball Players." *Boston Globe,* July 8, 1888, 6.

Murnane, Tim. "Never Give Up: Timely Suggestions by Tim Murnane." *Boston Globe,* July 23, 1888, 8.

Murnane, Tim. "Tim Murnane on Hanlon." *Boston Globe,* March 13, 1904.

Murnane, Tim. "Tim Murnane's Views on Managing a Team." *Boston Globe,* August 20, 1888, 8.

Murnane, Tim. "Tim Murnane Visits George Foster, Who Is a Real Farmer in Oklahoma." *Boston Globe,* January 16, 1916, 14.

Nason, Jerry. "Duffy's Hall of Fame Excursion Starts and Finishes in the Globe." *Boston Globe,* April 28, 1945.

National Archives and Records Administration. *Joint Address to Congress Leading to a Declaration of War Against Germany, April 2, 1917.* National Archives Milestone Documents, accessed December 20, 2025. https://www.archives.gov/milestone-documents/address-to-congress-declaration-of-war-against-germany.

National Army Museum. "Battle of the Somme." Accessed December 20, 2025. https://www.nam.ac.uk/explore/battle-somme.

National Baseball Hall of Fame and Museum. *BBWAA Career Excellence Award.* Accessed December 20, 2025. https://baseballhall.org/discover-more/awards/884.

New Britain Herald. "All-Stars Beaten in Benefit Game." September 28, 1917.

New York Times. "Cobb and Speaker Cleared by Landis: Verdict Exonerating Stars of Baseball Scandal." January 28, 1927. https://www.nytimes.com/1927/01/28/archives/cobb-and-speaker-cleared-by-landis-verdict-exonerating-stars-of.html.

New York Times. "Charles H. Taylor, Boston Editor, Dies." June 23, 1921. https://timesmachine.nytimes.com/timesmachine/1921/06/23/109809151.pdf.

New York Times, "The Death of Ray Chapman," August 17, 1920. https://archive.nytimes.com/www.nytimes.com/packages/html/sports/year_in_sports/08.17.html.

New York Times. "Out-Door Sports: The National Game." September 29, 1865.

New York Times. "Speaker Has Not Agreed; May Not Go To Cleveland – Seeks Explanation from Lannin." April 10, 1916. https://www.nytimes.com/1916/04/10/archives/speaker-has-not-agreed-may-not-go-to-cleveland-seeks-explanation.html.

New York Times. “Speaker Not a Holdout, Says Boston Has Great Team Without Him; Goes.” April 11, 1916. https://www.nytimes.com/1916/04/11/archives/speaker-not-a-holdout-says-boston-has-great-team-without-him-goes.html.

New York Times. “Tris Speaker Sold to Cleveland Club; Boston Red Sox to Get Two.” April 9, 1916. https://www.nytimes.com/1916/04/09/archives/tris-speaker-sold-to-cleveland-club-boston-red-sox-to-get-two.html.

Nowlin, Bill, ed. *Opening Fenway Park with Style: The World Champion 1912 Red Sox.* Associate editors Maurice Bouchard, Dan Desrochers, and Len Levin. Phoenix: Society for American Baseball Research, 2012.

Pitoniak, Scott. “MLB All-Star Game Created a Blueprint For Other Leagues to Follow,” June 6, 2023. https://baseballhall.org/discover/mlb-all-star-game-created-blueprint-for-other-leagues-to-follow.

Pittsburgh Press. “Harry Hooper Was Real Redsox Hero.” December 13, 1912.

Pittsburgh Press. “Tim Murnane Roasts Valentine—Morris Poorly Supported.” September 23, 1888.

Pittsburgh Press. “Tim Murnane’s Awful Break.” November 4, 1901.

Pomrenke, Jacob. “1917 Fenway Park Gamblers’ Riot.” *Jacob Pomrenke.* Accessed December 20, 2025. https://jacobpomrenke.com/black-sox/1917-fenway-park-gamblers-riot/.

Reading Eagle. “Harry Hooper Dies at 87.” December 18, 1974.

Retrosheet. “Babe Ruth.” Accessed December 20, 2025. https://www.retrosheet.org/boxesetc/R/Pruthb101.htm.

Retrosheet. “Box Score: Boston at Washington Senators, June 23, 1917.” Accessed December 20, 2025. https://www.retrosheet.org/boxesetc/1917/B06231BOS1917.htm.

Retrosheet. "Joe Wood." Accessed December 20, 2025. https://www.retrosheet.org/boxesetc/W/Pwoodj108.htm.

Retrosheet. "John Heydler." Accessed December 20, 2025. https://www.retrosheet.org/boxesetc/H/Pheydj901.htm.

Retrosheet, "Tim Murnane Player Page," accessed December 20, 2025, https://www.retrosheet.org/boxesetc/M/Pmurnt101.htm.

Rhodes, Greg. "June 14, 1870: The Atlantic Storm: Red Stockings Suffer First Defeat." *SABR Games Project*. Accessed December 20, 2025. https://sabr.org/gamesproj/game/june-14-1870-the-atlantic-storm-red-stockings-suffer-first-defeat/.

Richardson, Gary, Alejandro Komai, Michael Gou, and Daniel Park. "Stock Market Crash of 1929." *Federal Reserve History*. Accessed December 20, 2025. https://www.federalreservehistory.org/essays/stock-market-crash-of-1929.

Ritter, Lawrence S. *The Glory of Their Times*. New York: Macmillan, 1966.

Rosenzweig, Edward. "The Boston Fan Speaks." *Baseball Magazine* 14, no. 2 (February 1915): 90. Accessed July 11, 2025. https://digital.la84.org/digital/collection/p17103coll2/id/3844/rec/5.

Rumore, Kori, and Marianne Mather. "Vintage Chicago Tribune: We Started Baseball's First All-Star Game — 90 Years Ago." *Chicago Tribune*. July 6, 2023. Accessed December 20, 2025. https://www.chicagotribune.com/2023/07/06/vintage-chicago-tribune-we-started-baseballs-first-all-star-game-90-years-ago/?clearUserState=true.

Ryan, Bob. "Perfect Time When Game Was Young." *Boston Globe*. May 5, 1998.

Ryan, Bob. "Time to Stop Dodging Us." *Boston Globe*, June 11, 2004.

Ruth, Babe. "The Story of His Life" [Chapter VII]. *Boston Post*, August 15, 1920.

Sarnoff, Gary. "Sam West." *SABR BioProject.* January 4, 2012. Accessed December 20, 2025. https://sabr.org/bioproj/person/Sam-West/.

Sault Star. "What's What in Sport." February 15, 1933.

Sentinel-Record. "Boston Party of Players Here." March 12, 1912.

Seymour, Deb. "The Game of the Century." *BallNine.* July 20, 2022. Accessed March 4, 2026. https://ballnine.com/2022/07/20/the-game-of-the-century/.

Seymour, Harold, and Dorothy Seymour Mills. *Baseball: The Early Years.* New York: Oxford University Press, 1989.

Speaker, Tris. "Hurlers Work Was Wellnigh Perfect." *Pittsburgh Press.* October 14, 1915.

Sporting News. "1917 World Series." Archived February 10, 2006. Accessed December 20, 2025. https://web.archive.org/web/20060210012543/http://www.sportingnews.com/archives/worldseries/1917.html.

Sportsman. "Live Tips and Topics," *Boston Globe.* April 29, 1919.

Sportsman. "Live Tips and Topics." *Boston Globe.* August 15, 1914.

Sportsman. "Live Tips and Topics." *Boston Globe.* September 28, 1917.

Springfield Press. "Father of Scouts." March 20, 1933.

Stanley, Matthew E. "Ty Cobb and Tris Speaker Are Accused of Fixing Baseball Games." *EBSCO Research Starters,* 2022. Accessed December 20, 2025. https://www.ebsco.com/research-starters/history/ty-cobb-and-tris-speaker-are-accused-fixing-baseball-games.

Statue of Liberty–Ellis Island Foundation. *Passenger Record for Bridget Murnan. Ellen Austin,* arrived January 1, 1857. Accessed December 20, 2025. https://heritage.statueofliberty.org/passenger-details/czoxMzoiOTAxMjAwNzgzMTc5NyI7/czo4OiJtYW5pZmVzdCI7.

Stout, Glenn. *Fenway 1912.* Boston: Houghton Mifflin Harcourt, 2012.

Tacoma Daily Ledger. "Billy Sunday Comes Back at Tim Murnane." August 16, 1908.

The Deadball Era. "Prelude to Disaster." Accessed January 12, 2026. https://www.thedeadballera.com/prelude.html.

The Inter Ocean. "The Champion Slugger: John L. Sullivan Tells the Story of His Life to a Denver Reporter." January 1, 1884. Accessed December 20, 2025. https://www.newspapers.com/image/32570392/?clipping_id=7228862&fcfToken=eyJhbGciOiJIUzI1NiIsInR5cCI6IkpXVCJ9.eyJmcmVlLXZpZXctaWQiOjMyNTcwMzkyLCJpYXQiOjE3NjIxMDczNzEsImV4cCI6MTc2MjE5Mzc3MX0.4E6ldC2Jjd5ffiKElB1L-Oe8-LMX1S638mAA7WL5bMk.

The National Pastime: A Review of Baseball History. Edited by Society for American Baseball Research. Longmeadow, MA: LG "Baseball History," 2006. Accessed December 20, 2025. https://archive.org/details/nationalpastimer0000unse_i1t5/page/32/mode/2up.

Thorn, John. "George Wright — June 14, 1870." *Our Game.* April 21, 2025. https://ourgame.mlblogs.com/george-wright-june-14-1870-9a3ce11cbc48.

Thornley, Stew, comp. *Baseball Playing Rules Changes Year by Year Before 1950. Retrosheet.* Revised November 19, 2025. Accessed December 20, 2025. https://retrosheet.org/rules/PlayingRulesYearbyYearPre1950.pdf.

Toronto Star Weekly. "How Majority of Major League Clubs Were Named." November 4, 1933.

Tuchman, Barbara W. *The Guns of August.* New York: Macmillan, 1962.

Vincent, David, Lyle Spatz, and David W. Smith. *The Midsummer Classic: The Complete History of Baseball's All-Star Game.* Lincoln: University of Nebraska Press, 2001.

U.S. Bureau of Labor Statistics. "Consumer Price Index: History." September 6, 2023.Accessed March 8, 2026. https://www.bls.gov/opub/hom/cpi/archive/20230906/history.htm.

Wancho, Joseph. "Paul Waner." *SABR BioProject.* January 4, 2012. Accessed December 20, 2025. https://sabr.org/bioproj/person/Paul-Waner/.

Warrington, Robert D. "A Ballpark Opens and a Ballplayer Dies: The Converging Fates of Shibe Park and Doc Powers." *SABR Journal.* 2014. Accessed December 20, 2025. https://sabr.org/journal/article/a-ballpark-opens-and-a-ballplayer-dies-the-converging-fates-of-shibe-park-and-doc-powers/.

Whalen, Thomas J. *When the Red Sox Ruled: Baseball's First Dynasty, 1912–1918.* Lanham, MD: Rowman & Littlefield Publishers, Inc., 2011.

Wilson, Woodrow. *Address to Joint Session of Congress Requesting Declaration of War Against Germany,* April 2, 1917. National Archives and Records Administration. https://www.archives.gov/milestone-documents/address-to-congress-declaration-of-war-against-germany.

Wright & Ditson's Base Ball Guide. Boston: Wright & Ditson, 1884.

INDEX

A

Agnew, Sam, 62, 81, 83, 98, 119
Alexander, Grover Cleveland ("Pete"), 78
Alexandria, Texas, 8
American League, 22, 38, 39, 52, 56, 74, 92, 110, 114, 115, 126, 130, 131, 134, 136, 137
    see also Johnson, Ban
Anson, Adrian Constantine ("Cap"), 10, 30, 172
Averill, Earl, 136

B

Baltimore Orioles, 11
Barnard, Ernest, 126
Barrow, Edward, 57
Barry, Jack, 61, 81, 83, 88, 97, 98, 119,139, 202, 205
Barry, Tom, 88
Bartell, Dick, 135
Bechtel, George, 106
Bender, Charles Albert ("Chief"), 11
Berger, Wally, 135
Black Monday, 113
Black Sox, 100, 103, 107, 116, 127, 202
Black Tuesday, 113
Boston Globe, 3, 9, 10, 26, 31, 35, 37, 41, 44, 53, 67, 71, 72, 73, 77, 78, 81, 86, 89, 90, 119, 143, 164, 173, 177, 188
    Murnane as baseball editor, 24, 35 ,36, 37, 41, 72, 177
    publication of baseball reform commentary, 27, 53
    shaping public understanding of the game, 41, 44, 143
    sports coverage in early twentieth century, 67, 86, 173
Boston Red Sox, 2, 3, 20, 21, 22, 34, 44, 50, 52, 53, 54, 55, 57, 58, 59, 60, 62, 66, 68, 76, 77, 80, 81, 85, 86, 87, 97, 98, 110, 138, 139, 140, 149, 162, 173, 174
    1912 season, 15, 54, 55
    1917 season, 12, 14, 15, 61, 65, 119, 137
    history of, 51, 56, 60, 75, 116, 148
    see also Fenway Park
Brice, Fanny, 3, 68, 89

Briggs, Frank, 88
Brooklyn Atlantics, 27, 198
Brown, Mordecai ("Three Finger"), 10
Burns, Ken, 184

C

Carrigan, Bill ("Rough"), 59
Center of early baseball culture, 1, 20
Chadwick, Henry, 198
Chapman, Raymond Johnson, 2, 66, 67, 81, 83, 92, 98, 119, 139, 160
Chase, Charles E., 106
Chicago American Giants, 12
Cicotte, Eddie, 61, 101, 102
Cincinnati Red Stockings, 27, 28, 51, 87, 101, 102, 106
Civic gatherings at Fenway Park, 15, 51, 52
Civil War, 1, 6, 7, 86, 104, 134
Cobb, Tyrus ("Ty") Raymond, 2, 12, 21, 22, 46, 66, 68, 77, 81, 83, 86, 89, 92, 97, 98, 107, 110, 111, 112, 113, 119, 139, 160, 172, 173, 176, 203, 205, 210
Cochrane, Mickey, 114
Comiskey Park, 15, 115, 116, 128, 130, 131, 135, 136, 156, 157
Comiskey, Charles Albert, 30, 102
Coolidge, Calvin, 88
Craver, Bill, 106, 107
Cronin, Joe, 131, 135, 136
Crowder, General, 136
Cummings, E.E., 78
Curley, James Michael, 73, 76, 88, 147, 203, 213

D

Dean, Dizzy, 130
DeCamp, Joseph, 87
Delahanty brothers, 10
Detroit Tigers, 16, 46, 73, 78, 93, 110, 131, 160
Devyr, Thomas, 104
Diamond, Edwin, 156, 213
Dickey, Bill, 132
Dinneen, Bill, 135
Dos Passos, John, 78
Doubleday, Abner, 198, 199

Dovey, George, 52
Dowling, Mary Agnes, 32, 71, 73, 76
Doyle, Larry, 56
Dreyfuss, Barney, 73
Dykes, Jimmy, 131, 135

E

Ehmke, Howard, 92, 119
Elias, Al and Walter, 126
Evers, Johnny, 78

F

Fens, The, 20, 21, 54
Fenway Park, 2, 20, 51, 52, 70, 75, 79, 84, 85. 118, 132, 146, 148, 149, 158, 161, 162, 177
 see also Boston Red Sox
Ferguson, Bob, 27
Ferrell, Rick, 132, 135, 136
Fitzgerald, F. Scott, 103, 205
Fitzgerald, John ("Honey Fitz"), 55, 147, 213
Flood, Tim, 40
Forbes Field, 15, 206
Foster, Andrew ("Rube"), 12, 61
Foster, Bill, 12
Foster, George ("Rube"), 12, 34, 61, 119, 139, 146, 199, 212
Foxx, Jimmie, 114, 132
Freedman, Lew, 125, 129, 206
Frisch, Frank, 133, 136

G

Gainer, Del, 146, 212
Gallivan, James A., 73, 88
Gardner, Larry, 59, 81, 98, 119, 201, 202
Gehrig, Lou, 61, 131, 132, 156, 214
Gehringer, Charlie, 131, 135
Ginsburg, Daniel, 106
Goldsmith, Wallace, 92, 148, 164, 204, 205, 213, 214
Gomez, Lefty, 132, 135, 136
Grant, Ulysses, 104
Great War, 1, 204

Green, Monster, 15
Griffith, Clark, 73, 204
Grove, Lefty, 114, 136

H

Hafey, Chick, 135
Hallahan, William ("Wild Bill"), 133, 135, 136
Hallahan, John, 81
Hanlon, Ned, 30
Harridge, Will, 126, 127, 128
Hartnett, Gabby, 133, 206, 207
Hayes, Rutherford B., 105
Hermann, Sport, 88
Heydler, John, 11, 126, 127, 128
Hill, Pete, 12
Hoblitzell, Richard ("Dick") or ("Doc"), 81, 97, 98, 119, 120, 139
Holmes, George R., 56, 201
Hooper, Harry ("Hoop"), 50, 56,57, 58, 59, 61, 66, 67, 81, 97, 98, 119, 139, 201, 202, 210
Hulbert, William A., 29, 105, 107
Hurlburt, Archie, 88

J

Jackson, Joseph Jefferson ("Shoeless Joe"), 2, 12, 46, 47, 66, 67, 68, 77, 81, 97, 98, 102, 119, 120, 139, 150, 161, 172, 176, 210, 213
James, Bill, 11, 196
Janvrin, Hal, 66
Jefferies, E.J., 111
Jennings, Hughie, 2, 78, 93
Johnson, Byron Bancroft ("Ban"), 39, 52, 53, 73, 77, 78, 110, 126
Johnson, Walter Perry ("Big Train"), 2, 10, 21, 22, 47, 55, 67, 86, 111, 139, 161, 173, 176
Jones, Sam, 65
Joss, Addie, 74, 75

K

Kauff, Benny, 77, 78, 203
Keeler, Willie ("Wee Willie"), 10
Keliher, Jack, 41
Kelley, John Paul Santiago, 86

Kelly, Ed, 124, 125
Kelly, Jerome, 22
Kennedy, John F., 55
Klein, Chuck, 130, 135

L

Lajoie, Napoleon ("Nap"), 10, 42, 87
Landis, Kenesaw Mountain, 108, 109, 111, 112, 125, 126, 127, 128, 129, 136, 203
Lane, F.C., 75, 115
Leonard, Emil John ("Dutch"), 60
Leonard, Hubert Benjamin ("Dutch"), 60, 61, 68, 69, 110, 111
Lewis, George ("Duffy"), 50, 56, 58, 59, 61, 65, 66, 81, 83, 92, 97, 98, 118, 119, 120, 139, 166, 173, 174
Lieb, Fred, 33
Lloyd, John Henry ("Pop"), 12
Luce, Henry, 123
Lusitania, RMS, 17

M

Mack, Connie ("Cornelius McGillicuddy") 2, 93, 112, 113, 114, 132, 134, 160
MacLeish, Archibald, 78
Manning, Frances, 29
Maranville, Walter ("Rabbit"), 66, 81, 82, 83, 87, 92, 98, 119, 139
Marston, Charles A., 87
Martin, Pepper, 133, 136
Mathewson, Christy, 10
Mays, Carl, 61, 67, 92, 204
McCormick, Robert, 124, 125
McGraw, John, 30, 54, 55, 134, 136, 164
McInnis, Stuffy, 81, 92, 98, 119, 139
McNally, Mike, 66, 67
Middletown Mansfields, 28, 142, 143
Miller, Guy A., 111
Morrill, John F., 77, 87
Murderers' Row, 132
Murnan, Bridget, 26, 197
Murnan, Patrick, 26
Murnane, Emma Louise, 30, 41

Murnane, Mary Adelaide, 30
Murnane, Timothy Hayes ("Tim") or ("Silver King"), 3, 8, 9, 25, 31, 33, 34, 140, 168, 177
  advocate for baseball reform and fairness, 11, 13, 40, 93, 115
  author of instructional baseball guides, 41, 42, 43, 144, 145
  Boston Globe career, 10, 32, 35, 37, 39
  death, 3, 18, 25, 72, 75, 88, 158, 162, 165, 173, 174
  early professional baseball player, 27, 28, 29, 143
  Irish immigrant background, 30
  Murnan spelling, 26, 142
  president of New England League, 207
  public mourning by baseball community, 36, 44, 46, 52, 60, 62, 81, 73, 76, 77, 85, 89, 94, 101, 133, 134, 149, 154
  role in minor-league governance, 38
Murray, Miah, 87

N

National Association of Professional Base Ball Players, 28, 29, 38, 104
National League, 11, 12, 29, 30, 38, 39, 52, 53, 74, 77, 82, 105, 106, 122, 126, 128, 130, 133, 134, 201
  see also Hulbert, William A.
Navin, Frank, 73
Negro leagues, 12, 13, 61

O

O'Neill, Steve, 81, 92, 98, 119
Ott, Mel, 130
Owens, Brick, 62

P

Polo Grounds, 137
Powers, ("Doc"), 74, 75
Pulliam, Harry, 126

Q

Quinn, Bob, 44

R

Red Stockings, Boston, 28, 29, 51, 52, 87, 142, 143
Red Stockings, Cincinnati, 27, 28, 51, 87, 101, 102, 106
Rice, Grantland, 32
Rockne, Knute, 125
Rogers, Will, 3, 64, 68, 69, 88, 173
Role in development of professional baseball, 164
Roosevelt, Quentin, 78
Roosevelt, Theodore, 43
Roush, Edd, 78
Runyon, Damon, 32
Russell, Harry E., 77
Ruth, George Herman ("Babe"), 2, 3, 12, 33, 47, 57, 59, 60, 61, 62, 63, 66, 67, 69, 73, 78, 80, 81, 82, 83, 86, 97, 98, 107, 109, 113, 114, 115, 119, 130, 132, 135, 146, 154, 156, 161, 179

S

Sarajevo, 16
Schang, Wally, 92, 120
Scott, Everett ("Scoot"), 61, 81, 83, 98, 119, 131, 139, 140
    see also *Boston Globe*
    see also Hulbert, William A.
Shibe Park, 15, 74, 114
Shocker, Urban (Urbain Jacques Shockcor), 81, 92, 97, 98
Shore, Ernie, 61, 62, 146
Shubert Theatre, 3, 71, 174
Simmons, Al, 114, 130, 132, 156
Somme, Battle of the, 17
Spalding, Albert, 199
Speaker, Tristram Edgar ("Tris"), 2, 12, 21, 50, 56, 59, 65, 68, 77, 78, 81, 89, 96, 97, 98, 110, 160
Stout, Glenn, 55
Sullivan, John Lawrence ("John L."), 3, 68, 89, 144, 173
Sunday, Billy, 37

T

Taft, William Howard, 52
Talbot, Emory H., 71
Taylor, General Charles, 53, 200
Taylor, John I., 53, 54, 57, 77, 138, 140, 173

Tener, John, 77
Terry, Bill, 135
Thomas, Pinch, 62
Thompson, G.W., 105
Thorn, John, 27, 184
Titanic, RMS, 55
Torriente, Cristóbal, 12
Traynor, Pie, 133
Tuchman, Barbara, 16
Tweed, Boss, 104

V

Verdun, Battle of, 17

W

Waddell, Rube, 11
Wagner, Honus, 10, 11, 78
Walker, Clarence ("Tilly"), 65, 68, 81, 98, 119, 120, 139
Waner, Paul, 133
Ward, Arch, 115, 124, 130, 137, 155
Warneke, Lon, 130, 133, 136
Wartime military activity during WWI, 72, 73, 151
Washington Senators, 62, 73, 78, 112, 139, 161, 197
Weaver, George ("Buck"), 2, 81, 92, 97, 98, 102, 119, 161
West, Sam, 132
Williams, Claude ("Lefty"), 101
Wilson, Jimmie, 133
Wilson, Woodrow, 4, 17, 18, 73
Wood, Joe ("Smoky"), 55, 57, 59, 60, 110, 111, 201, 202, 204
World War I, 1, 124, 151, 197, 204
Wright, Beals, 87
Wright, George, 27, 28, 86, 87, 142, 198
Wright, Harry, 27, 28, 51, 87, 142, 198
Wright, Irving, 87

Y

Young, Denton True ("Cy"), 10, 42, 53, 54, 146

Z

Zimmerman Telegram, 18
Zimmerman, Henry ("Heinie"), 78

ACKNOWLEDGMENTS

As with many worthwhile endeavors, this book began with a moment of discovery that felt, at first, almost accidental. I was deep into another project—one that has occupied my mind on and off for more than a decade and will be published soon—when, late one night, I followed an online trail into a largely forgotten baseball game played in 1917. What struck me was not only the game itself, but the realization that something so rich in meaning—so resonant with the themes of community, purpose, and possibility that define the best of the American story—had never been fully brought to life for a general audience.

The more I sat with it, the less it felt like a curiosity and the more it felt like a responsibility. During a call about my other book with former Congressman Bob Mrazek, publisher of Compass Rose, I described the game. Even as I did, I knew this was not simply an aside; it was a story waiting to be told. I said as much, and soon after drafted a prologue and outline and shared them with Bob.

Tom Hurd, CEO of Compass Rose, soon joined the conversation. I hadn't known that Tom's father had once pitched for the Red Sox, but when that connection surfaced, the project took on an added sense of purpose. What began as a quiet discovery quickly gathered momentum. And just like that, here we are.

Reading teaches. Writing teaches even more. What began as a story about a single baseball game—made famous by the legends who took the field—gradually became a way of tracing how memory and meaning intertwine. The process allowed me to explore why the game mattered, how much meaning it could bear, and what its quiet disappearance revealed. It demanded attention not only to facts and dates, but to texture as well: how events were remembered, why certain stories endured, and why others receded from view.

As the research deepened, the game revealed itself less as an isolated spectacle than as a lens. Through it, I found myself looking not only backward into history, but outward toward the country itself, and toward the enduring role our national pastime plays in helping us understand who we are. In the course of this project, I learned far more than I expected. I learned how easily a single afternoon can slip from collective memory, how fragile civic rituals can be, and how much meaning can reside in moments that were never meant to be monumental. I also learned, again and again, how dependent historical understanding is on generosity—of archivists who preserve, writers who notice, and readers willing to linger.

No book is possible without the time, generosity, and patience of those who are willing to share their support and encouragement. The Compass Rose team has been a valued partner throughout the writing and publication process. I thank Bob and Tom for sharing my vision of what this book could be—and for their friendship. Both contributed meaningfully to its final form. And I'm grateful to my friend, former Congressman Steve Israel, for making the introduction to Bob.

James Bock has a superb editorial eye, and his friendly suggestion to "kill your darlings" helped me refine the points I sought to make in this book. I'm indebted to him for his insightful guidance. Maddie Mafilios is as cheerful a collaborator as they come. Working together on the cover design was a joy. I also thank Diane Kane and Cecilia Januszewski for their support in bringing this book to life.

My dear friend, David Eisenhower, is the biggest baseball aficionado I know, and I loved bouncing my early ideas off him and benefiting from his wisdom. The indefatigable Jen Tucholski has been a steadfast partner and source of support across many initiatives, and I'm grateful for her valuable work. I'm indebted as well to the individuals who support some of America's finest institutions, including the staff at the U.S. Library of Congress, the Boston Public Library, and the National Baseball Hall of Fame and Museum in Cooperstown, New York.

Over the years, I've been sustained by a remarkable circle of friends and extended family whose generosity, humor, loyalty, and encouragement have shaped my life far beyond this book. They know who they are, and my gratitude to them runs deeper than these pages can express.

Throughout this project, I was reminded how much I inherited myself—not just a love of baseball or history, but a way of paying attention: to stories, traditions, and the meaning carried in shared rituals. Those inheritances were passed down through time spent together, conversation, and example. They shaped the person I became long before I had words for it, and in many ways, they shaped the book you now hold. I'm grateful to have shared those inheritances with my siblings Leslie, Andrew, and Jesse, and I thank my parents and late grandparents for passing them along to us.

My grandparents—Beverly and Eddie Herschenfeld, and Betty and Marshall Reich—would have loved this book. Grandma Betty grew up near Ebbets Field and saw Jackie Robinson play. Grandpa Eddie tried out for the Dodgers and played catch with me throughout my childhood. In my mind, they're all standing at home plate somewhere.

My parents, Jamie and Danny, brought me into this world and showed me how to live in it. Whatever I've achieved is rooted in what they gave me. My dad's thoughtful feedback on drafts of this book was especially valuable and appreciated.

Ilissa has endured late nights, stacks of books, and more baseball stories than anyone should reasonably be expected to hear (although, to be fair, some of them are pretty good). More importantly, she has helped carry the much heavier things beyond these pages, which matter far more than any book ever could.

My children are the reason this book's themes of memory, belonging, and inheritance matter so deeply to me. Much of what I came to understand while writing was shaped simply by watching them—by thinking about what is passed down and what endures after its origins fade from view. If this book is a small act of preservation, it is written with them in mind. Emmy, Eli, and Dylan make every day feel like Opening Day.

Finally, a message for the young reader, whoever that may be, whether now or in the future: This world can be cynical. It can knock you down. You can get hurt. It can be messy. But if I've learned anything while writing this book, it's that we each have the power to supply our own meaning to the events around us. History is not only made by the famous names who appear in textbooks. It is shaped, every day, by ordinary people who choose courage over comfort, kindness over indifference, and hope over despair.

Baseball has always understood this. No game is perfect. Not every swing connects. Even the best players fail more often than they succeed. And yet they keep stepping back into the batter's box. They keep taking the field. They keep believing that the next pitch might be the one they've been waiting for. Life asks the same of us. So when your moment comes—whether on a field, in a classroom, or somewhere no one else is watching—step forward with courage, keep your eye on the ball, and take your swing, even—especially—when it's a curveball you didn't see coming. The world needs you.

SCOTT D. REICH is a nationally acclaimed author, historian, attorney, and nonprofit leader whose work explores how Americans make meaning—in history, sport, and public life—especially in moments of uncertainty and change.

He is the author of *The Power of Citizenship: Why John F. Kennedy Matters to a New Generation*; host of the podcast *Curveball*, which explores life's unexpected turns and the resilience they demand; and founder and CEO of Believe in a Cure, a global nonprofit supporting the rare disease community, which includes his son.

A graduate of the University of Pennsylvania and the University of Pennsylvania Law School, Reich has practiced law at Willkie Farr & Gallagher LLP and American Express and has taught at Penn. His work has been featured widely, including on *The Today Show*, in *The New York Times* and *People*, and across national television, radio, and major publications. More at **Scott-Reich.com.**

www.ingramcontent.com/pod-product-compliance
Lightning Source LLC
LaVergne TN
LVHW091301150826
845673LV00006B/1493

* 9 7 9 8 9 9 4 1 9 5 8 7 1 *